The Complete International
BREAKFAST
BRUNCH
COOKBOOK

The Complete International BREAKFAST BRUNCH COOKBOOK

Kay Shaw Nelson

STEIN AND DAY/*Publishers*/New York

For
My Favorite Brunch Bunch
Rae
and
Eileen, Francene, Katie, Mary Sue,
Nancie, Sandy, Sarah, Sue, and Wendy

FIRST PUBLISHED IN 1982
Copyright © 1982 by Kay Shaw Nelson
All rights reserved.
Designed by L.A. Ditizio
Printed in the United States of America
Stein and Day/*Publishers*
Scarborough House
Briarcliff Manor, N.Y. 10510

Library of Congress Cataloging in Publication Data

Nelson, Kay Shaw.
  The complete international breakfast/brunch cookbook.
  Includes index.
  1. Breakfasts. 2. Brunches. 3. Cookery,
International. I. Title.
TX733.N44   641.5'2   80-5714
ISBN 0-8128-2786-4   AACR2

Contents

Introduction

"Start the day right and all's well by night," is an old English jingle. What better way to do this than with an imaginative morning or midday meal prepared with inspiration and served with flair.

Given today's emphasis on relaxation, enjoyment of leisure time, and low-cost dining, more and more homemakers, hostesses, and hosts are discovering the pleasures of serving breakfasts and brunches as simple but good everyday meals or as planned special-occasion events.

Sydney Smith, the English writer, once opined that no one is conceited before one o'clock. Truly the best time to catch people in a convivial mood is when they've recently awakened to the duties or pleasures of the day.

Everything about an early meal, whether a breakfast or noonish brunch, should be easygoing and comfortable. And much can be said for a warm and congenial morning get-together to enjoy good food and drink and light conversation. Breakfast, from the Middle English *brekfast* or *breken faste*, literally means to "break fast," while our "brunch" is a colloquialism indicating a late first meal of the day, one that takes the place of both breakfast and lunch.

Breakfast customs have varied widely over the centuries. Ancient

1

Egyptians dined on buffets of breads and meats washed down with beer. Early Greeks and Romans preferred bread dipped in wine, eaten perhaps with honey, cheese, or olives. An early Chinese emperor began his day with a dish of crystal sugar and swallow's nests, and then enjoyed a second repast of delicacies—smoked chicken and Chinese cabbage, bamboo shoot-stuffed steamed dumplings, boiled duck and bean curd, swallows' nests and smoked duck, pickled vegetables, and rice cakes with honey.

The Japanese favored rice wafers, rice and soybean paste soups, and custards. Spiced tea and rice cakes were Indian staples. Central Asians preferred sour yogurt, or sharp cheese and hot breads. Russians "broke fast" with hot tea, cheese, smoked fish, and dark bread.

Early European breakfast tastes varied widely. Louis XIV ate only white bread, wine, and water. French workers subsisted on cereal beverages, gruels, or soups. Germans began the day with *schnapps* and gingerbread. Eastern Europeans preferred mead or heady fruit punches and dark breads.

The noted gastronome Grimod de la Reynière considered oysters essential for winter breakfasts but warned in one of his tomes that, "It is proved by experience that, beyond five or six dozen, oysters . . . cease to be enjoyable."

Brillat-Savarin consumed two dozen oysters for breakfast. He also liked an omelet made with blanched carp roe, tuna, shallots, parsley, chives, and lemon juice which, he wrote, "should be reserved for breakfasts of refinement, for connoisseurs in gastronomic art—those who understand eating, and where all eat with judgment; but especially let it be washed down with some good old wine, and you will see wonders."

While most of the French have long preferred a simple morning repast of *café au lait* (coffee with milk) and a croissant or other bread, there are some regional preferences. An ample dash of cognac or other spirit is often added to the coffee, for one thing. In Normandy a good snifter of Calvados or applejack is a common eye-opener. A strange combination dubbed hog wash (white wine and lemon syrup) is drunk with tripe and crusty white bread in the southwest. Catalans prefer their bread rubbed with garlic and sprinkled with olive oil.

The so-called Continental breakfast, a light repast of various coffees and breads, became traditional in Italy, Austria, Spain, and Switzerland, as well as in France. But in cold climates such as those of

Northern Europe it has long been customary to eat heartier breakfasts.

The Dutch still enjoy a meal of two or three cheeses, ham, sausage, boiled eggs, three or four kinds of breads and preserves and rich creamy coffee or chocolate. In northern Germany the fare is ham and cold cuts, cheese, boiled eggs, crisp dark rolls and breads.

Norway's breakfast is the most important meal of the day and a formidable groaning board, indeed, of fresh, cured, and smoked fish, seafood dishes, smoked and cured meats (including game and reindeer), cheese, eggs, breads, sour cream, fruits in season, and buttermilk, milk, hot chocolate, or coffee.

The Swedes eat a substantial breakfast of porridge and milk, breads, eggs, fish, and coffee. The Finns, however, enjoy two breakfasts: an early-morning coffee with breads or open-faced sandwiches, and a late-morning array of boiled potatoes, meat or fish, sour rye bread, cheese, and a traditional dessert of hot cooked cereal topped with fresh berries in season.

The famous English breakfast evolved through a long process and is so highly regarded that it is considered by many persons to be their finest meal. In fact, it is an institution. Somerset Maugham is said to have remarked that the best way to eat well in England is to have breakfast three times a day.

In the Tudor and Stuart eras breakfasts were massive meals of pottages, boiled beef and mutton, vegetables, herring, oatmeal, and tankards of ale. Queen Elizabeth I dined on poultry, rabbit, mutton, veal, and beef with wine and beer. In 1661 Samuel Pepys gave his friends a New Year's breakfast of "oysters, neats [oxen] tongues, meats, anchovies, wine, and Northdowne ale."

By the early 1700s tea began to replace the breakfast beer, and thereafter for a time meals were meager—coffee, chocolate, or tea with bread, rusk, or toast. For visitors there were light Wiggs (rectangles of baked raised dough), Curled Wiggs (rectangles of ginger-flavored baked raised dough), Bath Cakes, Sally Lunn, and various marmalades, jellies, and preserves.

Thereafter English society developed formidable breakfasts that remained convivial upper-class family and company meals until after World War I. Sideboards were covered with silver dishes filled with a prodigious variety of fare: cold roast meats, kidneys, bacon, sausages, game, kippers, smoked fish, ham, kedgeree, chicken livers, grilled sole, poached haddock, potted salmon or meat, steak and kidney pie, veal or game pie, curries, eggs, lamb chops, steaks, fresh trout, mushrooms, breads, scones, porridges, toasts, baked or stewed fruits, condiments, and tea.

Mrs. Beeton's "Book of Household Management" of 1912 listed pages of breakfast dishes, and she wrote that "The moral and physical welfare of mankind depends largely upon its breakfast."

Particularly festive were wedding breakfasts and hunt breakfasts held at country estates. Menus for the latter featured claret cups, *pâtes* of pheasant, coddled quail eggs, fish puddings, sweetbreads, herring, aspics, lamb, hot breads, creams, and cakes.

Today the English still enjoy substantial, although less elaborate, morning meals which generally include bacon with eggs, sausage with bacon, and grilled tomatoes and mushrooms, creamed fish, kippers with boiled potatoes, grilled kidneys on toast, oatmeal porridge, crisp toast with marmalade, and tea or coffee.

The English have also become noted for an institution called "Bed and breakfast" which means that at reasonable rates travelers can have a good place to sleep in private homes and a great morning meal, usually comprising such fare as stewed prunes, berries in season, homemade brown and oatmeal breads, poached or scrambled eggs, sausage or bacon, preserves, and tea.

The English breakfast owes a great deal to the Scots who have long eaten more substantial repasts than either the English, Welsh, or Irish. "If an epicure could remove by a wish in quest of sensual gratification, wherever he had supped, he would breakfast in Scotland," wrote Samuel Johnson after a visit there in 1776.

The earliest Scots breakfast featured solid basic fare such as ham, sirloin, barons of beef, venison, and "whets," strong ale, mead, and drams of Scotch. They also enjoyed their native Aberdeen sausage, Dundee orange marmalade, oatmeal porridge, and many breads like the bap (yeasted roll), bannock, and scone.

Scottish breakfasts were great social events often heralded by the skirl of bagpipes, and tables were laden with smoked salmon, kippers, Finnan haddie, smoked goose, mutton, game, porridges flanked by pitchers of cream and buttermilk, hot breads of many varieties, and marmalades, accompanied by tea.

In one of his novels Sir Walter Raleigh expressed his disdain for some changes in the traditions. "When I come to a friend's house of a morning, I used to be asked if I had my morning draught yet. I am now asked if I had my tea. And in lieu of the big quaigh [cup or bowl] with strong ale and toast, and after a dram of good wholesome Scots spirits, there is now the tea-kettle put to the fire, the tea-table and silver and china equipage brought in, and marmalade and cream."

Early American breakfasts inherited many dishes and traditions from the cuisines of Britain and northern Europe. Yet the colonists utilized New World foods to make innovative specialties. In New England family breakfasts were substantial meals featuring hot porridges, pancakes with maple syrup, meat hashes, pork cakes, codfish balls or cakes, fried trout, sausages, ham, beefsteaks wrapped in buckwheats, cold and hot baked beans, baked bean sandwiches with bacon, corn breads and mush, brown bread, doughnuts, and assorted pies. In coastal areas lobsters, oysters, and all kinds of fish were staple fare.

In "Down East Breakfast," Robert P. Tristam Coffin philosophized about his favorite meal. "Weather, mother of good poetry, is also mother of good breakfasts. The solider the weather, the solider the meal. The sharper the air, the sharper the appetite. Maine runs to fine breakfast as it runs to fine poetry.

"Maine breakfast . . . It is a symphony concert of the north, the proper prelude to manhood, a three-ring circus of dough, of meat, of sweet, of fat."

A celebrated breakfast in 1879 at Boston in honor of Dr. Oliver Wendell Holmes, the poet laureate of the breakfast table, was considerably more elegant. Holmes and his distinguished friends dined on littleneck clams, grilled trout, sautéed cucumbers, an omelet with mushrooms in cream, grilled plover, fillet mignon, asparagus with hollandaise sauce, ice cream, strawberries, cakes, and coffee.

Dutch settlers in New York ate what could best be described today as an old-fashioned American breakfast, one that started a family's day with a sense of well-being. Here is an apt description of the heart-warming fare: "Tart apples baked with maple syrup and currants; a porringer of oatmeal dotted with butter and covered with cream spooned out of a pitcher; fresh laid eggs fried in bacon fat, with home-cured, hickory-smoked ham or bacon on the side; or a brace of pork or lamb chops, or a small steak, beef or venison, or corned beef hash topped with a poached egg, or shad roe likewise decorated, or calves liver and bacon or kidneys, or creamed salt codfish or codfish cakes, or a mess of five-inch brook trout dredged in corn meal and fried in bacon fat, or succulent fried salt pork with milk gravy; with sidedishes of fried potatoes, or fried apple rings, or fried hominy, or fried corn meal mush—and always fresh doughnuts and buckwheat cakes, to fill up the chinks. Homemade peach or wild strawberry jam, apple butter, and maple syrup and honey to top off the appropriate items satisfied any lingering craving for a full meal. Descendants of the old Dutch settlers usually added a dish of mild cheese. With these vittles, according to a New York State 1959 booklet called "Year of History Dutch Treats," went a pot of boiling strong coffee, strong enough to float a lump of sugar!"

The Pennsylvania Dutch were also hearty eaters who relished potato pancakes, stewed dried fruits, preserves, sugar cakes, sticky and cinnamon buns, and their treasured crusty fried scrapple served with eggs, fried apples, applesauce, or maple syrup.

The most lavish early American breakfasts, however, were those served in antebellum days on Southern plantations. They began with eye-openers of bourbon, juleps, rum drinks, punches, cordials, shrubs, flips, claret cups, or other spirits. Then came cold turkey, country hams and sausage, cured meats, varieties of hominy, shrimp, potted salmon, creamed chicken, game birds, eggs by the platter full, batter cakes, waffles, sweet potato pies and puddings, a variety of hot breads, preserves, and cheese pies.

The closest resemblance to such repasts that one enjoys today are the Kentucky Derby breakfasts, held each year since 1875 on the morning of the race. Then elegant homes and restaurants set tables with fine appointments and offer such traditional fare as mint juleps, thinly sliced country ham, turkey and chicken hash, baked cheese grits, spoon bread, scrambled eggs, Kentucky scramble, thin corn-meal pancakes, sausage patties, fried apples, assorted sweet rolls, Derby chocolate pie, pecan pie, or bourbon balls.

To this day, Southerners also enjoy their famed hunt breakfasts which feature similar dishes but also game birds—broiled quail on toast, roast pheasant or pheasant hash. Emily Post was evidently not impressed with such entertaining which she dismissed in a few words. "A hunt breakfast is just a stand-up luncheon. It is a 'breakfast' by courtesy of half an hour in time. At twelve-thirty it is breakfast, at one o'clock it is lunch." Hunt breakfasts, however, have become the *dernier cri* in restaurants and feature many of the best dishes of the South.

In Charleston, South Carolina, traditional breakfasts are still served and include such dishes as cold and hot shrimp, shrimp paste, hominy with eggs and bacon, fish roe, creamed chicken on waffles, and beaten biscuits.

At opulent breakfasts enjoyed in the West and on trains around the turn of the century, diners could choose from a repertoire of the most expensive foods available—grilled salmon, oysters, beef fillets, racks of lamb, game, scallops of veal, hangtown fry (oysters and eggs), countless accompaniments, and sweet omelets and rich desserts.

America's colorful Diamond Jim Brady began his breakfast with a full gallon of orange juice, followed by eggs, hominy, chops, beefsteak, fried potatoes, corn bread, muffins, and flapjacks.

Those who fondly recall the marvelous and satisfying breakfasts of days gone by will agree with Nathaniel Hawthorne who wrote, "Life within doors has fewer pleasantries than a neatly arranged and well-provisioned breakfast table."

With the trend to rush after rising and the related emphasis on easy-to-prepare and convenience foods, the good breakfasts of yester-year began to disappear from the American scene in recent decades. Thankfully, the morning meal is back in style, both in the home and in restaurants that feature great "early riser specials" or similar presentations.

Certainly "Breakfast at Brennan's," a marvelous institution in New Orleans, did a great deal to popularize the glamour of this morning meal. The origins of the custom began, perhaps, in the mid-1800s when Begue's, a legendary and colorful coffee house operated by a local Creole, was open only for breakfast. Workers from the French Market across the street flocked to the eatery for a second breakfast in late morning. Soon it became a fashionable gathering place where the smart set enjoyed such Sunday breakfast fare as snails, crawfish, tripe, omelets, steaks, herbed tomatoes, desserts, fruits, coffee, and brandy.

Brennan's, founded in 1946 and now located in a lovely setting at 417 Royal Street, is world famous for its breakfast, believed to have been conceived by the late Lucious Beebe, and highly publicized with his help. As their extensive menu, decorated with the trademark of the colorful cock, explains: "Turn back the clock to the time when the

French aristocrats of New Orleans dined in leisurely elegance, when breakfast was served in the patio amidst the soft rustle of exotic plants, a refreshing breeze from the palmetto fans and the romantic aromatic of magnolia blossoms."

You begin breakfast on the spacious patio with a local eye-opener—Absinthse Suissesse, Sazerac, Milk Punch, or perhaps New Orleans gin fizz.

In one of the many charming dining rooms you agonize about what to choose from the lavish breakfast selections. Particularly noteworthy are the oyster and onion soups, grilled grapefruit with kirsch, Creole cream cheese with fresh fruit in season; omelets and eggs in sophisticated styles; entrées of pompano, chicken livers, meats such as veal grillades and steaks. Finally the marvelous desserts—sweet omelets, flambéed *crêpes*, bananas Foster, and then *café* Brûlot or *café au lait*. It is truly a marvelous way to enjoy breakfast.

Although Brennan's calls their lavish morning meal a breakfast, many devotees consider it brunch. Forerunners of today's brunch can be traced to late morning meals around the world. In China, for example, it has long been the practice to serve steamed filled dumplings and other tempting morsels of foods called *dim sum* with tea at a midday meal.

In France during the Revolution it became customary to take a second breakfast, *déjeuner,* including eggs and meat as well as coffee and breads, at about 11 A.M. Later the meal was extended into luncheon.

Austrians still relish their custom of pausing in mid-morning for a second, or fork, breakfast of goulash, sausages, or some other warming fare, with a glass or two of spirits, and in Germany there are several variations of the same idea. Once it was a substantial meal about 11 A.M. preceded by *schnapps.* Now it is generally beer with sausages, goulash soup or ham with bread. You can also have a "hangover repast" with spirits, herring of some kind with sour cream, or a hot soup or stew.

Where our modern brunch originated is a matter of conjecture. Some say the inspiration came from England, where the word was coined and where elegant post-wedding feasts and after-the-hunt morning meals have long been popular. Others say it was in New York. Many persons believe it originated in New Orleans from the *grand déjeuner* or "big breakfast" of the Louisiana Creoles. Possibly it was when elaborate dining and after-midnight parties were fashionable in the late 1800s. Lazy risers found the breakfast hour past and lunchtime imminent. The happy solution was a rather elegant combination of the two meals.

However it was named, Sunday brunch has become an American institution, the "conventional" brunches that had been favorite informal weekend meals for some time becoming an infatuation by the mid-1960s: Witness the popularity of this meal in every American city where cafes, restaurants and hotel dining rooms feature informal and formal meals with all kinds of drinks and food specialties. You can choose from Ye Olde Sunday Brunch, A Moveable Champagne Feast, A Bubbling Sunday Brunch, Brunch Louisiana Style, Brunch New York Style, Bruncheon, or Eat as Much as You Want Brunch.

In Washington, D.C., where brunch is now an acclaimed phenomenon, it was Clyde's, the stylish bar-restaurant in Georgetown, that initiated the area's craze for the lively meal. On Sunday the barrooms, omelet room, and New Orleans-like atrium are alive with a crowd that loves people-watching and conviviality, and relishes the spicy Bloody Marys, the orange and grapefruit Screwdrivers, Mimosas (freshly squeezed orange juice and champagne), champagne, burgers with multiple toppings, seafood specialties, omelets, egg dishes, sinfully rich desserts, and coffee creations.

At the recently opened Clyde's in Tysons Corner, Virginia, acclaimed as an architectural extravaganza, you can drink and snack at the central main bar or choose to dine on the Palm Terrace, in the Cafe, the Oyster Bar, or Grill. Popular brunch specialties include such innovative omelets and egg dishes as Ira's Eggs (slices of lox and cream cheese on a toasted bagel, topped with poached eggs and Hollandaise sauce), Kentucky Scramble (eggs scrambled with corn, bacon, onions, green and red peppers, and served in a popover), quiches, creamed chipped beef on an English muffin with fresh broccoli, an Oyster Fry, stuffed fillet of sole, or salads.

Desserts range from warm apple crisp served with Häagen Dazs ice cream and New York-style cheesecake with fresh strawberries to sorbets and chocolate strawberries Grand Marnier, fresh strawberries spiked with Grand Marnier, dipped in chocolate and served with fresh whipped cream.

Especially good are the Irish and Spanish coffees, espressos, and cappuccinos, like Cappucino L'Amore—a blend of crème de cacao, light rum, gin, brandy, Galliano, cloves, cinnamon, hot espresso and cocoa powder served topped with a dollop of whipped cream and a dash of cinnamon.

For many persons brunch is the most convenient—and afford-able—meal for entertaining. Everything about the event is flexible. It can be as early as 11 A.M. or as late as 1 P.M. The occasion may be a well-planned celebration for a special event or a casual get-together for no particular reason. You can have a brunch for two persons, for six or eight, or for as many guests as you wish. Generally the number of persons will depend on the type of meal and how many the entertaining area will accommodate.

While the brunch menu can be a simple one, similar to a breakfast, it may include three or four courses, after the fashion of a luncheon. Generally the food is satisfying but on the light side. You can serve it casually or formally, either indoors or out. While a brunch is a flexible meal, it should not be haphazard, and it is best to plan it so that much of the food preparation is done in advance, leaving only some minor last-minute cooking or reheating if it is for a large number of persons.

While brunch is now a congenial weekend happening, I wonder if it will ever be as treasured a meal as the breakfasts that inspired these writers to mention their favorite fare. Kenneth Roberts, for example, wrote: "Pork and wine wouldn't be bad for breakfast . . . a little pork and a lot of wine." On the other hand, Elizabeth Robins Pennell had different ideas: ". . . the tiny, round radish, pulled in the early hours of the morning, still in its virginal purity, tender, sweet, yet peppery, with all the piquancy of the young girl not quite a child, not yet a woman . . . on the breakfast table it is the gayest poem that uncertain March can sing . . . Bread and butter . . . will serve as sympathetic background, and enhance rather than lessen its charm."

Obviously we all have our own ideas about what to enjoy for breakfast or brunch. This book offers suggestions and recipes for as many tastes as possible. Some of the dishes can be prepared for a few persons; others for many. They encourage international experimenta-tion with all kinds of possibilities. While the range is limitless, selec-tions have been made to provide fare that is not only appealing but an interesting variation on the usual culinary repertoire. I hope that both the text and the recipes will enhance the pleasure of cooking and serving these marvelous morning and midday meals.

SUGAR SUBSTITUTES

Artificial or synthetic sweeteners with no- or low-calories come in several brands as liquids or solids and can be substituted for sugar in drinks, some desserts, and other dishes. For cooking and baking, it is preferable to use recipes specially designed for them. They do not give the same texture in baking and do not have the preservative quality of sugar. See the product package for equivalent amount.

1

Eye-Openers

The informal nature and relaxed atmosphere of breakfasts and brunches call for superb introductory drinks, eye-openers that will get the conversation flowing and lend gaiety and spontaneity to the gathering.

Everyone has his or her own favorite eye-opener. The choice can range from bottled mineral waters and fruit juices to mild apéritifs or mixed alcoholic drinks. The best are tangy, soothing, refreshing, and appropriate for the occasion and time of year.

Over the years people have created hundreds of drinks that would perk up or stimulate the appetite at any early hour. By now the selection offered at bars and restaurants or prepared in the home includes not only the traditional favorites but the modern creations with such off-beat names as Tropical Itch, Red Hot Mama, Suffering Bastard, Shark's Tooth, and Woozy Suzzy, all most often made as elaborate alcoholic concoctions and served in as grandiose a manner as possible.

More basic and excellent for breakfasts are fresh, canned, or frozen fruit and vegetable juices. You don't have to stick with the conventional orange, grapefruit, or tomato juice. Try papaya, mango or tangerine juice, singly or in combination. Also good are specialties such as bottled white grape or tangy apple juice, either American or imported. Serve chilled in pitchers or bottles to be drunk alone or with a nip of alcohol for those who wish it.

Many purists contend that the most palatable and suitable early day drink is chilled *brut* or *blanc de blancs* champagne, or a mixture thereof, that can be served before and throughout the meal. It goes with almost all kinds of food, requires only one glass, and can be easily and attractively served.

Also appealing are white wine on the rocks or a spritzer—two-thirds chilled white wine and one-third chilled club soda. Reliable standbys are also chilled sherry, preferably *finos* (amontillado or manzanilla), red or white Dubonnet and aromatized dry or sweet white and red vermouths (including French Noilly Prat and Italian Cinzano), served straight over ice cubes with a twist of lemon or orange peel or a dash of bitters.

If you're looking for drinks that are low in alcohol and appealing in taste, consider the many kinds of apéritifs based on aromatic wines. Much in vogue now are Lillet, made from white wine, brandy and herbs; the lesser known French Byrrh, flavored with quinine and spiked with brandy; and Italian Cynar, made from artichokes—all served with club soda on the side.

Also increasingly popular in our country are the so-called bitter apéritifs, based on wine, quinine, aromatic roots, and other flavorings. Try Italian Campari and Punt e Mes, or French Amer Picon on the rocks with a twist of lemon peel and a splash or more of club soda or water.

For a different drink, serve licorice- or anise-based drinks such as French Pernod, American Herbsaint, or Greek ouzo which, when mixed with water, turn milky. Or you can enjoy Scandinavian caraway-flavored aquavit, made from potato or grain spirits and drunk straight and ice-cold from small glasses. For further attraction, freeze the aquavit bottle in a block of ice and serve from the bottle.

There are a number of delicious mixed alcoholic drinks suitable for morning and midday. Particularly popular, in addition to the fizzes, coolers, punches, and slings, are those made with fruit and vegetable juices. Many "recipes" call for non-alcoholic beverages, spirituous liquors, or wines and "smoothing agents" such as cream, milk, eggs, fruit, and sweet syrups.

Many hostesses and hosts prefer to set up a bar and let everyone choose and make his or her own drink. On the other hand, you can offer a prepared punch or a particular drink that goes with the type of food, say a Margarita with Mexican fare or a May Wine Bowl with German dishes.

There is now no limit to the kinds and quantity of drink ingredients that one can offer, since our stores are stocked with specialties from around the world. Generally, however, cost of the selections, entertaining space, and the number of guests must be considered.

As for equipment, you can have an elaborate array or a few necessary items. Drinks can be served in cocktail, champagne, wine, sherry, old-fashioned, highball, collins, or sour glasses, as well as in mugs, cups, large goblets or even, a current fashion, mason jars. You also need some bar equipment such as a shaker and mixing glass, strainer, stirrers, shot glasses, corkscrew, and perhaps a lemon/lime squeezer and ice crusher.

Proportions and preferences for drinks may vary according to the taste of the individual maker and drinker. Given below are suitable standard directions, and suggestions for international drinks that I think are the best of hundreds of possibilities and that are currently in fashion for breakfasts and brunches.

Alcoholic Eye-Openers

Here are my suggestions for breakfast and brunch drinks. As a guideline:

> 1 jigger = 1½ ounces or 3 tablespoons
> 1 pony = 1 ounce or 2 tablespoons
> 4 ounces = ½ cup
> 1 ounce = 2 tablespoons
> 1 highball glass = 6 to 9 ounces
> 1 collins or tall glass = 10 to 12 ounces
> 1 old-fashioned glass = 6 ounces or large, 10 ounces
> 1 cocktail glass = 3 to 4 ounces

Bloody Mary

This is America's most popular morning and midday drink. There are many tales about when, where, and how it was created. Most authorities say it was the inspiration of a bartender, Fernand Petiot, who brought the drink from Paris to New York in 1934. By the end of World War II it had become a great favorite across America and was highly touted as a hangover "remedy." Since then the drink has become increasingly celebrated, and numerous variations of the basic vodka-tomato juice formula have been devised. Seemingly every devotee of the libation has an opinion about what should be used to make it, and how it should be done. Most agree that it is best to make the drink with fresh top-quality ingredients and to combine them just before serving. Here are my suggestions and a good traditional recipe.

Alcohol: Use any kind of vodka; a recommended amount is 1½ ounces vodka with 3 ounces tomato or other kind of juice.

Juice: Most drinks are made with tomato juice; the best kind is a heavy variety such as Sacramento or one made with fresh tomatoes. You can also use V-8 juice, Beefamato juice or Clamato juice. Substitute sauerkraut juice, clam juice or bouillon for half the tomato juice, if desired.

Seasonings: Purists use Tabasco or hot sauce, Worcestershire sauce, salt and freshly ground pepper to taste; some persons like celery salt or seed or cayenne pepper; do not use soy sauce, mustard, or other "strangers."

Lime or Lemon Juice: While either lime or lemon juice may be used, lime is preferable as it is less tart. Squeeze just before making the drink.

To shake or stir: There are two schools of thought about making a Bloody Mary: the stirrers and shakers. Purists contend that the drink is not well mixed if the ingredients are put in a glass and stirred. They maintain that the drink is best blended by shaking by hand in a cocktail shaker but not in a blender which makes it too foamy.

1½ *ounces vodka*
3 *ounces heavy tomato juice, or other juice*
Juice of ½ lime or lemon
3 *to 4 dashes Tabasco sauce*
2 *to 3 dashes Worcestershire sauce*
Salt and freshly ground pepper to taste
1 *lime or lemon wedge or slice*

Put ingredients, except lime or lemon wedge or slice, with ice in a cocktail shaker; cover; shake well; strain into a chilled highball or old-fashioned glass over ice cubes. Add lime or lemon wedge or slice. Makes 1 drink.

Champagne Cocktail

This is an elegant drink for a special-occasion breakfast or brunch.

1 *lump sugar*
2 *dashes orange bitters*
1 *twist of lemon or orange peel*
1 *split (about 6 ounces) chilled dry champagne*

Put sugar in a chilled champagne or large wine glass; sprinkle with bitters. Add lemon or orange twist. Fill glass with champagne. Makes 1 drink.

Daiquiri

The most celebrated rum drink in America is the refreshing and tart daiquiri which is generally made with light rum, lime juice, and sugar. It was created by an American engineer living in Cuba near the town of Daiquiri in the 1890s. Since then the classic drink has been made in many colorful variations with ingredients ranging from bananas to ice cream, as well as the popular "frozen" drink that is whirled in an electric blender. Here are some appealing daiquiris.

Basic Daiquiri

2 *teaspoons freshly squeezed lime juice*
1 *teaspoon powdered sugar*
1½ *ounces light rum*

Combine ingredients with ice in a cocktail shaker, cover, shake well, and strain into a chilled cocktail glass. Makes 1 drink.

Frozen Daiquiri

> 4 teaspoons freshly squeezed lime juice
> 2 teaspoons sugar, Triple Sec or Cointreau
> 3 ounces light rum
> 2 cups crushed ice

Combine ingredients in an electric blender container, cover, and blend 60 seconds or until consistency of fine snow. If mixture freezes around blades they will stop revolving. Remove cover and, with a rubber spatula, carefully break surface, scraping frost from sides of container into center. Spoon into large chilled stemmed glasses. Serve with short straws. Makes 2 drinks.

Banana Daiquiri

> 2 ounces light rum
> 1 tablespoon banana liqueur, sugar or Cointreau
> 1 tablespoon freshly squeezed lime juice
> ½ banana, peeled and cut up
> ½ cup crushed ice

Combine ingredients in an electric blender container, cover, and blend several seconds, until smooth. Spoon into a chilled stemmed glass. Makes 1 drink.

Frozen Pineapple Daiquiri

> 1½ ounces light rum
> 4 canned pineapple chunks
> 1 tablespoon freshly squeezed lime juice
> 1 teaspoon sugar
> 1 cup crushed ice

Combine ingredients in container of an electric blender; blend as in frozen daiquiri. Serve in a chilled champagne glass. Makes 1 drink.

Gin Fizz

The original gin fizz was created in the late 1800s by Henry C. Ramos. He had a bar in New Orleans where it became an attraction to pass the drinks in shakers down along a line of barmen each of whom gave the drink another shake until it became a creamy and fizzy sensation. In New Orleans the drink became known as the Ramos gin fizz and it is still one of the city's most popular libations. Over the years a great many other fizzes have been created; called about every possible name from Apple Blow to Violet, and using numerous kinds of alcohol with or without an egg white. All are tangy and refreshing, and particularly good in the early morning or at midday. An electric blender is now generally used as a replacement for the "shaker boys."

Basic Gin Fizz

    1 tablespoon freshly squeezed lemon juice
    1 teaspoon powdered sugar
    2 ounces dry gin
      Cold soda water
    1 thin slice of lemon

Combine lemon juice, sugar and gin with ice in a cocktail shaker, and shake well. Strain into a highball glass over two ice cubes, fill with soda water and stir. Garnish with lemon slice. Makes 1 drink.

Ramos Gin Fizz

    1 tablespoon freshly squeezed lemon juice
    1 teaspoon powdered sugar
    1 tablespoon cream
    ½ teaspoon orange flower water
    1 egg white
    2 ounces dry gin
      Cold soda water

Combine ingredients, except soda water, with ice in a cocktail shaker, cover, shake vigorously about 10 times, strain into a highball glass over two ice cubes, fill with soda water, and stir. Makes 1 drink.

Mimosa

This popular eye-opener combines two great early day beverages, orange juice and champagne.

    1 split (about 6 ounces) chilled dry champagne
    2 ounces freshly squeezed orange juice
    1 tablespoon Cointreau

Pour ingredients into a chilled large stemmed glass; stir. Makes 1 drink.

Piña Colada

This frothy refreshing drink, made with rum, coconut cream, and pineapple juice, was created by a Puerto Rican bartender in the early 1950s and is now made in fascinating variations that include bananas, peaches, and strawberries or other fruits, as well as ice cream. You can serve the drink in a tall glass, or in a hollowed coconut or pineapple shell attractively garnished with fresh fruit or flowers. This is the classic Puerto Rican recipe.

3 *ounces light rum*
3 *tablespoons coconut cream*
2 *tablespoons heavy cream*
3 *tablespoons crushed pineapple*
2 *cups crushed ice*
1 *pineapple spear*

Combine ingredients, except pineapple spear, in the container of an electric blender. Cover and blend several seconds, until smooth. Pour into a tall glass. Garnish with pineapple spear. Makes 1 drink.

Note: For a richer drink, add vanilla ice cream to taste.

Margarita

Almost everyone thinks of this drink as Mexican because it is made with tequila, a Mexican alcoholic beverage named for the town where it is made. According to legend, however, it was created by a Virginia City, Nevada, bartender in memory of his girl friend who died in his arms after being shot by a stray bullet during a saloon brawl.

Salt
1½ *ounces tequila*
½ *ounce Triple Sec or Cointreau*
1 *ounce freshly squeezed lime or lemon juice*

To prepare the glass, moisten the rim by rubbing with lime or lemon rind; turn upside down and press the rim into a mound of salt on a small plate, giving glass a spin so the salt clings to it. Combine ingredients with ice in a cocktail shaker, cover, shake well, and strain into the prepared glass. Sip the drink over the salted edge. Makes 1 drink.

Milk Punch

You can make up a large quantity of this drink beforehand and chill until ready to serve.

> 2 *ounces bourbon, rum, or brandy*
> 1 *cup cold milk*
> 1 *teaspoon sugar*
> *Dash vanilla extract*
> *Freshly grated or ground nutmeg*

Combine ingredients, except nutmeg, with ice in a cocktail shaker. Cover, shake well, and strain into a chilled mug or glass. Sprinkle top with nutmeg. Makes 1 drink.

Screwdriver

Some devotees of the popular orange-vodka drink called a screwdriver insist that it was created in the historic and enchanting city of Istanbul, Turkey. Who knows? It has a colorful name and has long been a favorite morning libation.

> 2 *ounces vodka*
> 6 *ounces freshly squeezed orange juice*
> *Dash orange bitters or orange-flower water (Optional)*

Pour vodka into a tall or stemmed glass over ice cubes. Add orange juice, stir, and add bitters or flower water, if desired. Makes 1 drink.

Some Other Good Alcoholic Eye-Openers

Absinthe Frappé

In New Orleans during the mid 1800s drinks made with absinthe—a potent green liqueur flavored with wormwood—were the rage in bars of the city's French Quarter. Later the sale of absinthe was banned in America and other countries but the name lingered on in several drinks of New Orleans. This and the following eye-opener are now made with an absinthe substitute.

> *½ teaspoon sugar syrup*
> *1½ ounces absinthe substitute (Pernod, Herbsaint or Ojen)*
> *1½ ounces chilled club soda*

Fill an old-fashioned glass with crushed ice. Add syrup and absinthe substitute. Slowly add soda water, frappéing with a spoon while adding, until glass is chilled. Makes 1 drink.

Absinthe Suissesse

> *1½ ounces absinthe substitute (Pernod, Herbsaint, or Ojen)*
> *2 tablespoons light cream*
> *1 egg white*
> *1 tablespoon orgeat (almond-flavored) or sugar syrup*

Combine ingredients with ½ cup crushed ice in a cocktail shaker. Cover, and shake vigorously until frothy and smooth. Pour into a chilled cocktail glass. Makes 1 drink.

Americano

This Italian apéritif can be served with or without club soda.

> *2 ounces Campari*
> *2 ounces sweet vermouth*
> *Club soda (optional)*
> *1 twist of lemon peel*

Pour Campari and vermouth into an old-fashioned glass over two ice cubes. Add a splash or more of soda, if desired. Add lemon peel. Makes 1 drink.

Bacardi

This drink is named for the light Bacardi rum.

> 1½ ounces light rum
> 1 tablespoon freshly squeezed lime juice
> ½ teaspoon grenadine

Combine ingredients with ice in a cocktail shaker; cover, shake well, and strain into a cocktail glass. Makes 1 drink.

Batida

In Brazil a national drink called a *batida* is made with fruit juice, with or without alcohol. The name means "whipped" or "beaten," since the drink is shaken until frothy. This is one popular version.

> 1½ ounces light rum
> ½ teaspoon sugar
> 1 tablespoon freshly squeezed lemon juice
> 1 egg white
> ½ thin slice of lemon

Combine ingredients, except lemon slice, with ice in a cocktail shaker. Cover, shake vigorously, and strain into a chilled cocktail glass, the rim previously moistened with water and dipped in sugar, if desired. Make a small slit in the lemon slice and place on the edge of the glass. Makes 1 drink.

Black Russian

This is a colorful vodka-coffee liqueur drink.

> 1½ ounces vodka
> ¾ ounce Kahlùa or coffee liqueur

Pour ingredients into an old-fashioned glass over ice cubes; stir. Makes 1 drink.

Black Velvet

This English stand-by is made of equal parts of chilled champagne and stout. The drink takes its name from the dark color of the stout. You will find that it's an interesting combination.

> 6 *ounces chilled stout*
> 1 *split (about 6 ounces) chilled dry champagne*

Pour stout into a chilled silver mug or tall glass. Carefully pour champagne over it so the two liquors do not mix. Do not stir. Serve at once. Makes 1 drink.

Bull Shot

You can serve this drink either cold or hot.

> 1½ *ounces vodka*
> 3 *ounces strong cold beef bouillon*
> 1 *or 2 dashes Worcestershire sauce*
> *Dash salt and pepper*

Combine ingredients with ice in a cocktail shaker. Cover, shake well, and pour into an old-fashioned glass over two ice cubes. Makes 1 drink.

Note: Another version is to combine vodka or bourbon with hot bouillon and to serve the drink hot.

Cuba Libre

The name of this drink means "free Cuba" and it was created by American soldiers in Cuba during the Spanish-American War when Cuban rum was readily available and cola was a comparatively new American beverage.

> 1 *tablespoon freshly squeezed lime juice*
> 2 *to 3 ounces light rum*
> 6 *ounces cola (approximately)*
> 1 *thin slice of lime*

Pour lime juice into a tall glass over two ice cubes. Add rum, fill glass with cola. Garnish with lime slice. Makes 1 drink.

Daisy

You can make this colorful sweet drink with any kind of alcohol.

1 tablespoon freshly squeezed lime or lemon juice
½ teaspoon powdered sugar
1 teaspoon grenadine or raspberry syrup
2 ounces gin or other alcohol
   Club soda (optional)
   Fresh fruit spears

Combine ingredients, except soda and fruit spears, with ice in a cocktail shaker. Cover, shake well, and strain into a chilled mug or tall glass over ice cubes. Add a little soda water and garnish with 1 or 2 fruit spears. Makes 1 drink.

Fish House Punch

This classic punch which originated in Philadelphia is a superb drink for a large brunch.

   Juice of 12 lemons
   Powdered sugar
1½ quarts brandy
 1 pint peach-flavored brandy
 1 pint dark rum
 1 quart soda water
 1 pint strong tea (optional)

Combine lemon juice with sugar to taste; pour over a block of ice in a punch bowl. Add remaining ingredients. Decorate the top with whole or sliced fresh fruits of your choice, if desired. Serve in punch glasses. Makes 4 quarts.

Floradora Cooler

This refreshing tall drink is a good summer eye-opener.

1 tablespoon freshly squeezed lime juice
½ teaspoon powdered sugar
1 tablespoon grenadine or raspberry syrup
2 ounces club soda
2 ounces gin
   Ginger ale to taste

Combine lime juice, sugar, grenadine or syrup, and soda water in a tall glass over two ice cubes; stir. Add gin and fill glass with ginger ale; stir again. Makes 1 drink.

Gimlet

This sweet gin-lime drink originated in the Far East where it has long been a great favorite. Its name derives from the sharp tart taste that is said to resemble that of a gimlet, a sharp small tool used for boring.

> *1 ounce Rose's lime juice*
> *2 ounces gin*

Combine ingredients with ice in a cocktail shaker; cover; shake well; strain into a chilled stemmed glass. Add a little cold water, if desired. Makes 1 drink.

Golden Dream

> *½ ounce Triple Sec*
> *1 ounce Galliano liqueur*
> *1 tablespoon light or heavy cream*
> *1 tablespoon freshly squeezed orange juice*

Combine ingredients with ice in a cocktail shaker; cover; shake well; strain into a cocktail glass. Makes 1 drink.

Harvey Wallbanger

> *1½ ounces vodka*
> *6 ounces freshly squeezed orange juice*
> *½ ounce Galliano liqueur*

Pour vodka and orange juice into a tall glass over ice cubes. Float Galliano on top. Makes 1 drink.

Hot Buttered Rum

This is an excellent winter drink.

1 lump or 1 teaspoon sugar
Boiling water
1 teaspoon butter or margarine
2 ounces light rum
1 cinnamon stick (optional)
Freshly grated or ground nutmeg

Put sugar in a mug or a large old-fashioned glass. Fill ⅔ full with boiling water. Add butter or margarine and rum; stir. Add cinnamon stick. Top with nutmeg. Makes 1 drink.

Hurricane

In New Orleans this traditional drink is served in a tall glass shaped like a hurricane lamp.

1 ounce dark rum
1 ounce light rum
1 tablespoon passion fruit syrup
2 teaspoons freshly squeezed lime or lemon juice

Combine ingredients with ice in a cocktail shaker; cover; shake well; strain into a cocktail shaker. Garnish with an orange slice and Maraschino cherry, if desired. Makes 1 drink.

Jack Rose

This is a flavorful pink-colored drink made with applejack that has long been popular in America.

2 ounces applejack
1 tablespoon freshly squeezed lemon juice
1 teaspoon grenadine

Combine ingredients with ice in a cocktail shaker; cover; shake well; strain into a chilled cocktail glass. Makes 1 drink.

Kir

This French drink, named for Canon Felix Kir, the late mayor of Dijon, the city where it was created, was originally called *Vin blanc Cassis* as it is made with dry white wine and *crème de cassis,* a black currant liqueur.

> *6 ounces chilled dry white wine*
> *1 to 1½ ounces cassis liqueur*

Pour wine into a large wine glass. Add cassis to taste; stir. Serve at once. Makes 1 drink.

Le Gare du Nord

This apéritif was popular in Parisian cafes in the 1920s.

> *1½ ounces dry vermouth*
> *1½ ounces sweet vermouth*
> *1 twist of lemon peel*

Pour vermouths into an old-fashioned glass over ice cubes. Add lemon peel. Makes 1 drink.

Mai-Tai

This colorful potent drink from Polynesia and Hawaii is made in many fascinating variations that are generally garnished attractively with fresh fruit and/or flowers. You can serve it in a large stemmed glass or a coconut shell.

> *2 ounces dark rum*
> *1 ounce light rum*
> *1 ounce Curacao or Triple Sec*
> *1 tablespoon freshly squeezed lime juice*
> *1 tablespoon orgeat (almond-flavored syrup) or sugar syrup*
> *1 ounce 151 proof rum*

Combine ingredients, except 151 proof rum, in an extra-large glass or other container about ⅓ full of cracked ice; stir. Top with 151 proof rum. Garnish with a wedge of fresh pineapple and a sprig of fresh mint or float a fresh flower on top, if desired. Serve with small straws. Makes 1 drink.

May Wine Bowl

This delicate German wine punch is flavored with woodruff, a woodland herb with an appealing sweet scent, that is grown in America and sold at herb shops and nurseries. This is a traditional spring drink.

½ cup woodruff (optional)
½ cup sugar
2 bottles (⁴/₅ quart each) dry white wine
3 cups whole strawberries, washed and stemmed
1 bottle (⁴/₅ quart) dry champagne, chilled

Combine woodruff, ¼ cup sugar, and wine in a large bowl. Leave at room temperature. Combine 2 cups strawberries and ¼ cup sugar; chill. When ready to serve, strain wine mixture over a block of ice in a punch bowl. Add sweetened strawberries, remaining strawberries, and champagne. Serve in punch cups. Serves 12.

Mint Julep

Few persons agree on the proper way to make a mint julep and controversies have raged for years over whether or not the mint should be crushed, the kind of whiskey to be used, and the proper method of serving. Consequently, there are innumerable "recipes" for this drink which, of course, is traditional at Kentucky Derby breakfasts and brunches but is also good for other occasions. Here is one version from Kentucky. Always serve ice-cold.

1 heaping teaspoon powdered sugar
2 teaspoons water
6 small tender fresh mint leaves
2 to 3 ounces bourbon whiskey

Dissolve sugar in water in a chilled silver mug or cup or a tall glass. Add 4 sprigs mint and bruise gently with a muddler or spoon. Fill mug, cup or glass with crushed ice; stir. Add whiskey. Put in refrigerator or freezer until well frosted, if desired. Just before serving, add a final dollop of whiskey and garnish with 2 mint leaves. Serve at once with or without a small straw. Makes 1 drink.

Mojito

This is a refreshing Cuban rum drink.

½ teaspoon sugar
1 tablespoon freshly squeezed lime juice
2 ounces light rum
2 drops orange bitters
 Cold club soda
2 sprigs fresh mint

Combine sugar and lime juice in a tall glass. Add rum, bitters, and 2 or 3 ice cubes. Fill glass with soda. Garnish with mint. Makes 1 drink.

Moscow Mule

Despite its name, this is an American drink that was dreamed up to promote the sale of vodka in the United States.

2 to 3 ounces vodka
1 tablespoon freshly squeezed lime juice
4 to 6 ounces cold ginger beer

Pour vodka and lime juice in a mug or tall glass over ice cubes. Fill with ginger beer to taste. Garnish with a lime wedge, if desired. Makes 1 drink.

Negroni

This is an Americano laced with gin or vodka.

¾ ounce dry gin or vodka
¾ ounce sweet vermouth
¾ ounce Campari
 Club soda (optional)
1 twist of lemon peel

Combine gin or vodka, vermouth, and Campari with ice in a cocktail shaker; cover; shake well; strain into an old-fashioned glass over two ice cubes. Add a little soda water, if desired. Add lemon peel. Makes 1 drink.

Orange Blossom

This drink originated during Prohibition when it was made with bathtub gin.

1½ ounces gin
1½ ounces freshly squeezed orange juice
½ teaspoon powdered sugar
1 half slice orange

Combine gin, orange juice, and sugar with ice in a cocktail shaker; cover; shake well; strain into a cocktail glass. Garnish with orange slice. Makes 1 drink.

Orange Nog

This vodka-orange drink also includes an egg.

2 ounces vodka
1 cup freshly squeezed orange juice
1 egg
Few drops lemon juice

Combine ingredients in an electric blender container. Blend 30 seconds. Pour into a large old-fashioned glass over ice cubes. Makes 1 drink.

Pisco Sour

This stimulating Peruvian drink is made with Pisco brandy, a fragrant, nearly clear liquor unique to Peru and Chile but sold in America. Hot and cold drinks made with the brandy have been popular in America since the mid-1800s.

2 ounces Pisco brandy
1 teaspoon sugar syrup
1 egg white
1 or 2 dashes orange bitters
1 teaspoon freshly squeezed lime or lemon juice

Combine brandy, syrup, egg white, and bitters with ice in a cocktail shaker; cover; shake well; add lime or lemon juice; shake vigorously until frothy. Strain into a chilled cocktail glass. Makes 1 drink.

Planter's Punch

This traditional Caribbean drink is made with just about any kind of rum, generally dark, but also with light, or a combination of both, and fruit juice. The classic recipe is given in a popular Island Jingle: "One of sour, two of sweet, three of strong, and four of weak," or one part lime juice, two parts sugar, three parts rum, and four parts water or ice. This is one good version.

> *1 tablespoon freshly squeezed lime juice*
> *2 teaspoons sugar*
> *3 ounces dark rum*
> *1 or 2 dashes orange bitters*
> *Cold club soda*
> *Garnishes: 1 lime or lemon slice, 1 stick fresh pineapple, 1 Maraschino*
> *cherry*

Combine lime juice, sugar, rum, and bitters with ice in a cocktail shaker; cover; shake well; pour into a chilled tall glass over ice cubes. Add soda water to taste. Add garnishes. Top with grated nutmeg, if desired. Makes 1 drink.

Prairie Oyster

This zesty drink has long been touted as an effective hangover "remedy" and is a good eye-opener for any "ailing" guests.

> *1½ to 2 ounces brandy*
> *2 teaspoons catsup*
> *2 teaspoons Worcestershire sauce*
> *1 teaspoon vinegar*
> *1 grinding black pepper*
> *Dash hot pepper sauce*
> *1 egg*

Combine ingredients with ½ cup crushed ice in an electric blender container; cover; whirl several seconds. Serve in an old-fashioned glass over ice cubes. Makes 1 drink.

Red Eye

This tomato juice-beer drink was popular years ago in America and is now featured in many restaurants as a popular brunch eye-opener.

2 *ounces cold tomato juice*
4 *ounces cold beer*

Pour tomato juice over ice cubes in a stemmed or large old-fashioned glass. Top with beer. Stir. Makes 1 drink.

Rob Roy

This Scottish drink takes its name from a famous Highland outlaw. It has been a popular drink in America for devotees of Scotch whisky.

1½ *ounces Scotch whisky*
¾ *ounce sweet vermouth*
2 *dashes orange bitters*

Combine ingredients with ice in a cocktail shaker; cover; shake well; strain into a cocktail glass. Makes 1 drink.

Salty Dog

This drink with an innovative name does include salt.

2 *ounces gin or vodka*
4 *to 5 ounces grapefruit juice*
  Salt to taste

Pour gin or vodka into a large old-fashioned or tall glass over ice cubes; add grapefruit juice and a dash or more of salt; stir.

Sangria

This great Spanish and South American punch can be easily prepared beforehand, refrigerated, and attractively served in a pitcher.

1 *bottle (.75 liter) dry red wine*
  Juice of 1 orange
  Juice of ½ lemon
¼ *to* ⅓ *cup sugar*
1 *orange, peeled and sliced*
  Spiral of orange and lemon peel
  Cold club soda to taste

Combine wine, orange and lemon juices, and sugar in a large

pitcher; stir. Add orange slices and orange and lemon peels. Refrigerate 1 hour or longer. Stir before serving. Add soda to taste. Pour into chilled wine glasses. Serves 4 to 6.

Sangrita

This Mexican drink is called "little blood" for its red color. It is made with a spicy combination of tomato, orange and lime juices and is drunk with an accompaniment of tequila.

> 2 *ounces tomato juice*
> 2 *teaspoons freshly squeezed orange juice*
> 2 *teaspoons freshly squeezed lime juice*
> 1 *teaspoon grated onion*
>   *Pinch cayenne pepper or few drops hot sauce*
> 1 *shot glass of tequila*

Combine ingredients, except tequila, in a large glass; chill to blend flavors. Serve in an old-fashioned glass over ice cubes accompanied by tequila. Or add tequila to juice mixture to make a cocktail, if desired. Makes 1 drink.

Sazerac

This distinctive potable is the best known New Orleans drink. It is named for the Sazerac-le-Forge brandy with which the drink was originally made in 1859 in the Sazerac Coffee House, a flourishing bar in the French Quarter. In 1870 absinthe was added to the drink, and later American rye whiskey replaced the brandy. Now a Sazerac is made with an absinthe substitute and rye or bourbon. To mix the drink, you need two glasses.

> 1 *lump sugar*
> 2½ *ounces rye or bourbon whiskey*
> 2 *or 3 drops orange bitters, preferably Peychaud of New Orleans*
> 1 *drop Angostura bitters*
> 2 *dashes absinthe substitute (Pernod, Herbsaint or Ojen)*
> 1 *twist of lemon peel*

Combine sugar with a little water to moisten it in a mixing glass; stir to dissolve the sugar. Add rye or bourbon, bitters, and 3 ice cubes; stir. Pour absinthe substitute into a chilled cocktail or old-fashioned glass;

tip from side to side to "perfume" the inside of the glass. Strain the whiskey mixture into the glass. Squeeze lemon peel over the drink so that a little oil from peel is added. Serve at once. Makes 1 drink.

Sidecar

This tart drink was invented in Paris during World War I and was named after a motorcycle sidecar in which an American Army captain was driven to his favorite bar where the drink was created and christened. Over the years the ingredients have been changed.

2 teaspoons freshly squeezed lemon juice
1 ounce Cointreau or Triple Sec
2 ounces brandy

Combine ingredients with ice in a cocktail shaker; cover; shake well; strain into a chilled cocktail glass. Makes 1 drink.

Singapore Sling

Drinks called "slings" are sweetened combinations of alcohol to which a liqueur and lemon juice are added. They have long been favorite morning libations. The name comes from a German word meaning "to swallow." This version is said to have been created in the Raffles Hotel in Singapore by a bartender who added cherry brandy to the usual gin drink.

1 tablespoon freshly squeezed lemon juice
1 teaspoon powdered sugar
2 ounces gin
1 ounce cherry brandy
 Cold water or club soda

Combine ingredients, except water or soda, with ice in a cocktail shaker; cover; shake well; strain into a tall glass over ice cubes. Fill with water or soda. Garnish with a slice or spear of fresh fruit, if desired. Makes 1 drink.

Tequila Mockingbird

This appealing green-colored drink can be served either as a cocktail or a tall drink.

 1½ *ounces tequila*
 ¾ *ounce green* crème de menthe *(cream of mint)*
 1 *tablespoon freshly squeezed lime juice*
  Cold club soda (optional)
 1 *thin slice of lime*

Combine tequila, cream of mint, and lime juice with ice in a cocktail shaker; cover; shake well; strain into a cocktail glass or tall glass; add soda to taste to the latter. Garnish with lime slice. Makes 1 drink.

Tequila Sunrise

This popular Mexican or Western drink is a colorful potable that was supposedly named because someone looked at a sunrise, made a drink to look like it, and enjoyed the taste.

 2 *ounces tequila*
 4 *ounces freshly squeezed orange juice*
 ½ *ounce grenadine*
 1 *thin slice of lime or orange*

Pour tequila and orange juice into a tall glass over ice cubes. Slowly add grenadine and allow to settle. Stir before drinking. Make a small slit in a lime or orange slice and place on the side of the glass. Makes 1 drink.

Tom Collins

This well known drink was originally made with Old Tom gin, once sold as a sweet gin and considered to be the perfect liquor for making a Collins. A lesser known drink, John Collins, was and is made with Dutch gin, or genever.

 1 *tablespoon freshly squeezed lemon juice*
 1 *teaspoon powdered sugar*
 2 *ounces dry gin*
  Cold club soda
  Garnishes: 1 thin slice of lemon, 1 thin slice of orange, and 1
   maraschino cherry

Combine lemon juice, sugar, and gin with ice in a cocktail shaker; cover; shake well; strain into a tall glass over ice cubes. Fill glass with soda water. Garnish with fruit. Serve with a straw. Makes 1 drink.

Velvet Hammer

1½ ounces vodka
1 ounce white crème de cacao *(cream of chocolate)*
1 tablespoon light or heavy cream

Combine ingredients with ice in a cocktail shaker; cover; shake well; strain into a cocktail glass. Makes 1 drink.

Vermouth Cassis

3 ounces dry vermouth
About 1 ounce cassis liqueur
Cold club soda (optional)

Pour vermouth over ice cubes in an old-fashioned glass; add cassis to taste and a little soda water, if desired; stir. Makes 1 drink.

Whiskey Sour

Drinks called "sours" are made with lemon juice, sugar, and any of the basic liquors. They are appealing and tart. Some versions also include an egg white or a whole egg.

2½ ounces blended whiskey or bourbon
1½ tablespoons freshly squeezed lemon juice
1 teaspoon powdered sugar
½ thin slice of orange
1 maraschino cherry

Combine whiskey or bourbon, lemon juice, and sugar with ice in a cocktail shaker; cover; shake well; strain into a sour glass. Garnish with orange slice on side of glass. Add cherry to drink. Makes 1 drink.

Non-Alcoholic Eye-Openers

Apricot Shake

1 cup cold milk
1 cup apricot nectar
½ cup vanilla ice cream

Combine ingredients in the container of an electric blender; blend smooth. Makes 2 drinks.

Banana Smoothee

¾ cup milk
½ ripe banana, peeled and cut-up
½ cup vanilla ice cream

Combine ingredients in an electric blender container; blend smooth. Makes 1 drink.

Coffee Shake

1 cup strong coffee
½ cup coffee ice cream
Dash cinnamon

Combine ingredients in an electric blender container; blend smooth. Makes 1 drink.

Cider, Spiced

1 quart sweet cider
¼ cup sugar
6 whole cloves
¼ inch piece stick cinnamon
8 whole allspice
⅛ teaspoon salt

Combine ingredients in a large saucepan; bring to a boil; cool and let stand overnight. When ready to serve, strain and reheat. Serve hot. Serves 4.

Egg Nog

1 *cup milk*
1 *egg*
2 *teaspoons sugar*
¼ *teaspoon vanilla extract*
   Grated nutmeg

Combine all ingredients except nutmeg in an electric blender container; blend smooth. Sprinkle on the grated nutmeg. Makes 1 drink.

Grapefruit Pecos

1 *egg separated*
1 *cup chilled grapefruit juice*
1 *tablespoon honey*
   Dash salt
   Grated nutmeg

Beat egg yolk in a small bowl until creamy. Gradually add grapefruit juice, beating constantly. Add honey and salt. Beat egg white until stiff but not dry in a medium-sized bowl. Add grapefruit mixture. Pour into a chilled glass. Top with nutmeg. Makes 1 drink.

Lemonade, Old-Fashioned

4 *large lemons*
¾ *cup hot water*
½ *cup sugar*
6 *cups cold water*

Roll lemons on a flat surface. Cut in halves; squeeze juice into a pitcher. Slice halves and put in a small bowl. Cover with hot water; cool. Strain and add to lemon juice. Add the sugar and cold water; stir to dissolve sugar; chill. Makes 6 drinks.

Orange Punch

3 *cups orange juice*
2 *cups pineapple juice*
2 *bottles (12 ounces each) ginger ale*

Combine juices in a pitcher; chill. Just before serving add ginger ale. Serve in a punch bowl. Makes 7 to 8 drinks.

Strawberry Nog

1 cup milk
1 egg
½ cup partially thawed strawberries

Combine ingredients in an electric blender container; blend smooth. Makes 1 drink.

Tomato Cocktail

1 cup tomato juice
1 tablespoon lemon juice
½ teaspoon Worcestershire sauce
⅛ teaspoon celery salt
  Dash Tabasco

Combine ingredients; chill 1 hour or longer. Makes 1 drink.

Tomato-Yogurt Pick-Up

½ cup chilled tomato juice
½ cup chilled plain yogurt
2 tablespoons chopped fresh parsley
1 teaspoon fresh lemon juice

Combine ingredients in a glass; mix well. Makes 1 drink.

2

Good Beginners

Good beginners, such as canapes, dips, relishes, fruits, vegetables, pastries and other imaginative dishes, are very important overtures to breakfasts and brunches since they set the scene for the rest of the meal, and for the occasion. They should stimulate the appetite, please the palate, and attract the eye.

Fortunately we have a wide variety of selections to serve before the meal, or as the first course, but the choice should be made carefully so that the offering is compatible with the food to follow. Each must contrast with or complement the other in color, taste, and texture.

Individual and national tastes differ considerably about what's good to eat as morning or midday fare. While fruit and fruit juices are popular in North and South America, in the Middle East the morning staples are cubes of white cheese, unleavened bread, raw vegetables, and yogurt. In Japan and Korea soup is a traditional part of breakfast. The Chinese have long savored an array of *dim sum,* or appetizers, as midday fare; while in Scandinavia and Israel the day begins with a number of tangy dishes, including those made with cheese, fish, and vegetables.

Although there are no hard and fast rules about what to serve as appetizers, the choice of fare should generally be light rather than

41

heavy, a few rather than several dishes, and foods that are not too highly seasoned or overpowering and are easy to serve and handle. Some can create a special atmosphere, such as a Spanish appetizer before a Spanish meal, while also being appropriate for the season— such as a cold soup before an outdoor event in summer.

Specialties featuring fruit juices and fruit are always excellent choices for breakfasts and brunches. Consequently, many suggestions and recipes are given for making and serving them. While there are many well known traditional fruit appetizers, the old standbys can be made more attractive and palatable with additions and garnishes.

Seafood, particularly shellfish such as oysters, lobsters, clams, shrimp, and crabmeat, are also treasured selections for morning or midday meals. They can be served simply with lemon juice or a piquant sauce, as cocktails, in salads and soups, or in special dishes. Caviar or fish roe, tuna and salmon are also good choices.

Because these meals are intended to be enjoyed at leisure, most of the beginners in this chapter can be totally or partially prepared beforehand and served without a great deal of trouble.

The following is an assortment of international specialties, designed and selected to enlarge the scope of your possibilities.

Fruit

Fruit, whether fresh, dried or cooked, is a superb beginner for any breakfast or brunch. While just about any kind can be served, certain fruits have particular appeal for these meals. Therefore, I have only given specific data and recipes for avocados, grapefruit, melons, oranges, pineapples and strawberries, as well as suggestions for serving other fruits.

AVOCADOS

The avocado is a superb fruit because it is very adaptable. Its rich, nutlike taste blends with both bland and strong flavors and is appealing at an early hour. The fruit has a particular affinity for seafood, especially crabmeat, and combines well with artichoke hearts, chicken, citrus fruits, mushrooms, pineapples, and tomatoes. It can be served simply in the half-shell, with only a little vinegar and oil, salt and pepper; or a half-shell can be filled with diced fresh fruit, marinated seafood, dilled cucumbers and sour cream, chicken or vegetable salad. Use seasoned mashed avocados to make dips or spreads; cubed or sliced avocados for cocktails and canapes. It is essential that the avocado be fully ripe. Here are two easy avocado recipes.

California Avocado-Tomato Cocktail

2 *large ripe avocados*
2 *tablespoons fresh lemon juice*
3 *large tomatoes, peeled and chopped*
2 *tablespoons prepared horseradish*
2 *tablespoons chopped chives*
1 *cup dairy sour cream*
  Salt, pepper to taste

Peel avocados; remove seeds; cut into bite-size cubes; sprinkle with lemon juice. Combine with remaining ingredients in a large bowl; refrigerate. Serve in the bowl or in individual small dishes. Serves 8.

Mexican Avocado Dip

1 *large ripe avocado*
2 *tablespoons fresh lemon juice*
1 *tablespoon grated onion*
1 *clove garlic, crushed*
1 *cup chopped peeled tomatoes*
2 *teaspoons chili powder*
  Salt, pepper to taste

Peel avocado; remove seed; mash with a fork or purée in an electric blender. Put in a small bowl; add lemon juice and remaining ingredients; mix well; refrigerate. Serve with corn chips or raw vegetables. Makes about 2 cups.

GRAPEFRUIT

Here are some recipes and suggestions for serving white or pink grapefruit.

Broiled Grapefruit

Halve 1 grapefruit crosswise; remove any seeds; loosen grapefruit sections. Sprinkle with any of the following: 1 to 2 tablespoons sugar and ½ teaspoon ground cinnamon; 1 to 2 tablespoons honey and 1 tablespoon light rum; 2 to 3 tablespoons honey, jelly or maple syrup, dotted with butter or margarine; or 1 to 2 tablespoons brandy or sherry. Put under preheated broiler a few minutes, until topping melts and grapefruit is browned around edges. Serves 2.

Brennan's Grilled Grapefruit

Halve 1 grapefruit crosswise; remove any seeds; loosen grapefruit sections. Sprinkle each top with 2 tablespoons sugar and 2 tablespoons kirsch. Put under preheated broiler a few minutes, until top begins to brown. Garnish each with a maraschino cherry and 2 sprigs fresh mint. Serves 2.

Grapefruit-Crab Cocktail

3 cups grapefruit sections
2 cans (7¾ ounces each) crabmeat, cleaned
   Salad greens
   About ¾ cup Russian or Italian dressing

Combine grapefruit sections and crabmeat in a bowl; refrigerate. Serve in sherbet glasses lined with salad greens. Top with dressing. Serves 6.

Fruit Topped Grapefruit

Halve 1 grapefruit crosswise; remove any seeds; loosen grapefruit sections. Top with sliced fresh strawberries or preserves; or add champagne or dry sherry; refrigerate until ready to serve. Serves 2.

Fruit-Filled Grapefruit

Fill 2 cleaned grapefruit halves with a combination of chopped grapefruit sections and orange sections and fresh berries. Add champagne or a liqueur, if desired; refrigerate until ready to serve. Serves 2.

MELONS

You can make any number of appealing beginners with canta-loupes, casabas, cranshaws, honeydews or watermelons.

Melon with Port

Pour 2 ounces of port wine into the cleaned cavity of half a canta-loupe, or other kind of melon; let stand 30 minutes before serving.

Melon with Prosciutto

Top thin slices or strips of any kind of melon with 2 or 3 thin slices of prosciutto (or other kind of ham) for each serving. Serve with a wedge of lime or lemon and freshly ground pepper, if desired.

Note: Substitute 2 fully ripe white or purple-skinned fresh figs for the melon, if desired.

Melon Balls with Sherbet

Arrange an assortment of melon balls in small bowls or stemmed glasses. Top with a spoonful of raspberry or orange sherbet and a sprig of fresh mint.

Melon Halves with Sherbet

Place a scoop of pineapple or raspberry sherbet in a cleaned melon half. Top with 2 tablespoons puréed raspberries.

Garnished Melon Circles

Cut a cantaloupe or honeydew melon into halves, crosswise. Remove seeds; cut fruit into circular slices. Put fresh berries or halved seedless grapes in center; sprinkle with fruit juice or a liqueur.

Melon Delight

1 cantaloupe
2 cups fresh blueberries
½ cup honey
2 tablespoons fresh lemon juice
1 tablespoon chopped candied ginger

Cut cantaloupe in half; remove seeds; cut out flesh into balls. Combine melon balls with blueberries in a bowl. Combine remaining ingredients; pour over fruit; mix. Serve in small bowls. Serves 4.

Tipsy Watermelon

Make a plug in a large watermelon and fill with an alcoholic beverage such as champagne, brandy or rum. Replug. Leave 24 hours, turning several times so beverage will penetrate the fruit. Cut as you wish.

Watermelon Bowl

> 1 *round watermelon*
> ½ *to ¾ cup sugar*
> ¼ *cup water*
> 10 *cups prepared melon balls: use any kind*
> 1 *cup chilled dry white wine or champagne*

Cut a slice of rind from one end of watermelon so it will stand upright. Stand watermelon on cut end. Cut off top of watermelon and make a scalloped or rick-rack edge with a sharp knife around the rim. Cut melon balls from melon and scoop out remaining fruit to make a bowl. Refrigerate melon and balls. Combine sugar and water in a small saucepan; bring to a boil; cool and chill. Just before serving, pile watermelon balls and other balls into shell; add sugar syrup and wine or champagne. Garnish with sprigs of fresh mint. Serves 12.

Note: The exact amount of melon balls will depend of the size of the melon so the number of cups may vary.

ORANGES

The popular sweet orange can be served attractively sliced or in sections sprinkled with sugar and Cointreau, with whipped cream and a little orange marmalade or grated coconut and light rum. Here are some other suggestions.

Mexican Orange Appetizers

Arrange peeled and cleaned thinly sliced seedless oranges on a platter or individual serving plates, allowing 1 orange per serving.

Sprinkle with orange juice, powdered sugar and a little ground cinnamon.

Orange "Flowers"

Cut an unpeeled orange into 8 wedges or "petals" and separate into sections. Garnish with a whole fresh strawberry and sprinkle with powdered sugar.

Caribbean Orange-Fruit Cups

Cut a half-inch slice from the top of each orange. Scoop out segments and any remaining membrane with a curved grapefruit knife. Scallop edges. Fill cups with chopped orange segments, bananas, and dates or nuts. Sprinkle with orange juice or light rum. Refrigerate 3 or 4 hours. Garnish with a fresh mint leaf.

Note: A variation is to fill each cup with a combination of chopped orange segments and fresh berries. Sprinkle with dry sherry or Marsala wine.

PINEAPPLES

One of our most appealing fruits is the pineapple, a popular canned food but more delectable when eaten fresh. Here are some ideas for serving it.

Fresh Pineapple

With a sharp knife cut a ripe pineapple through fruit and crown in half lengthwise, then cut halves lengthwise to make four quarters. Cut away hard fibrous core leaving the crown on. Loosen fruit by cutting close to rind to separate fruit from shell, preferably with a carved grapefruit knife. Replace in shell. Cut fruit crosswise through loosened fruit, then cut lengthwise to make bite-size pieces. Serve plain or with other fruits, sprinkled with orange juice, rum, or a liqueur, and sweetened with brown sugar, if desired.

Fresh Pineapple In Shell

Cut a thick slice, including crown, from top of a ripe pineapple. Discard any blemished leaves from crown and set aside to use as a lid.

Cut around fruit between pulp and shell with a sharp knife, prefera- bly curved, and make a deep criss-cross down through bottom of fruit and lift out four quarters. Discard center core; cut fruit into finger shapes; return to shell. Sweeten fruit to taste, if desired, add about ⅓ cup light rum, brandy or a liqueur. Refrigerate several hours.

Note: Add fresh berries, seedless grapes or cut-up fresh fruit to fresh pineapple, if desired.

Hawaiian Pineapple-Seafood Appetizer

1 fresh ripe pineapple
2 cups cleaned chopped cooked shrimp, crabmeat or lobster
½ cup chopped peeled tart apples
⅓ cup mayonnaise or dairy sour cream
1 tablespoon fresh lemon juice
  Salt, pepper to taste

Cut pineapple according to directions under fresh pineapple. Remove and dice fruit. Combine with remaining ingredients and spoon into pineapple shell with crown still on. Refrigerate until ready to serve. Serves 4.

STRAWBERRIES

Firm, well shaped fresh strawberries with a full red color are superb beginners.

Fresh Strawberries

Allow 6 washed strawberries with stems per person; put in a circle on a small serving plate, perhaps over a large fresh green leaf on the plate, around a mound of powdered sugar or sweet or sour cream for dipping. Or arrange in a large bowl with small side dishes of sugar and cream for everyone to help him- or herself.

Fresh Strawberry Fruit Cup

Strawberries have an appealing tart flavor and combine superbly with such fruits as bananas, rhubarb, melons, oranges, and/or pineapples in fruit cups. This is one idea.

1½ *cups sliced fresh strawberries*
1½ *cups diced fresh pineapple*
1½ *cups diced fresh oranges*
  Sugar to taste (optional)
  Cointreau, Triple Sec or champagne

Combine fruits in a large bowl; sweeten to taste, if desired. Add liqueur or champagne to taste. Refrigerate 1 hour or longer. Serve in stemmed glasses. Garnish with a fresh mint leaf, if desired. Serves 6.

OTHER FRUITS

Apples: Serve fresh apple wedges or slices with Cheddar cheese cubes; hot baked apples, filled with chopped nuts, topped with cream or sprinkled with honey or cinnamon sugar; applesauce, sweetened with honey or cinnamon sugar, topped with cream or chopped nuts and raisins.

Apricots: Serve canned or fresh apricots topped with slivered almonds, or whipped cream, fresh berries, or a spoonful of sherbet. Serve poached apricots with heavy cream and a liqueur.

Bananas: Serve sliced bananas with orange juice and brown sugar, or sweet or sour cream. Serve sliced bananas and another fresh fruit sprinkled with fruit juice and chopped nuts.

Berries: Serve berries in a cantaloupe half or orange "basket" sprinkled with powdered sugar; serve berries with brown sugar or maple syrup and sweet or sour cream; or with Cointreau and a spoonful of vanilla ice cream.

Cherries: Serve cooked or canned cherries with plain or whipped cream and kirsch, if desired.

Cranberries: Serve sweetened canned or cooked cranberries with sour cream and grated nutmeg.

Figs: Serve sliced fresh or canned figs with heavy cream and slivered almonds; or combine with cooked rhubarb and top with whipped cream.

Grapes: Serve whole seedless grapes over melon wedges or topped with sour cream and brown sugar.

Kiwi fruit: Serve sliced fresh kiwi fruit with a dash of lime or lemon juice and sugar, if desired; or combine fresh fruit slices with sliced fresh strawberries and pineapple and sprinkle with a little lime or lemon juice.

Mango: Serve sliced fresh mangos with grated coconut or a liqueur.

Papaya: Fill fresh papaya halves with fresh berries and top with whipped cream.

Peaches: Serve sliced fresh or canned peaches with dry red or white wine or light rum; serve baked or poached peaches with fruit juice or Cointreau and candied ginger.

Pears: Serve honey covered baked pears with cream; serve poached pears with candied ginger and cream, or sour cream or yogurt and chopped nuts.

Plums: Serve fresh pitted or canned prune-plums with whipped cream and grated nutmeg; or serve stewed plums with lemon juice and ground cinnamon.

Prunes: Serve canned or cooked prunes with brown sugar, ground cinnamon, and sour cream or in orange juice.

Rhubarb: Serve canned or cooked rhubarb with diced fresh apples or applesauce or with strawberries and cream.

Mixed Fruits: Serve a mixture of fresh fruits with a topping of sherbet; make a fruit platter with cut-up and whole small fresh fruit around a small bowl of cream cheese or yogurt, powdered sugar, and honey and lemon juice, for dipping. Garnish with fresh mint leaves.

Seafood Beginners

Here are some seafood suggestions and recipes.

Angels on Horseback

Wrap strips of thin bacon around small oysters; fasten with tooth-picks. Arrange in a shallow baking dish. Bake in a preheated 400° F.

oven or cook under broiler a few minutes, turning once, until bacon is crisp. Serve hot.

English Grilled Oysters

Arrange oysters in half shells, in pie pans, or shallow baking dish, allowing 4 to 6 per person. Top each with a spoonful of melted butter or margarine mixed with a little Worcestershire sauce, minced fresh parsley, salt, and pepper. Put under broiler until edges begin to curl. Serve with lemon wedges.

Clams or Oysters on Half Shell

Arrange clams or oysters in half shells, allowing 6 per person, on a bed of crushed ice in individual shallow bowls or on a large platter, with a container of cocktail sauce in the center. Garnish with lemon wedges.

Belgian Herbed Seafood Cocktail

Put chilled cooked shrimp, crabmeat, and/or diced lobster, allowing ½ cup per person, over shredded lettuce in stemmed glasses. Top with a spoonful of cocktail sauce made with ¾ cup chili sauce or mayonnaise, 1½ tablespoons fresh lemon juice, 2 tablespoons minced chives, 2 teaspoons horseradish, and 2 tablespoons minced fresh parsley or dill, seasoned with salt and pepper.

Southern Pan Roast Oysters

2 pints oysters, drained
½ cup butter or margarine, melted
Salt, pepper to taste
8 slices hot buttered toast

Arrange oysters in a buttered shallow baking dish; pour butter or margarine over them. Season with salt and pepper. Bake in a preheated 400° F. oven about 10 minutes, until edges curl. Serve at once on toast. Serve with lemon wedges and one or two dashes Worcestershire sauce on each, if desired. Serves 8.

Oysters Casino

You can also make this traditional dish with clams.

   24 *oysters on half shell*
    8 *slices thin bacon, chopped*
   1/3 *cup minced onions*
   1/3 *cup minced green pepper*
   ½ *cup chopped fresh parsley*
    1 *lemon*

Remove oysters from shells; scrub shells with a wire brush to remove any sand. Return oysters to shells. Place shells on a baking pan. Fry bacon in a small skillet to partially cook or until translucent; remove bacon from skillet; cut each slice into three pieces; set aside. Add onions and green pepper to bacon fat; sauté 1 or 2 minutes; stir in parsley. Spoon vegetable mixture over oysters. Top with a little lemon juice and a piece of bacon. Bake in a preheated 450° F. oven about 8 minutes, or until oysters are hot and bacon is crisp. Serve at once. Serves 4 to 6.

Other Beginners

Dutch Cheese Truffles

These bread-covered cheese balls, *kaastruffels*, can easily be made beforehand.

   ¼ *pound butter or margarine, softened*
   ¼ *pound grated Gouda, Edam, or other yellow cheese*
   ¼ *teaspoon paprika*
     Dash grated or ground nutmeg
     Salt and pepper to taste
  3-4 *slices pumpernickel*

Cream butter or margarine in a small bowl; add cheese, paprika, nutmeg, salt, and pepper; mix well; chill 20 minutes. Shape into tiny balls. Toast pumpernickel twice and whirl in an electric blender or crush with a rolling pin to make crumbs. Roll each cheese ball in crumbs; chill 2 hours or longer. Makes about 20.

Mexican Bean Dip

1 can (about 1 pound) pinto or red beans
1 medium-sized onion, finely chopped
2 tablespoons vegetable oil
½ teaspoon dried oregano
2 tablespoons chili powder
1 8 ounce can tomato sauce
   Salt and pepper to taste

Mash or purée beans; put in a medium-sized bowl. Sauté onion in heated oil in a small skillet until tender; add oregano and chili powder; cook 1 minute. Stir in tomato sauce; salt and pepper; cook slowly, uncovered, 10 minutes. Add to beans; mix well. Refrigerate until ready to serve. Serve with corn chips. Serves 8 to 10.

Canadian Cheddar Cheese Toasties

You can prepare these small open-face sandwiches beforehand and cook just before serving.

1 cup grated Cheddar cheese
2 tablespoons mayonnaise
2 teaspoons light cream or milk
1 teaspoon minced onion
½ teaspoon dry mustard
1 teaspoon Worcestershire sauce
   Dash of cayenne
4 slices white toast
2 slices thin bacon

Combine cheese, mayonnaise, cream or milk, onion, mustard, Worcestershire sauce, and cayenne in a small bowl; mix well. Remove crusts from toast and spread each with some of cheese mixture. Cut each slice into 5 strips. Cut bacon into small pieces and put on strips. Just before serving, put in a preheated 450° F. oven 5 minutes. Serve hot. Makes 20.

Spanish Garnished Tuna Appetizer

A good appetizer to serve at a small outdoor brunch.

 2 *cans tuna (about 7 ounces each), drained*
 1 *large red onion, sliced and separated into rings*
 1 *cup chopped red and green peppers*
 2 *tablespoons olive oil*
 1 *tablespoon red wine vinegar*
  Salt and pepper to taste
 8 *black olives*
 8 *green olives*

Break tuna into chunks and arrange on a serving plate. Top with onion rings and peppers. Sprinkle with oil, vinegar, salt, and pepper. Garnish with olives. Serves 8.

Indian Vegetable-Yogurt Dip

This is a good low-calorie dip.

 1 *medium-sized onion, chopped*
 1 *garlic clove, crushed*
 2 *tablespoons vegetable oil*
 1 *to 2 tablespoons curry powder*
 1 *teaspoon chili powder*
 2 *medium-sized tomatoes, peeled and chopped*
 1 *teaspoon minced hot green chilis (optional)*
 1 *cup diced, peeled, seeded cucumber*
 2 *cups plain yogurt*
  Salt and pepper to taste
 2 *tablespoons chopped fresh coriander or parsley*

Sauté onion and garlic in heated oil in a small skillet until tender. Add curry and chili powders; cook 1 minute. Remove from heat and combine with remaining ingredients, except coriander or parsley, in a serving bowl. Refrigerate 1 hour or longer. Serve, garnished with coriander or parsley, with Indian unleavened bread (*chapati*) or crackers. Serves 8.

Austrian Liptauer

This is an attractive tangy cheese mound that is prepared before hand and chilled to blend flavors.

 12 *ounces cream cheese*
 ½ *cup butter or margarine, softened*
 ¼ *cup chopped drained capers*
 2 *tablespoons chopped chives*
 2 *tablespoons finely chopped onions*
 4 to 6 *flat anchovy fillets, drained and minced*
 1½ *tablespoons prepared sharp mustard*
 3 *teaspoons paprika*
    Pepper to taste

Cream cheese and butter or margarine in a large bowl. Add remaining ingredients; mix well. Chill 2 hours or longer. Shape into a mound on a large serving plate. Serve with thin pumpernickel or rye bread slices. Serves 10 to 12.

Dutch Meatballs

These traditional Dutch appetizers are called *bitterballen* or meatballs, but are actually small croquettes.

 ¼ *cup butter or margarine*
 ¼ *cup all-purpose flour*
 1 *cup beef bouillon*
 1½ *cups minced or ground cooked meat (beef or veal)*
 3 *tablespoons grated onion*
 2 *tablespoons chopped fresh parsley*
 1 *teaspoon Worcestershire sauce*
    Dash freshly grated or ground nutmeg
    Salt and pepper to taste
    Fine dry breadcrumbs
 2 *eggs, beaten*
    Shortening or vegetable oil for frying

Melt butter or margarine in a small saucepan; stir in flour; cook 1 minute. Gradually add bouillon; cook slowly, stirring, until thickened and smooth; stir in meat, onion, parsley, Worcestershire sauce, nutmeg, salt, and pepper. Cook slowly, stirring occasionally, 15 minutes.

Remove from heat; spoon into a greased pie plate, spreading evenly. Chill 2 to 3 hours. Shape into small bite-size balls. Roll each in breadcrumbs, then in beaten egg and again in breadcrumbs. Refrigerate at least 1 hour. Fry in hot deep fat, 390° F. on frying thermometer, a few minutes, until golden brown. Drain on paper toweling. Serve hot with sharp mustard. Makes about 35.

French Stuffed Mushrooms

These are elegant appetizers that can be served on small toast rounds, if desired.

> 1 *pound large fresh mushrooms*
> *About 1/3 cup butter or margarine*
> *¼ cup minced shallots or scallions*
> 2 *cloves garlic, crushed*
> 1 *tablespoon olive oil*
> 2 *medium-sized tomatoes, peeled, seeded, and finely chopped*
> *½ teaspoon dried basil*
> *1/3 cup chopped fresh parsley*
> *Salt and pepper to taste*

Rinse mushrooms quickly or wipe with wet paper toweling to remove any dirt. Pull off stems and cut off any tough woody stems. Mince stems and set aside. Brush caps with about 2 tablespoons melted butter or margarine; arrange, hollow sides up, in a shallow baking dish.

Sauté shallots or scallions and garlic in 2 tablespoons heated butter or margarine and the oil in a small skillet until tender. Add minced mushroom stems; sauté 1 minute. Stir in tomatoes and basil; cook slowly about 4 minutes. Remove from stove; stir in parsley; season with salt and pepper. Spoon into mushroom caps, filling as full as possible. Bake in a preheated 375° F. oven about 12 minutes, until mushroom caps are tender. Serve hot. Makes about 20, the number depending on the size of the mushrooms. Use any leftover stuffing as a spread for crackers.

English Sausage Rolls

These fried sausages in flaky pastry "coats" are superb beginners.

24 *link pork sausages*
1½ *cups all-purpose flour*
¾ *teaspoon salt*
½ *cup shortening*
4 *tablespoons cold water*
1 *egg, beaten*

Partially cook sausages by frying in a large skillet to release almost all of the grease. Drain on paper toweling; cool. Sift flour and salt into a medium-sized bowl; cut in shortening with a pastry blender or two knives. Add water, enough to make a firm dough. Roll out on a lightly floured board or surface to make a thin pastry; cut into 24 strips, each 2½ x 3 inches. Place a sausage link in center of each strip; roll up, leaving ends of sausage out; seal pastry edges with a little cold water. Make a couple of small slashes across top of each roll. Brush tops with beaten egg. Arrange on a greased cookie sheet. Bake in a preheated 425° F. oven about 20 minutes, until pastry is crisp and golden. Serve hot. Makes 24.

Jewish Chopped Chicken Liver Appetizer

You can serve this traditional appetizer with matzo, crackers, or lettuce leaves.

1 *pound chicken livers*
2 *medium-sized onions, finely chopped*
¼ *cup butter or margarine*
3 *hard-cooked eggs, chopped*
   Salt and pepper to taste
3 *tablespoons chopped fresh parsley*

Drop chicken livers in boiling water in a medium-sized saucepan. Simmer a few minutes, until done; drain; chop finely; set aside. Sauté onions in heated butter or margarine in a skillet until tender. Add chopped chicken livers and remaining ingredients; mix well. Remove from heat and mash or blend to make a smooth paste. Chill. Serve with matzo or lettuce leaves. Serves 6 to 8.

Mexican Tacos

A good beginner for a brunch featuring Mexican food.

 2 *medium-sized onions, finely chopped*
 ¼ *pound Jack or Cheddar cheese, shredded or diced*
 1 *can (4 ounces) green chilies, seeded and chopped*
 2 *cups shredded lettuce*
 2 *medium-sized tomatoes, peeled and chopped*
    Salt and pepper to taste
 12 *hot prepared taco shells*
 2 *cups hot tomato sauce*

Combine onions, cheese, chilies, lettuce, and tomatoes in a medium-sized bowl. Season with salt and pepper; mix well. To serve, spoon filling into hot taco shells and top with tomato sauce. Makes 12.

Provençal Onion-Olive Pizza

 8 *medium-sized onions (about 6 cups), sliced*
 2 *or 3 garlic cloves, crushed*
 ½ *cup olive oil or mixture of olive and vegetable oil*
 2 *tablespoons butter or margarine*
    Salt and pepper to taste
 1 *package pizza dough mix (6¾ ounces) or equivalent homemade yeast dough for 1 12-inch pizza*
 1 *can (2 ounces) flat anchovies, drained*
 12 *pitted black olives*

Sauté onions and garlic in heated oil and butter or margarine in a medium-sized skillet until soft, being careful not to brown. Remove from heat; season with salt and pepper. Cool. Prepare and roll out dough; put in an oiled 12-inch pizza pan and push evenly with fingers until stretched to fit the pan. Crimp edges to form a rim. Let rest 10 minutes. Spread onion mixture evenly over dough. Make a lattice pattern with anchovies over onions. Place an olive in center of each square. Brush lightly with oil. Bake in a preheated 425° F. oven about 25 minutes, until crust is golden and filling is bubbly hot. Cool slightly. To serve, cut into pie-shaped wedges. Serves 10 to 12.

Russian Pirozhki

You can make these mushroom-stuffed small plump round pastries beforehand and freeze them, if desired. Serve as appetizers or with soup.

> 1 *envelope active dry yeast*
> ¼ *cup lukewarm water*
> ½ *cup butter or margarine*
> 1 *cup lukewarm milk*
> 1 *teaspoon salt*
> 2 *teaspoons sugar*
> 4½ *to 5 cups all-purpose flour*
> 3 *eggs*
> *Mushroom Filling (recipe below)*
> 1 *egg yolk*
> 2 *tablespoons cold water*

Sprinkle yeast in lukewarm water in a large bowl; let stand until dissolved. Put butter or margarine in lukewarm milk and leave until melted; add, with salt and sugar, to yeast. Stir in 1 cup flour and eggs, beating after each addition. Add remaining flour, enough to make a soft dough. Turn out on a lightly floured board or surface; knead until smooth and elastic. Form into a large ball; put into a large greased bowl; turn over. Cover with a clean light cloth and let rise in a warm place until double in bulk, about 1½ hours. Punch down dough. Turn out onto a lightly floured board; knead until smooth and elastic. Cut off small pieces of dough and flatten into thin circles, about 2½ inches in diameter. Place about 1 teaspoon of Mushroom Filling in center of each circle. Bring up dough around filling to secure completely and shape into a smooth round. Place on greased cookie sheets. Let rise, covered, with a clean light cloth, in a warm place for 20 minutes, or until *pirozhki* are light and somewhat larger. Mix egg yolk with water; brush tops with it. Bake in a preheated 400° F. oven about 20 minutes, until tops are golden and dough is baked. Serve warm. Makes about 3½ dozen.

Note: Or cool and place in plastic bags in freezer. When ready to use, brush with melted butter or margarine and warm in preheated 350° F. oven 20 minutes.

Mushroom Filling

½ *pound fresh mushrooms*
½ *cup finely chopped scallions, with some tops*
3 *tablespoons butter or margarine*
  Dash grated or ground nutmeg
  Salt and pepper to taste
¼ *cup dairy sour cream, at room temperature*
3 *tablespoons chopped fresh dill or parsley*

Rinse mushrooms quickly or wipe dry with wet paper toweling to remove any dirt; cut off any tough stem ends. Chop mushrooms finely. Sauté scallions in heated butter or margarine in a small skillet until tender. Add mushrooms; sauté 4 minutes. Season with nutmeg, salt, and pepper. Remove from heat; stir in sour cream and dill or parsley. Cool.

Greek Cheese-Filled Pastries

These squares or diamonds are made with sheets of a paper-thin pastry called *phyllo* that is sold in supermarkets and specialty food stores in 1-pound boxes or packages. It is better fresh than frozen.

½ *pound farmers' or feta cheese, crumbled*
4 *cups small-curd cottage cheese*
4 *eggs, beaten*
2 *tablespoons light cream or milk*
½ *cup chopped fresh parsley*
½ *pound prepared phyllo pastry in standard-sized sheets*
½ *pound butter or margarine, melted*

Combine cheeses, eggs, cream or milk, and parsley in a large bowl; mix well. Line a buttered 8-inch square baking dish with half the phyllo pastry sheets, brushing each sheet with melted butter or margarine and handling quickly, before putting in dish. Spread cheese mixture over phyllo sheets. Top with remaining sheets after brushing each with butter or margarine. Spread top with butter or margarine. Trim off any overhanging pastry. Mark off pastry into squares or diamonds. Bake in a preheated 350° F. oven about 1¼ hours, until filling is set and top is golden. Serve hot or lukewarm. Makes 12 pieces.

German Herring Appetizer

This tangy appetizer featuring pickled herring and sour cream can be served plain or with rye bread.

4 pickled herring, drained
1 cup sour cream
1 large dill pickle, chopped
2 tart apples, peeled, cored and chopped
2 large onions, chopped
  Salt and pepper to taste
3 tablespoons chopped chives

Cut herring into 1-inch pieces. Combine with sour cream, chopped pickle, apples, and onions; mix well. Season with salt and pepper. Refrigerate. Serve garnished with chives. Serves 4.

Middle Eastern Kibbe

This national Lebanese-Syrian appetizer is a mixture of cracked wheat (bulgur), raw meat, and seasonings. It is an innovative beginner for a small brunch.

1 cup fine cracked wheat (bulgur)
1 pound top quality lean ground lamb or beef, ground 2 or 3 times
1 large onion, finely chopped
½ teaspoon ground allspice
¼ teaspoon ground nutmeg or cloves
  Salt and pepper to taste
1 tablespoon butter or margarine, melted
2 tablespoons finely chopped scallions

Soak cracked wheat in water to cover 30 minutes. Drain off water. Squeeze grains by pressing between palms of the hands. Combine with meat, onion, spices, and salt. Turn out onto a wooden surface or put in a large bowl and combine thoroughly with the hands or a wooden spoon. Moisten hands with cold water to mix well. Place on a serving plate and shape into a mound. Refrigerate 1 hour before serving, if desired. Garnish top with melted butter or margarine and scallions. Serve with lettuce leaves or pita bread to use as "scoops." Serves 8.

Note: Have the meat freshly ground by a butcher or grind it in the home.

Polish Mushrooms In Sour Cream

2 *pounds fresh mushrooms*
1 *cup sliced scallions, with some tops*
¼ *cup butter or margarine*
2 *tablespoons fresh lemon juice*
2 *tablespoons all-purpose flour*
  Salt and pepper to taste
2 *cups dairy sour cream, at room temperature*
¼ *cup chopped fresh dill*

Rinse mushrooms quickly or wipe with wet paper toweling to remove any dirt; cut off tough stem ends. Slice lengthwise through stems. Sauté mushrooms and scallions in heated butter or margarine and lemon juice in a skillet 4 minutes, or until tender. Stir in flour and cook slowly, stirring, 1 minute. Season with salt and pepper. Mix in sour cream and dill; leave over low heat long enough to heat. Serve on small hot toast rounds. Serves about 12.

Provençal Anchoïade

You can make this pungent anchovy paste and keep it in the refrigerator to serve with crusty white or dark bread as an impromptu appetizer.

2 *2 ounce cans flat anchovy fillets, drained*
2 *large garlic cloves, crushed*
2 *tablespoons minced shallots or scallions*
3 *tablespoons finely chopped fresh parsley*
1 *tablespoon olive oil*
1 *teaspoon red wine vinegar*
  Freshly ground pepper

Mash anchovies in a small dish. Add remaining ingredients; mash to form a paste. Put in a small container or bowl and leave at room temperature to blend flavors. Refrigerate until ready to serve. To serve, spread bread with a little of the mixture. Makes about ⅔ cup.

Bulgarian Eggplant-Vegetable Caviar

Serve this colorful appetizer as a dip with crusty dark or white bread.

1 *medium-sized eggplant, about 1¼ pounds, washed*
2 *large green peppers, cleaned and minced*
2 *medium-sized tomatoes, peeled, seeded and minced*
2 *to 3 garlic cloves, crushed*
1 *small hot red or green pepper, seeded and minced (optional)*
⅓ *cup olive oil*
3 *tablespoons fresh lemon juice or red wine vinegar*
3 *tablespoons chopped fresh parsley*
  Salt and pepper to taste

Prick eggplant in several places with a fork; put on a cookie sheet. Bake in a preheated 400° F. oven until soft, about 50 minutes. When cool enough to handle, peel off and discard skin. Put pulp in a medium-sized bowl; chop with a wooden spoon or knife. Pour off any excess liquid. Add remaining ingredients; mix well. Cool. Refrigerate until ready to serve. Serve in a bowl or as a mound on a plate. Serves about 8.

Indian Appetizer Meatballs

1 *pound lean ground lamb or beef*
1 *small onion, finely chopped*
2 *cloves garlic, crushed*
1 *tablespoon ground turmeric*
1 *teaspoon ground coriander*
½ *teaspoon ground cumin*
¼ *teaspoon chili powder*
1½ *teaspoons salt*
½ *teaspoon pepper*
2 *tablespoons plain yogurt*
1 *teaspoon lemon juice*

Combine ingredients in a large bowl; mix well. Divide mixture into 24 portions. Shape each portion into a small sausage-shaped cylinder. String 2 cylinders onto each of twelve 7- or 8-inch wooden skewers. Cook over hot coals on a hibachi or broil in a preheated broiler about 6 minutes, until done. Turn once or twice during cooking. Serve at once. Serves 12.

English Potted Herbed Cheese

Keep this beginner in an attractive small pot or crock to serve as needed.

    ½ *pound grated Cheddar cheese*
      Dash cayenne
    3 *tablespoons softened butter or margarine*
      Pinch dry mustard
    ¼ *cup port or sherry*
    2 *tablespoons crushed fresh herbs (parsley, basil, oregano, thyme)*

Combine ingredients in a bowl; beat until smooth. Spoon into a small pot or crock; cover, refrigerate 24 hours or longer before serving. Leave at room temperature a short time before serving. Serve with crackers or crusty bread. Makes 1¼ cups.

A Jewish Bagel Brunch

Bagels are doughnut-shaped rolls made of a non-sweet leavened dough. First simmered in water and then baked, they have a hard glazed crust, chewy white interior, and bland flavor. The name presumably comes from *bongel*, an old German word for ring.

Bagels have an important and distinctive role in Jewish cuisine. They are staples in delicatessens and have long been traditional fare, split, spread with cream cheese and lox (smoked salmon), for Sunday breakfast.

In the United States, at first primarily in New York but now across the country, a home and restaurant brunch for Jews and non-Jews has come to mean bagels with as many accompaniments as one wishes. The food is usually and principally purchased from a delicatessen or neighborhood grocery.

Both water and egg bagels are available fresh and frozen everywhere. Besides these classics (water or egg), there are many other kinds seasoned with cinnamon, garlic, onions, poppy seeds, raisins, sesame seeds, or extra salt, and some relatively new ones—pumpernickel, rye and whole wheat. Purists scorn all of the faddist types.

You can eat bagels plain, split, or toasted, and spread with butter, cream cheese, orange marmalade, strawberry or cherry preserves.

For a Jewish, sometimes called a New York, brunch the bagels are halved, spread lavishly with top-quality cream cheese and topped with sliced lox and chopped onions and/or capers. The richness of lox calls for the blandness of cream cheese to neutralize its flavor. Instead of the rich fat belly lox, cut from the thick underside of the salmon, you can use the more delicate and less salty pale pink Nova Scotia salmon, cut in paper-thin slices. Other smoked fish such as carp, sable, sturgeon or whitefish, shiny gold on the outside, may be used.

Another bread that is often served at these brunches is the bialy, a flat round baked roll with a crisp texture, topped with onion flakes. The name comes from Bialystok, a city in northeast Poland.

It is very difficult to duplicate the goodness of commercially made bagels and bialys in the home kitchen. Thus it is best to buy top quality types of your choice rather than attempt to prepare them, unless you are an expert. (It goes without saying that fresh bagels and bialys are superior to the frozen varieties.)

MENU

Purchase and/or prepare an array of selections from the following and arrange attractively on a table with plates and serving implements for guests to help themselves. Buffet style is convenient.

Drinks: Orange juice, Mimosa or Screwdrivers

Breads: Bagels and bialys with side dishes of sweet butter, orange marmalade, cherry or strawberry preserves.

Cheese: Cream cheese, cream cheese spreads.

Fish: Lox, Nova Scotia salmon, smoked whitefish or sturgeon, herring (in wine, pickled, or in sour-cream sauce).

Vegetables: Sliced tomatoes, onions, cucumbers and/or green peppers.

Accompaniments: Black olives, capers, pickles.

Dessert: Jewish honey cake° and/or fresh fruit.

°See recipe on page 238.

A Chinese Dim Sum Brunch

The ancient custom of enjoying *dim sum,* an array of appetizers or bite-size foods, has become popular in America in Chinese restaurants as a week-end brunch. You can serve a similar meal at home.

Dim sum means "touch the heart" or "heart's delight." The term derives from the fact that the foods, prepared in small but satisfying pieces, are served whenever the heart, and stomach. craves them. While dim sum are served in China throughout the day as snacks, they are eaten as a meal at midday in tea houses.

Most people think of dim sum as an assortment of light and dainty savory or salted and sweet little dumplings, stuffed with meat, seafood, sweet pastes or preserves, and enclosed in a thin translucent dough or flaky pastry, made in an incredible variety of shapes, sizes, and colors, and baked, fried, or steamed.

While these dumplings are a form of dim sum, they are only one element of the many varieties. Also included might be spring rolls, shrimp toast, meatballs, deep fried puffs, spareribs, braised marinated meats, noodle dishes, soups, thick porridge-like dishes called congee, exotic specialties such as duck flippers with oyster sauce, and desserts—custards, puddings, and sweet dumplings.

In Chinese restaurants you choose whichever dim sum you wish, from menus or large trays or rolling carts. The whole idea is to try a number of the small portions. Small cups of fragrant green tea accompany the dim sum.

The art of making the intricate dim sum dumplings is complex, as you need special Chinese foods and equipment for preparing and cooking them. There is also considerable chopping, wrapping, and folding which requires a great deal of time. Unless you are an expert in preparing the dumplings, you should purchase selections that can be reheated, if necessary, from a Chinese restaurant; serve them with the following foods and dishes that have either been purchased or made at home. Serve as many as you wish, at one large or several small tables with the dishes of foods arranged in the center for diners to help themselves. Set the table with Chinese dishes and implements, if desired.

MENU

Drinks: Fruit juice, dry white wine or Bloody Marys as beginners; hot green tea with the meal.

Beginners: Hot spring or egg rolls with mustard; shrimp toast,* braised spareribs, meatballs.

Soup: Chinese Velvet Corn-Chicken Soup* or Black Mushroom Soup.*

Dumplings: White meat-filled steam buns (*bow* or *bao*), shrimp "bonnets" in translucent dough (*har gow*), steamed meat dumplings (*shiu*), or any others.

Noodles: Chinese Wor Mein,* Chinese Pork and Vegetables over Soft Noodles.*

Dessert: Chinese Stuffed Sweet Dumplings or canned Mandarin oranges and almond cookies.

Shrimp Toast

> 1 *pound deveined shelled raw shrimp, minced*
> 1 *can (8 ounces) water chestnuts, drained and minced*
> ¼ *cup minced onion*
> 2 *tablespoons cornstarch*
> 1 *teaspoon sugar*
> ½ *teaspoon salt*
> 1 *egg, beaten*
> 1 *tablespoon soy sauce*
> 1 *tablespoon rice wine or dry sherry*
> 12 *slices firm white sandwich bread*

Combine shrimp, water chestnuts, onion, cornstarch, sugar, and salt in a medium-sized bowl. Add egg, soy sauce, wine or sherry; mix to form a paste. Or, with metal blade of a processor in place, blend ingredients, turning machine on and off rapidly for several seconds. Trim crusts from bread and spread shrimp mixture over one side of

---

*Consult index for these recipes.

each slice. Cut each slice into quarters or triangles. Drop, about 6 at a time, shrimp side down, in hot deep fat or oil (375° F. on frying thermometer) and fry about 1 minute, until golden brown. Gently turn and fry several seconds. Remove from oil and drain on paper toweling. Serve at once. Makes 48.

Note: The toast can be made ahead and kept warm, or reheated in a preheated 375° F. oven about 7 minutes.

An Israeli Breakfast Buffet

In Israel the sabra breakfast, a buffet meal, was initiated on the kibbutz as a daily morning get-together to enjoy an assortment of hearty and nutritious fare. It became so popular in that country that city hotels began offering their guests a lavish spread of similar foods and dishes.

You can serve such a repast at home by offering any of the following: freshly squeezed orange juice, fresh fruit in season, hot cereals or porridge, sliced raw vegetables (cucumbers, tomatoes, green peppers, scallions, radishes), smoked or marinated fish, hard-cooked eggs, spinach or eggplant specialties, salads, relishes, cheeses, olives, yogurt, sweet rolls, breads, preserves, honey, and coffee.

3

Soups

Soup is superb for breakfast or brunch. You can serve elegant light soups to whet the appetite or as first courses. More substantial creations are excellent one-dish meals, especially at midday.

A generous serving of soup can be a marvelous pick up and it can also satisfy nutritional needs at any hour. Furthermore, soups are easy and inexpensive to make.

The art of making soup dates back to the beginnings of cooking, and over the centuries cooks, utilizing the available bounty of land and sea, created a galaxy of national favorites, each prepared and flavored according to local tastes. We have acquired a rich heritage of appealing soups from them.

In the Orient people have long enjoyed soups for breakfast and as morning snacks. Europeans and Middle Easterners have drunk soups as restoratives and sometimes enjoy them with a glass or two of wine. In recent years more and more Americans have discovered that cold or hot soups in the morning are appealing and easy-to-make nutritious drinks.

In considering soups for breakfast or brunch, it is generally best to choose clear or light ones rather than heavy or rich varieties. For more substantial soup choices, those made with poultry or seafood are usually preferable to those made with red meats. Go light with seasonings and avoid those with exotic ingredients, which are more suitable later in the day.

You can easily make tempting clear soups with purchased or homemade broths, bouillons and consommés to which garnishes such as fresh herbs, lemon slices, julienne strips of raw or cooked vegetables, croutons, cooked rice, or pasta are added. Or combine chicken broth, beef bouillon or consommé with clam broth, mushroom bouillon, fruit, or vegetable juices for impromptu soups.

It is not difficult to make soups from scratch, but shortcuts may be used to good effect. You can make appealing variations with canned, dehydrated, or frozen soups, with or without the addition of other foods and seasonings. Many persons achieve variety by combining two or more canned soups.

For summer meals, chilled or jellied soups, previously prepared and ready in the refrigerator, are attractive and refreshing. In the winter, chowders and vegetable soups provide warmth and goodness.

Appetizer or first course soups should be in perfect harmony with the rest of the menu and served at the proper temperature if they are to be hot, well chilled if they are to be cold.

Serve soups attractively in cups, mugs, glasses, or bowls with appropriate garnishes. One-dish soups can be conveniently ladled from large bowls, casseroles, or tureens.

Here is an inviting collection of round-the-world appetizer and one-dish soups that you will find good for breakfast and brunch.

Beginner Soups

Given below are recipes for soups to serve as appetizers or first courses. They can be prepared beforehand and reheated and served hot, or chilled and served cold.

Swiss Mushroom Soup

¾ *pound fresh mushrooms*
3 *tablespoons butter or margarine*
8 *cups beef bouillon*
⅛ *teaspoon freshly grated nutmeg*
  Salt and pepper to taste
1 *cup dry sherry*
2 *tablespoons sliced scallions, with some tops*

Rinse mushrooms quickly or wipe them with wet paper toweling to remove any dirt. Cut off any tough stem ends. Sauté in heated butter or margarine in a large saucepan for 2 minutes. Add bouillon, nutmeg, salt, and pepper. Bring to a boil. Reduce heat; cook over moderate heat 10 minutes. Add sherry and scallions. Remove from heat. Serves 8.

Portuguese Chicken Soup

Serve in mugs for a large brunch.

1 *cup chopped cooked ham*
12 *cups rich chicken broth*
1 *cup long-grain rice*
  Salt and pepper to taste
½ *cup fresh lemon juice*
½ *cup chopped fresh mint (approximately)*

Put ham and chicken broth into a large saucepan. Bring to a boil; stir in rice; reduce heat; cook slowly, covered, about 20 minutes, until rice is tender. Season with salt and pepper. Add lemon juice; remove from heat. Serve garnished with mint. Serves 12.

French Onion Soup

This is a good soup for a winter meal.

1½ *pounds (about 5 cups sliced) onions, thinly sliced*
3 *tablespoons butter or margarine*
3 *tablespoons vegetable oil*
1 *teaspoon sugar*
  Salt and pepper to taste
6 *cups beef bouillon*
½ *cup dry white wine*
6 *or more slices toasted French bread*
1½ *cups grated Gruyère or Swiss cheese (approximately)*
  Melted butter or margarine

Sauté onions in heated butter or margarine and oil in a large saucepan until limp. Add sugar; mix well. Season with salt and pepper. Pour in bouillon; bring to a boil. Reduce heat and simmer, covered, 20 minutes. Add wine and continue to cook slowly 10 minutes. Ladle into earthenware or other ovenproof bowls. Top with one or more slices toasted French bread. Sprinkle generously with cheese. Sprinkle top with melted butter or margarine. Put in a preheated 375° F. oven 20 minutes, or until cheese is melted. Slide under broiler a few minutes, until golden and crusty on top. Serve in same dishes. Serves 6.

Chinese Velvet Corn-Chicken Soup

Serve as a first course at a brunch featuring Chinese dishes.

1 *chicken breast, skinned, boned and minced*
6 *cups rich chicken broth*
  Salt to taste
2 *cans (about 8 ounces each) cream-style corn*
2 *tablespoons cornstarch*
¼ *cup water*
4 *egg whites, slightly beaten*
½ *cup minced cooked ham*

Put minced chicken, chicken broth, and salt into a large saucepan. Bring to a boil. Add corn, stirring constantly; bring again to a boil. Mix in cornstarch, dissolved in water, and cook over medium heat, stirring, until thickened and clear. Remove from heat and quickly stir in egg whites; mix well. Serve at once in a tureen or soup bowls garnished with ham. Serves 8.

Note: Partially prepare beforehand; add egg whites just before serving.

Spanish Gazpacho

A colorful cold soup for a large summer meal.

6 *cups coarsely chopped peeled ripe tomatoes*
3 *cups coarsely chopped peeled cucumbers*
2 *large green peppers, cleaned and chopped*
3 *or 4 cloves garlic, crushed*
1 *cup water*
⅔ *cup olive oil*
½ *cup wine vinegar*
1 *cup soft bread cubes*
 Salt and pepper to taste
 Garnishes: Finely chopped cucumbers, scallions, and croutons

Combine ingredients, except garnishes, in a large bowl; chill. Serve in chilled mugs or soup bowls topped with garnishes. Serves 12.

Old-Fashioned Oyster Stew

An excellent soup for a holiday or winter meal.

2 *pints shucked oysters with liquor*
6 *cups light cream or half cream and milk*
 Salt, pepper, cayenne to taste
8 *teaspoons butter or margarine*

Cook oysters in their liquor in a large saucepan until edges curl, about 5 minutes. Add cream or cream and milk and seasonings. Leave over low heat until hot. Do not boil. Put a teaspoon of butter or margarine into each of eight warm soup bowls. Ladle soup into bowls and serve at once, with oyster crackers, if desired. Serves 8.

Easy Tomato Bouillon

Serve hot or cold.

4 cups tomato juice
4 cups beef bouillon
2 tablespoons fresh lemon juice
2 teaspoons Worcestershire sauce
2 or 3 dashes Tabasco sauce
2 teaspoons sugar (optional)
  Salt, pepper to taste
¼ cup chopped fresh dill or parsley

Combine ingredients, except dill or parsley, in a large saucepan; bring to a boil; reduce heat and cook slowly 5 to 7 minutes to blend flavors. Serve hot; or chill and serve cold. Serves 10 to 12.

Vichyssoise

This marvelous traditional soup is a good summer brunch dish.

4 large leeks, white parts only, well washed, cleaned, and thinly sliced
1 medium-sized onion, chopped
3 tablespoons butter or margarine
5 medium-sized potatoes, peeled and thinly sliced
4 cups chicken broth
1½ teaspoons salt
1 cup light cream
1 cup heavy cream
  White pepper to taste
2 tablespoons finely chopped chives (approximately)

Sauté leeks and onion in butter or margarine in a large saucepan until tender. Add potatoes, chicken broth, and salt. Bring to a boil; reduce heat and cook slowly, covered, about 30 minutes, or until potatoes are tender. Stir in the broth. Purée vegetables in a food mill, blender, or food processor. Combine broth and purée in a large container. Add creams and season with pepper and more salt, if needed. Chill several hours. Serve garnished with chives. Serves 8 to 10.

Maine Clam Chowder

A good winter soup.

 4 *pounds (about 7 dozen) medium-sized soft- or hard-shelled clams*
 ½ *pound salt pork, diced*
 2 *large onions, peeled and chopped*
 4 *medium-sized potatoes, peeled and cut into small cubes*
  Salt and pepper to taste
 4 *cups light cream or 2 cups evaporated milk and 2 cups milk*
 8 *unsalted soda crackers, split in halves (optional)*

Scrub clams under running water to remove any sand. Put into a large kettle to which ½-inch water has been added. Steam, tightly covered, about 10 minutes, or until shells partly open. Strain broth through cheesecloth and reserve. Remove clams from shells, clean and chop. Fry salt pork in a large kettle to release all fat and until crisp. Add onions and sauté until tender. Add reserved broth and potatoes; cook until tender, about 10 minutes. Add clams. Season with salt and pepper. Pour in cream or milk and leave on stove long enough to heat through. Serve over crackers, if desired. Leave to mellow in refrigerator and reheat, if desired. Serves 8.

Consommé Madrilene

This is a superb cold soup for summer dining.

 2 *envelopes (2 tablespoons) unflavored gelatin*
 2 *cups tomato juice*
 2 *cups chicken or beef consommé*
 1 *teaspoon grated onion*
 1 *tablespoon fresh lemon juice*
 2 *tablespoons dry sherry*
 1½ *teaspoons salt*
 ½ *teaspoon pepper*
 ½ *cup dairy sour cream*
 ⅓ *cup finely chopped chives*

Sprinkle gelatin over ½-cup cold tomato juice in a large bowl to soften. Heat remaining 1½-cups tomato juice, consommé, and onion to boiling. Pour over gelatin; stir until dissolved. Strain into a large bowl.

Add lemon juice, sherry, salt, and pepper. Pour into six individual soup bowls or cups. Chill at least 4 hours or longer, until thoroughly chilled and firm. Serve garnished with a tablespoon of sour cream and a sprinkling of chives on top of each cup of soup. Serves 6.

Chinese Black Mushroom Soup

This flavorful soup is made with large black dried *shiitake* mushrooms that are sold in specialty or Oriental stores.

    12 medium-sized dried black mushrooms
     2 quarts beef bouillon
     ½ cup minced scallions, with some tops
     ½ cup chopped bamboo shoots
     4 water chestnuts, sliced
     2 to 3 tablespoons soy sauce
       Pepper to taste

Soak mushrooms in lukewarm water to cover for 20 minutes; drain, retaining the liquid; slice thickly. Heat bouillon to boiling in a large saucepan. Add mushrooms with liquid, scallions, bamboo shoots, and water chestnuts. Reduce heat; simmer, covered, 30 minutes. Add soy sauce to taste and pepper. Remove from heat. Serves 8.

Note: The strongly flavored *shiitake* mushrooms go well with a beef bouillon, but you could use chicken consommé.

Balkan Cold Yogurt Soup

This flavorful soup includes cucumbers, walnuts, and fresh dill. A good summer soup.

     2 medium-sized cucumbers, peeled, seeded & diced
       Salt
     4 cups plain yogurt
    ⅔ cup chopped walnuts
     2 or 3 cloves garlic, crushed
     2 tablespoons red wine vinegar
     ¼ cup olive oil
     ¼ cup minced fresh dill
       White pepper to taste

Put diced cucumbers into a colander; sprinkle with salt; leave to drain 30 minutes. Combine with remaining ingredients in a container. Chill two hours or longer. Serve in chilled cups or mugs. Serves 8.

Senegalese Soup

This is an easy version of a favorite breakfast or brunch soup.

2 cans (10½ ounces each) condensed cream of chicken soup
2 soup-cans light cream
2 teaspoons curry powder
2 teaspoons paprika
¼ teaspoon ground cinnamon
2 cups crushed ice

Put soup, cream, curry powder, paprika, and cinnamon into an electric blender container. Blend, covered, 15 seconds. Add ice and blend 15 seconds. Serve cold garnished with grated coconut or chopped nuts, if desired. Serves 8.

Purée Mongole

2 cans (10½ ounces each) condensed tomato soup
2 cans (11¼ ounces each) condensed green pea soup
2 soup-cans milk
2 soup-cans water
2 teaspoons curry powder

Combine soups, milk, and water in a large saucepan; mix to blend well; heat to boiling. Stir in curry powder; remove from heat. Serves 8.

Southern Black Bean Soup

2 cans (10½ ounces each) condensed black bean soup
2 soup-cans hot water
2 tablespoons bourbon whiskey
Salt and pepper to taste
8 thin lemon slices
¼ cup finely chopped onions

Combine soup, water, and whiskey in a large saucepan; mix well;

bring to a boil; season with salt and pepper. Put 1 slice lemon in each of 8 soup cups or bowls. Pour in soup. Garnish each with a little minced onion. Serves 8.

Chilled Tomato Soup

2 cans (10¾ ounces each) condensed tomato soup
2 soup-cans water
2 cups dairy sour cream or yogurt
1 tablespoon horseradish
2 teaspoons paprika
2 large tomatoes, peeled, seeded, and chopped
¼ cup chopped fresh dill or parsley

Put soup, water, sour cream or yogurt, horseradish, and paprika into container of an electric blender. Blend, covered, until smooth. Pour into a container and chill 2 hours or longer. Add chopped tomatoes; mix well. Serve in chilled cups garnished with dill or parsley. Serves 8.

Swiss Cheese-Onion Soup

A good first course for a winter brunch.

4 medium-sized onions, thinly sliced
½ cup butter or margarine
4 cans (10¾ ounces each) condensed Cheddar cheese soup
2 soup-cans milk
2 soup-cans water
2 teaspoons dried basil

Sauté onions in butter or margarine in a large saucepan until tender. Add remaining ingredients; mix well. Heat through a few minutes. Serve garnished with croutons, if desired. Serves 8.

Boula Boula

This is an easy-to-prepare version of the traditional pea-green turtle soup, an elegant first course for a brunch.

4 cans (10½ ounces each) condensed pea soup
2 cans (10 ounces each) green turtle soup
½ cup dry sherry
1 cup whipped cream

Combine soups in a large saucepan; heat to boiling. Remove from heat; stir in sherry. Pour into ovenproof cups or bowls. Top each with 2 large spoonfuls of whipped cream. Put under heated broiler until light golden. Serves 8.

One-Dish-Meal Soups

Soupe au Pistou

A good French vegetable soup for a summer brunch. Serve with warm crusty French bread.

    1 large onion, diced
    2 leeks, white parts only, cleaned and sliced
    3 tablespoons butter or olive oil
    2 large tomatoes, peeled and chopped
    3 quarts water
      Salt and pepper to taste
    2 cups diced, peeled raw potatoes
    2 cups cut-up green beans
    2 unpeeled medium-sized zucchini, washed and diced
    1 can (1 pound) cannellini or navy beans, drained, or 1½ cups cooked
        dried white beans (pea or navy)
    ½ cup broken spaghettini or vermicelli
    3 cloves garlic, crushed
    ½ cup chopped fresh basil, or 1½ tablespoons dried basil
    ½ cup freshly grated Parmesan cheese
    ¼ cup olive oil

Sauté onion and leeks in heated butter or oil in a kettle until tender. Add tomatoes and cook 2 minutes. Add water; bring to a boil. Season with salt and pepper. Mix in potatoes and green beans. Reduce heat and simmer, uncovered, 15 minutes. Add zucchini, cannellini or beans, and spaghettini or vermicelli; cook another 15 minutes, or until vegetables are tender. While soup is cooking, prepare *pistou* sauce. Pound garlic and basil to form a paste in a mortar with a pestle, or mash in a bowl with a wooden spoon. Stir in cheese. Add oil, 1 tablespoon at a time, and beat to make a thick paste. Slowly stir into hot soup and serve at once. Pass grated Parmesan with soup, if you like. Serves 12.

Shrimp Gumbo Filé

You can serve this superb soup for a small outdoor meal. It's ladled over hot cooked rice. Serve with warm croissants or crusty white bread. Double recipe for a larger meal, if desired.

> 7 *tablespoons shortening or salad oil*
> 1/3 *cup all-purpose flour*
> 1 *large onion, chopped*
> 1 *or 2 cloves garlic, crushed*
> 1/3 *pound sausage, chopped*
> 2 *bay leaves*
> ¼ *teaspoon ground red pepper*
> ½ *teaspoon dried thyme*
>   *Salt and pepper to taste*
> 2 *cups boiling water*
> 1 *pound raw or fresh shrimp, shelled and deveined*
> 2 *teaspoons filé powder*

Heat 5 tablespoons shortening or oil in a kettle. Gradually add flour, stirring, and cook very slowly to make a dark brown *roux*, about 30 minutes. Sauté onion and garlic in 2 tablespoons heated oil in a small skillet. Add sausage, bay leaves, red pepper, thyme, salt, and pepper; cook 1 or 2 minutes. Add this mixture, with water and the shrimp, to *roux*. Cook slowly, uncovered, until shrimp are bright pink, about 8 minutes. Remove from heat and add filé powder, stirring slowly to mix thoroughly. Serve over hot cooked rice in soup bowls. Serves 4.

Mexican Tortilla Soup

You can serve this innovative soup with warm corn bread at a brunch featuring Mexican dishes.

> 12 *corn tortillas, cut in thin strips*
> ½ *cup salad oil (approximately)*
> 6 *scallions, with some tops, cleaned and sliced*
> 2 *large tomatoes, peeled and chopped*
> ½ *cup minced green pepper*
> 2 *green chilies (fresh or canned), washed, seeded, and minced*
> 8 *cups rich chicken broth*
> 1 *cup shredded Jack or Cheddar cheese*

Fry tortilla strips in heated oil in a large skillet until golden and crisp. Drain on paper toweling. Remove all but 2 tablespoons oil from pan. Add scallions, tomatoes, and green pepper; sauté until scallions are tender. Add chilies and chicken broth; mix well. Bring to a boil. Divide tortilla strips among 8 large soup plates; sprinkle with cheese. Ladle soup over them. Serve at once. Serves 8.

California Cioppino

Serve this colorful seafood soup-stew for a summer outdoor brunch with hot garlic bread.

 1 *large onion, chopped*
 2 *or 3 cloves garlic, crushed*
 1 *medium-sized green pepper, cleaned and diced*
 ⅓ *cup olive oil*
 2 *cans (1 pound each) tomatoes, undrained and chopped*
 1 *can (8 ounces) tomato sauce*
 1 *bay leaf*
 ¼ *teaspoon dried oregano or thyme*
   Salt and pepper to taste
 2 *pounds firm white-fleshed fish (bass, halibut, cod, haddock)*
 1 *large Dungeness crab or lobster*
 1 *dozen fresh clams in shells*
 1 *pound large shrimp in shells*
 2 *cups dry white or red wine (approximately)*

Sauté onion, garlic and green pepper in heated oil in a saucepan until onion is tender. Add tomatoes, tomato sauce, bay leaf, and oregano or thyme. Season with salt and pepper. Bring to a boil. Reduce heat and cook slowly, uncovered, 30 minutes. While sauce is cooking, cut fish into serving pieces. Clean and crack crab or lobster and put in a large kettle. Scrub clams to remove all dirt. Cut shrimp shells down the backs and remove any black veins. Put clams and shrimp over crabs. Add fish. Pour sauce over seafood; add wine. Cook slowly, covered, 20 to 30 minutes, until clams open and seafood is cooked. Add more wine while cooking, if needed. Remove and discard bay leaf. Serves 6 to 8.

Brazilian Chicken-Rice Soup

Serve any time of the year with warm corn muffins or bread.

1 broiler-fryer, about 3 pounds, cut up
1 large onion, chopped
1 or 2 cloves garlic, crushed
½ cup diced cooked ham
3 to 4 tablespoons salad oil
2½ quarts water
¾ cup uncooked long-grain rice
3 tomatoes, peeled and chopped
1 cup scraped, diced carrots
Salt and pepper to taste
3 tablespoons chopped fresh parsley

Wash chicken pieces and dry. Sauté onion, garlic, and ham in heated oil in a large kettle until onion is tender. Add chicken pieces, a few at a time, and fry until golden. Add water; bring to a boil. Reduce heat and cook slowly, covered, 25 minutes. Add rice, tomatoes, carrots, salt, and pepper. Continue cooking about 20 minutes longer, until chicken and rice are tender. Remove chicken pieces with tongs. When cool enough to handle take meat from bones. Discard skin and bones. Cut meat into bite-size pieces and return to kettle. Add parsley. Reheat if necessary. Serves 8 to 10.

Basque Fish-Onion Soup

Make this flavorful soup-stew with any kind of white-fleshed fish and serve with hot garlic bread.

4 large onions, sliced
4 cloves garlic
⅔ cup olive oil
4 large tomatoes, peeled and chopped
3 quarts water
¾ cup dry white wine
1 teaspoon dried thyme
2 bay leaves
3 tablespoons chopped fresh parsley
Salt and pepper to taste

6 large and thick pieces boneless white-fleshed fish (cod, haddock,
*   flounder)*
6 thick slices crusty white bread

Sauté onions and garlic in ⅓ cup heated oil in a kettle until tender. Add tomatoes and cook 2 minutes. Add water, wine, thyme, bay leaf, and parsley. Season with salt and pepper. Bring to a boil. Reduce heat; cook slowly, uncovered, 10 minutes. Add fish and continue cooking, covered, about 25 minutes, until fish is tender. Meanwhile, fry bread in remaining heated oil until golden on both sides. Rub with a cut clove of garlic, if you like. To serve, put a slice of fried toast in each of six or eight soup plates. Top with fish. Ladle broth over fish. Serves 6 to 8.

Scotch Cock-a-Leekie

Serve this famous Scotch soup, featuring chicken, leeks and barley, with hot scones or oat cakes. A good winter dish.

1 stewing chicken, about 5 pounds
5 quarts water
12 leeks, white parts and 2 inches green stems, washed and cut into
*   ¼-inch lengths*
4 parsley sprigs
1 bay leaf
½ teaspoon dried thyme
1 tablespoon salt
½ teaspoon pepper
½ cup pearl barley
¼ cup chopped fresh parsley

Put chicken and water into a large kettle. Bring to a boil; skim. Add remaining ingredients, except chopped parsley, and reduce heat. Cook slowly, partially covered, about 2½ hours, until chicken is tender. Remove chicken to a platter. When cool enough to handle, remove chicken, discarding skin and bones, and cut into bite-size pieces. Remove and discard parsley sprigs and bay leaf from liquid; skim liquid. Return chicken to kettle. Put soup back on stove long enough to heat through. Serve garnished with parsley. Serves 10 to 12.

Chinese Hot and Sour Soup

Serve this colorful soup at a meal featuring Chinese dishes.

> *4 dried Chinese black mushrooms*
> *½ cup warm water*
> *1 quart chicken broth*
> *¼ pound boneless pork, trimmed of fat and finely shredded*
> *½ cup shredded canned bamboo shoots*
> *1 to 2 tablespoons soy sauce*
> *¼ teaspoon pepper*
> *2 ounces bean curd, washed and finely sliced (julienne)*
> *2 to 3 tablespoons rice or white vinegar*
> *2 tablespoons cornstarch mixed with 3 tablespoons cold water*
> *1 egg, lightly beaten*
> *2 to 3 teaspoons sesame oil (optional)*
> *2 scallions, with some tops, cleaned and sliced*

Put mushrooms in a small bowl; add water; leave to soak 20 minutes; drain. Cut off and discard stems. Cut mushrooms into thin strips. Put chicken broth into a large saucepan; bring to a boil. Add mushrooms, pork, bamboo shoots, soy sauce, and pepper. Reduce heat to medium and cook, covered, 5 minutes. Add bean curd and vinegar. Stir cornstarch-water mixture and pour into soup, stirring. When slightly thickened, remove from heat. Pour in egg and stir until cooked. Add sesame oil, if used. Serve at once garnished with scallions. Serves 4 to 6.

Mulligatawny

This version of a spicy chicken soup that originated in India but was popularized by the British is a good year-round dish. Serve with unleavened *chapati* or toasted whole wheat bread.

> *1 frying chicken, about 3 pounds, cut up*
> *1 medium-sized onion stuck with 4 cloves*
> *2 medium-sized carrots, scraped and thickly sliced*
> *1 stalk celery, thickly sliced*
> *6 cups chicken broth*
> *1½ teaspoons salt*
> *¼ teaspoon pepper*
> *¼ cup butter or margarine*

1 *large onion, thinly sliced*
2 *teaspoons turmeric powder*
1 *teaspoon ground coriander*
1 *teaspoon cayenne pepper*
1 *clove garlic, crushed*
⅓ *cup all-purpose flour*
1½ *cups grated coconut, preferably unsweetened*
2 *cups hot cooked rice (approximately)*
1 *large lemon, sliced*

Put chicken in a large kettle. Add onion with cloves, carrots, celery, chicken broth, salt, and pepper; bring to a boil. Lower heat and cook slowly, covered, about 30 minutes, until chicken is tender. Take out chicken pieces with tongs and when cool enough to handle remove meat from bones. Cut meat into bite-size pieces; discard skin and bones. Strain and reserve broth. Melt butter or margarine in a large kettle. Add onion; sauté until tender. Add turmeric powder, coriander, cayenne, and garlic; cook slowly 1 minute. Stir in flour; cook 1 or 2 minutes. Gradually add strained broth and then the coconut. Cook slowly, stirring often, 10 minutes. Add cooked chicken pieces and leave on stove long enough to heat through. Serve in wide soup bowls. Put hot cooked rice in a bowl and lemon slices on a plate. Pass them to each person to be added to soup. Serves 6.

Finnish Vegetable Soup

A good summer soup to make with fresh vegetables or at other times with fresh and frozen vegetables. Serve with dark crusty bread.

2 *cups thinly sliced onions*
1 *cup thinly sliced scraped carrots*
2 *cups cut-up cauliflower*
2 *cups cut-up green beans*
1 *cup green peas*
5 *cups boiling water*
1 *tablespoon sugar*
  Salt and pepper to taste
6 *tablespoons all-purpose flour*
6 *cups hot milk*
2 *tablespoons butter or margarine*
⅓ *chopped fresh parsley*

Put vegetables and boiling water into a kettle. Add sugar, salt, and pepper. Bring to a boil. Reduce heat and cook slowly, covered, until vegetables are just tender, about 25 minutes. Combine flour and milk; mix until smooth. Gradually stir into soup; mix well. Continue to cook several minutes longer, until liquid has thickened and vegetables are tender. Remove from heat. Stir in butter or margarine and parsley. Serves 10 to 12.

Julio's Portuguese Bouillabaisse

Heck's Cafe, which has two locations on the outskirts of Cleveland, Ohio, one in Ohio City and another in Woodmere, serves an exceptional Sunday brunch with intriguing appetizer soups and seafoods, glorious entrée crêpes and sinfully rich desserts. Here is a specialty of their chef, Julio Reverendo.

> 1 *pound mussels in shell*
> 2 *dozen clams in shell*
> 1 *pound shrimp in shell*
> 1 *pound crab legs in shell*
> 3 *pounds white-fleshed fish*
> 4 *medium-sized green peppers, cleaned and diced*
> 6 *ripe tomatoes, diced*
> 3 *Spanish onions, cut in halves and diced*
> 2 *pounds potatoes, peeled and sliced*
> 3 *tablespoons chopped fresh parsley*
> 5 *bay leaves*
> 5 *garlic cloves, minced*
>   *Salt to taste*
> 1 *tablespoon white pepper*
> 1 *cup olive oil*
> 2 *cups dry white wine*
> 3 *tablespoons tomato paste*

Wash and clean seafood; cut crab legs and fish into large chunks. Combine chopped vegetables and arrange in layers in a deep pot. Sprinkle with seasonings; top with a layer of fish; sprinkle with additional seasonings. Repeat layers, using remaining vegetables, fish, and seasonings. Pour oil, wine, and tomato paste, previously mixed, over ingredients. Simmer, covered, 20 minutes. Add shellfish and simmer about 10 minutes longer, or until shells pop open and shrimp turn pink. Do not overcook. Ladle into bowls and serve with French bread. Makes 12 servings.

4

Egg Dishes, Omelets, and Soufflés

The egg is a fundamental ingredient of many breakfast and brunch offerings. A wealth of imaginative culinary creations can be made with eggs. They are easy to prepare, elegant and economical, and a boon to any cook looking for attractive and nutritious dishes.

One of nature's almost perfect foods, the egg is highly valued for the amount and high quality of protein it contains. Eggs are important to all aspects of cookery, as they are used in every type of dish. The basic methods of cooking eggs by themselves, however, are few: they are baked, soft- or hard-cooked, fried, poached, or scrambled.

People have been enjoying eggs since they first domesticated poultry, and the food has long been important in the everyday diet. Virtually all important cuisines have notable basic egg dishes as well as innovative egg specialties, prepared and seasoned according to local preferences.

Culinary experts have always been intrigued with perfecting egg cookery. Early French cookbooks dealt with the subject of how best to "boil" an egg, and there is still considerable disagreement about what the proper method is. In fact, controversies surround all the basic techniques of egg cookery. Continued interest, however, has led to a marvelous repertoire of dishes: By the early 1800s, the Parisian gastronome and food writer, Grimod de la Reynière, recorded that "they know in France 685 ways of dressing eggs . . ."

One of the best and most popular of the world's egg dishes is the omelet or *omelette*, a word taken from the old French word for a thin plate. The omelet is an ancient dish, glorified and popularized by the French who have developed hundreds of superb recipes for making unsweetened and sweetened kinds. Omelets in various forms (including a flat pancake type), and ingeniously flavored, have become an element of almost all cuisines, and are international favorites.

The soufflé is another remarkable and renowned egg dish. The name of this inflated light creation derives from the French word *soufflér*, meaning to puff up or inflate.

Eggs should be cooked over low or moderate heat so the nutrients will not be lost. High temperatures toughen the whites and cause the eggs to cook unevenly.

Here is some basic data which is vitally important for the preparation of good egg dishes. And here, too, is a collection of international recipes for everyday and special occasion dining.

Baked or Shirred Eggs

Eggs should be at room temperature. For baking, use individual ovenproof baking dishes such as custard cups, cocottes, or ramekins, or a large shallow baking dish. Grease dishes well with 1 teaspoon butter or margarine. Carefully break 2 eggs into each small dish, more into the larger. Top with butter or margarine, salt, and pepper. Bake in preheated 350° F. oven about 12 minutes, until whites are set and yolks are the way you wish. To shirr eggs, cook in a greased skillet over low heat on top of stove until whites begin to set. Top with a teaspoon of butter or margarine, salt, and pepper. Put into preheated 350° F. oven 5 minutes.

Variations:

1. Add 1 tablespoon light cream, dot with butter or margarine, sprinkle with fine dry breadcrumbs, salt and pepper.
2. Line dish with 1 or 2 spoonfuls of grated cheese, mashed cooked potatoes, creamed chicken, chopped cooked spinach, cooked asparagus spears, stewed tomatoes, sliced mushrooms, 1 or 2 thin slices of boiled ham or partially cooked bacon strips before adding eggs.
3. Top with a tomato, mushroom, curry or cheese sauce before baking.

Spanish Eggs, Flamenco Style

This is a colorful main dish that can be partially prepared beforehand.

> 2 medium-sized onions, chopped
> 2 or 3 garlic cloves, crushed
> 1/3 cup vegetable oil
> 2 cups diced chorizo (Spanish sausage) or cooked ham
> 4 medium-sized tomatoes, peeled and chopped
> 1 cup beef bouillon or chicken broth
> Salt and pepper to taste
> 16 eggs
> 2 cups cooked green peas
> 16 cooked or canned asparagus tips
> 2 canned pimentos, drained and julienne-cut
> ¼ cup chopped fresh parsley

Sauté onions and garlic in heated oil in a medium-sized skillet until tender. Add chorizo or ham; cook 1 or 2 minutes; stir in tomatoes; add bouillon or broth. Cook slowly 5 minutes. Season with salt and pepper. Spoon mixture into 8 individual medium-sized ramekins or ovenproof baking dishes or a large shallow baking dish. Carefully break 2 eggs into each individual dish, or break all eggs into the large dish over the ingredients. Arrange peas, asparagus, and pimento strips around eggs. Sprinkle tops with parsley. Bake in a preheated 350° F. oven about 15 minutes, or until eggs are set to desired degree of doneness. Serves 8.

Provençal Baked Eggs in Vegetables

A good dish for a small brunch.

1 medium-sized eggplant, about 1 pound
1 cup olive or vegetable oil (approximately)
2 garlic cloves, crushed
   Salt and pepper to taste
1 large onion, chopped
6 large tomatoes, peeled and chopped
8 eggs
½ cup chopped fresh parsley

Wash eggplant; wipe dry; cut off stem; dice but do not peel. Heat ½ cup oil in a large skillet. Add 1 clove garlic and eggplant, several pieces at a time; fry until golden and soft. Add more oil as needed. Season eggplant with salt and pepper. Remove to a bowl; set aside. Add 1 clove garlic and onion to drippings; sauté until tender. Stir in tomatoes; cook 3 or 4 minutes. Season with salt and pepper. Spoon eggplant into center of a large shallow baking dish; surround with onion-tomato mixture. Make 8 depressions with back of a large spoon in vegetables; break an egg into each depression. Sprinkle eggs with parsley. Bake in a preheated 350° F. oven about 12 minutes, until eggs are set. Serves 4.

Fried Eggs

A good fried egg should be relatively compact in shape, golden on the bottom and shiny on top, with no hard edges or tough whites. It can be cooked with firm or soft yolks, sunny-side-up, or turned to cook on both sides. The eggs should be at room temperature before cooking.

To cook, melt 1 tablespoon butter, margarine, or vegetable oil for each egg in a skillet. Break egg into a cup or small bowl and carefully slip into hot fat or oil. Cook over low heat to desired degree of firmness. If you wish the white over yolks to be firm, baste with hot fat or oil while cooking; or turn egg over with a spatula when whites are partially set. Sprinkle with salt and pepper. Or add a little water to pan after the addition of the egg; cover and steam. The steam helps to form a coating over the yolk.

Serve plain, with fried ham, bacon, or sausages; in a nest of cooked vegetables, or over a grilled tomato slice or fried breaded eggplant slice.

Mexican Huevos Rancheros

Serve this attractive main dish with hot refried beans at a Mexican brunch.

    1 *large onion, finely chopped*
    1 *tablespoon vegetable oil*
    1 *8-ounce can tomato sauce*
    1 *10-ounce can red chili sauce*
    ½ *teaspoon dried oregano*
      Salt and pepper to taste
    6 *hot fried corn tortillas*
    12 *hot fried eggs*
    ½ *cup grated Jack or Cheddar cheese*
    12 *avocado slices*

Sauté onion in heated oil in a medium-sized skillet until tender. Add tomato and chili sauces, oregano, salt, and pepper; cook slowly, uncovered, 15 minutes, stirring occasionally. Dip hot tortillas in sauce to cover on both sides. Arrange on individual serving plates or a large platter. Top with sauce and fried eggs. Sprinkle with cheese; garnish with avocado slices. Serves 6.

French Black Butter Eggs

This is a different way to fry eggs.

    3 *tablespoons butter*
    4 *eggs*
    2 *to 3 teaspoons vinegar*
      Salt and pepper to taste
    4 *slices hot toast*
      Garnishes: 4 teaspoons chopped fresh parsley or 2 teaspoons drained
        capers

Heat 2 tablespoons butter until hot in a medium-sized skillet. Carefully break eggs, one at a time, into a cup and slide gently into hot butter. Fry, covered, to desired degree of firmness. Remove eggs and keep hot. Add remaining 1 tablespoon butter to skillet and heat until brown but not burned. Add vinegar to taste; heat. Season with salt and pepper. Put eggs on toast; top with sauce and garnish. Serve at once. Serves 4.

Scrambled Eggs

You can cook scrambled eggs several ways. They can be slightly mixed, or the whites and yolks can be well mixed. The amount of liquid added to them can vary. Scrambled eggs cooked in a skillet will be fluffy; those cooked in the top of a double boiler will be creamy. Do not overstir or overcook; serve at once. Have eggs at room temperature before cooking.

BASIC RECIPE

8 eggs
1/3 to ½ cup light cream, milk or water
   Salt and pepper to taste
1/3 cup butter or margarine

Break eggs into a medium-sized bowl; add cream, milk, or water. Season with salt and pepper. Mix with a fork or wire whisk to combine thoroughly if a uniform color is desired, or mix slightly if streaks of white and yellow are desired. Heat butter or margarine until hot in a medium-sized skillet or in the top of a double boiler. Pour in the egg mixture all at once. Reduce heat to moderate, and as soon as mixture begins to set, stir, scraping from sides and bottom. Cook until eggs are thickened but still moist and shiny, about 5 minutes. Serve plain, over hot buttered toast, English muffins, or any variation suggested below. Serves 4.

Variations:

An interesting variety of one or more cooked or raw foods and seasonings can be added to eggs before or immediately after they are scrambled. The possibilities range from asparagus to cooked wild rice.

Bacon: Serve garnished with ½-pound sliced bacon, fried and drained.

Cheese: Add ½-cup grated Cheddar, Parmesan, or Swiss cheese to eggs before cooking.

Curried: Add 1 teaspoon curry powder to egg mixture. Garnish cooked eggs with chutney and/or toasted almond slivers.

Herbed: Add 1 tablespoon grated onion, 1 tablespoon chopped chives, and 1 tablespoon chopped fresh parsley, dill, or other herbs to eggs before cooking.

Meat: Brown 1 cup shredded dried beef, chopped boiled ham, or leftover cooked meat in butter or margarine before adding egg mixture.

Mushroom: Sauté 1 cup chopped fresh mushrooms in butter or margarine before adding egg mixture.

Seafood: Sauté 1 cup chopped cooked shrimp, oysters, lobster, crabmeat, salmon or tuna in butter or margarine before adding egg mixture.

Tomato: Sauté 2 chopped scallions and 1 large tomato, peeled and chopped, and ½ teaspoon dried basil in butter or margarine before adding egg mixture.

Vegetable: Add 1 cup cooked vegetables and 1 tablespoon chopped fresh herbs to eggs before cooking.

Western: Sauté 1 small onion, peeled and minced; ¼ cup chopped green pepper and 1 cup chopped cooked ham in butter or margarine before adding egg mixture.

Greek Scrambled Eggs

8 *eggs*
½ *cup diced feta or farmer's cheese*
⅓ *cup golden raisins*
⅓ *cup milk*
   Salt and pepper to taste
3 *tablespoons butter or margarine*

Break eggs into a medium-sized bowl; mix well. Add remaining ingredients, except butter or margarine; mix well. Heat butter or margarine in a medium-sized skillet; pour in egg mixture. Cook over moderate heat, stirring occasionally, until thickened but still moist. Serve on toasted crusty dark bread, if desired. Serves 4.

Kentucky Scramble

This old-fashioned egg-vegetable dish is a good breakfast or brunch entrée. Serve with warm corn bread.

2 *cups canned whole-kernel corn, drained*
⅓ *cup butter or margarine*
1 *cup finely chopped green pepper*
½ *cup chopped canned pimento, drained*
12 *eggs, beaten*
   Salt and pepper to taste
¼ *cup chopped fresh parsley*
12 *slices hot bacon, grilled or fried, drained*

Sauté corn in butter or margarine in a large skillet until hot. Add pepper and pimento; sauté 1 minute. Season eggs with salt and pepper; add to vegetables. Cook over moderate heat, stirring occasionally, until set. Mix in parsley. Serve garnished with bacon. Serves 6.

Basque Piperade

This well-known vegetable-egg dish can be served with thick slices of grilled or fried ham, if desired.

2 large onions, halved and thinly sliced
2 to 3 garlic cloves, crushed
⅓ cup vegetable oil
4 large tomatoes, peeled and chopped
2 large green peppers, seeded and chopped
3 canned pimentos, drained and chopped
1 teaspoon dried basil
Salt and pepper to taste
12 eggs, beaten
½ cup chopped fresh parsley

Sauté onions and garlic in heated oil in a large skillet until tender. Stir in tomatoes, peppers, pimentos, and basil. Season with salt and pepper. Cook slowly, stirring occasionally, 5 minutes. Add eggs and cook over moderate heat until mixture is set but softly scrambled. Stir in parsley. Serves 6.

Caracas Eggs

This recipe was popular in American cookbooks several decades ago.

¼ cup butter or margarine
2 2½-ounce jars dried beef, shredded
1 tablespoon grated onion
⅓ cup grated Swiss or Cheddar cheese
2 cups chopped, peeled fresh or canned tomatoes, drained
8 eggs, beaten
Dash cayenne pepper
Salt and pepper to taste

Heat butter or margarine until hot in a large skillet. Add dried beef, onion, and cheese; cook until beef is slightly frizzled. Add tomatoes; cook 1 or 2 minutes. Season eggs with cayenne, salt and pepper. Pour over beef mixture. Cook over moderate heat, stirring occasionally, until eggs are set but moist. Serves 8.

Scotch Woodcock

This popular egg dish is said to have been created when a clever Scottish cook did not have a woodcock to serve his guests. Instead he gave them this appealing specialty.

    8 *slices firm white bread*
    5½ *tablespoons butter or margarine*
    4 *teaspoons anchovy paste (approximately)*
    12 *eggs, beaten*
    ½ *cup light cream or milk*
    ⅛ *teaspoon cayenne pepper*
        Salt and pepper to taste
    ⅓ *cup chopped fresh parsley*

Toast bread; spread each slice generously with butter or margarine, and then spread lightly with anchovy paste. Keep warm. Combine eggs, cream or milk, cayenne, salt, and pepper in a bowl. Heat about 3 tablespoons butter or margarine until hot in a large skillet; add egg mixture. Cook over moderate het, stirring frequently, until set but still moist. Mix in parsley. Spoon over toast. Serve at once. Serves 8.

Soft- or Hard-Cooked Eggs

It is not easy to cook a soft- or hard-cooked egg well, and almost everyone has an opinion about how to do it. There are several ways to cook eggs in the shell. The eggs should not be boiled. Cook on gentle heat. The length of time to cook the eggs in the shell cannot be determined exactly since it depends on several factors—the size of the egg, its temperature when put in the pan, and how many eggs are in the pan. It is best to have the eggs at room temperature because they will cook more evenly than chilled eggs. Some tips: Extremely fresh eggs are more difficult to peel; and if eggs are moved a few times during cooking it will help to keep the yolks centered. Prick the small end of each egg with a needle before cooking to prevent the shell cracking. For hard-cooked eggs the object is to have a smooth and attractive egg with a perfectly centered yolk, well-cooked whites, and no black line between the yolk and white. You do not want cracked and leaking shells, lop-sided yolks and gaps at the end.

To cook, lower egg or eggs carefully into rapidly boiling water (enough to cover well). Reduce heat at once to below the boiling point and let simmer. For soft-cooked eggs, remove from water after 2 to 3 minutes; for medium-cooked eggs, after 4 to 5 minutes; for hard-cooked eggs, after 10 to 12 minutes. Plunge cooked eggs into cold water. Gently crack shell and peel. Refrigerate if not used at once.

French Baked Eggs In Mornay Sauce

This appealing casserole made with mushrooms and hard-cooked eggs may be prepared beforehand for a small brunch.

1 *pound fresh mushrooms*
6 *tablespoons butter or margarine*
2 *tablespoons fresh lemon juice*
6 *hard-cooked eggs, shelled*
¼ *cup cooked green peas*
½ *teaspoon ground turmeric*
1 *tablespoon mayonnaise*
   Salt and pepper to taste
3 *tablespoons all-purpose flour*
1½ *cups light cream or milk*
¾ *cup grated Swiss cheese*

Clean mushrooms by rinsing quickly under cold water, or wiping with wet paper toweling to remove any dirt; wipe dry. Sauté in 3 tablespoons butter or margarine and lemon juice for 4 minutes; remove from heat.

Cut hard-cooked eggs in halves lengthwise. Remove yolks and mash with peas in a small bowl. Mix in turmeric and mayonnaise. Season with salt and pepper. Spoon into the egg whites. Arrange in a buttered shallow baking dish, leaving spaces between them, and spoon sautéed mushrooms into the spaces. Melt remaining 3 tablespoons butter or margarine in a saucepan. Stir in flour; cook slowly, stirring, 1 minute. Gradually add cream or milk, stirring constantly, and cook slowly, stirring, until thickened and smooth. Stir in cheese and cook slowly until it melts. Season with salt and pepper. Remove from stove and pour over stuffed eggs and mushrooms. Bake in a preheated 350° F. oven about 30 minutes, until hot and bubbly. Serves 6.

Belgian Eggs With Shrimp

This traditional dish called *Oeufs Meulemeester* is from Flanders in northern Belgium where tiny shrimp are a specialty. It's a good brunch dish.

12 hard-cooked eggs, shelled
 1 pound cooked, cleaned, shelled shrimp
1½ cups light cream or milk
 3 tablespoons chopped fresh parsley
 2 teaspoons minced chives
 1 tablespoon prepared sharp mustard
 1 cup grated Parmesan cheese
   Salt and pepper to taste
 1 tablespoon butter or margarine (approximately)

Cut eggs into thin shreds. Cut shrimp, if large, into bite-size pieces. Combine shrimp, eggs, cream or milk, parsley, chives, mustard, and ⅓ cup cheese in a medium-sized bowl. Season with salt and pepper; mix. Spoon into a shallow baking dish. Sprinkle with remaining cheese; dot with butter. Bake in a preheated 400° F. oven 10 minutes, or until mixture is hot and bubbly, and golden on top. Serves 8.

Swedish Anchovy Eggs

This piquant specialty is called "anchovy hash."

 2 medium-sized onions, finely chopped
 ¼ cup butter or margarine
20 flat anchovy fillets, drained and minced
 8 hard-cooked eggs, shelled and chopped
   Black pepper to taste
   Triangles of white toast

Sauté onions in butter or margarine in a medium-sized skillet. Stir in anchovies and eggs; sauté quickly over fairly high heat until flavors are blended and mixture is hot. Season with pepper. Serve on toast triangles. Serves 8.

Poached Eggs

It is important to have fresh eggs for poaching, so the white will remain around the yolk when the egg is broken. To test for freshness, put eggs in a bowl and cover with cold water. If they lie flat at the bottom, they are fresh. Cold eggs poach better than those at room temperature. A good poached egg has a well-centered yolk and does not have strings or "streamers." The best way to keep an egg shapely while poaching is to dip the egg in the shell in boiling water for 8 to 10 seconds. Then break egg into a small saucer or cup before slipping it into simmering water.

BASIC RECIPE

Put water to a depth of about 1½ inches into a skillet. Add ½ teaspoon salt for each 2 cups water and 1 teaspoon white vinegar, if desired. The vinegar will help to keep the egg firm. Bring water to the boiling point, then reduce heat to hold at simmering. Stir water with a wooden spoon until it whirls to create a small whirlpool. Add egg in a small saucer or cup by slipping quickly into the water. Lift white around yolk with a wooden spoon, keeping the water simmering, not boiling. Cook 3 to 5 minutes, until whites are thoroughly set and the yolks as you wish. Remove eggs at once with a slotted spoon; drain. Trim edges with a knife or cookie cutter, if desired.

Note: Eggs can be poached in an egg poacher or in buttered muffin rings set in water.

Eggs can also be poached in milk, bouillon, or vegetable juice in place of water, if desired. But do not add vinegar, then; and serve the liquid with the egg, if desired.

If a quantity of eggs is required, you can poach them in advance, leaving them slightly undercooked, and put them into a bowl of cold water; then refrigerate, covered, several hours, or up to 2 days. When ready to use, transfer eggs to a dish of hot, not boiling, water and leave 2 to 3 minutes.

Serve plain or on rounds of hot buttered toast or English muffins. Top with melted butter and breadcrumbs, grated cheese, Hollandaise, mushroom, tomato, or cheese sauce. Serve over sautéed or puréed vegetables; in nests of cooked rice, macaroni, spinach, or corned-beef hash; in hollowed baked potatoes or whole tomatoes; or in the recipes below.

Eggs Benedict

This celebrated breakfast and brunch specialty is an American creation that has gained international fame. It has even been entitled one of the "timeless classic egg dishes." Now it is prepared in many variations. Here is the traditional recipe.

> *2 English muffins, split*
> *4 slices hot broiled or pan-cooked ham, cut into rounds to fit over muffins*
> *4 hot poached (soft or medium) eggs, drained*
> *1 cup warm Hollandaise sauce (recipe below)*
> *Garnish: 4 thin slices black truffles or 4 sprigs parsley*

Toast English muffins. Cover each half with a ham slice and 1 poached egg. Top with Hollandaise sauce and a garnish. Serves 4.

Variations:
1. Substitute Canadian bacon for ham.
2. Substitute a broiled thick slice of tomato for ham, and top eggs with a cheese sauce.
3. Put a fried breaded thick tomato slice over the ham before topping with other ingredients.
4. Substitute crabmeat or lobster for ham.

Hollandaise Sauce

> *¾ cup butter*
> *3 egg yolks*
> *1½ tablespoons fresh lemon juice*
> *¼ cup boiling water*
> *Pinch cayenne or white pepper*

Have all ingredients at room temperature. Soften butter in top of a double boiler over very low heat. Whisk in egg yolks and then lemon juice with pan over simmering, not boiling, water. Slowly add boiling water, whisking as adding, and cook, whisking constantly and vigorously, until sauce thickens. Add cayenne or pepper; whisk again. Remove from heat. Makes about 1 cup.

Poached Eggs Florentine

Here is an inviting easy recipe for making individual servings of cooked spinach topped with poached eggs and cheese sauce.

    2 10-ounce packages frozen chopped spinach
    ¼ cup butter or margarine
    ⅛ teaspoon grated or ground nutmeg
      Salt and pepper to taste
    16 warm poached eggs (soft or medium), drained
    2 cups warm Mornay sauce (recipe below)
    ¼ cup grated Parmesan cheese

Cook spinach according to package directions; drain thoroughly. Add butter or margarine, nutmeg, salt, and pepper; mix well. Divide into 8 individual ovenproof baking dishes. Top with 2 eggs in each dish. Cover with Mornay sauce. Sprinkle with Parmesan. Slide under heated broiler until bubbly hot and golden on top. Serves 8.

Mornay Sauce

    ¼ cup butter or margarine
    ¼ cup all-purpose flour
    2 cups light cream or milk
    ¾ cup grated Swiss cheese
      Salt and pepper to taste

Melt butter or margarine in a small saucepan; add flour; cook 1 minute. Gradually add cream or milk and cook slowly, stirring, until smooth and thickened. Stir in cheese and seasonings. Continue cooking until cheese melts. Makes 2 cups.

Eggs Sardou

Poached eggs served over creamed spinach on artichoke bottoms and topped with Hollandaise sauce are a specialty in several New Orleans restaurants. They are excellent for a small brunch.

    2 tablespoons butter
    2 tablespoons all-purpose flour
    1 cup light cream
    2 cups finely chopped cooked spinach, thoroughly drained
      Salt and pepper to taste

8 *hot cooked or canned artichoke bottoms, drained*
8 *warm poached eggs (soft or medium), drained*
1 *cup warm Hollandaise sauce**

Melt butter in a medium-sized saucepan; add flour; cook 1 minute. Gradually add cream, stirring as adding. Cook slowly until thickened and smooth. Season with salt and pepper. Spoon creamed spinach into artichoke bottoms. Top each with a poached egg and Hollandaise sauce. Serve at once. Serves 4, allowing two to each person.

Brennan's Eggs Hussarde

2 *thin slices Canadian bacon, grilled*
2 *Holland rusks*
¼ *cup* marchand de vin *sauce (recipe below)*
2 *poached eggs*
¼ *cup Brennan's Hollandaise Sauce (recipe below)*
1 *grilled tomato*

On a dinner plate place Canadian bacon slices on rusks. Cover each with marchand de vin sauce, and top each with a poached egg. Cover with Hollandaise. Garnish with tomato. Top with paprika and chopped parsley, if desired. Serves 1.

Marchand de Vin Sauce

¾ *cup butter*
¾ *cup finely chopped fresh mushrooms*
½ *cup minced cooked ham*
¹/₃ *cup finely chopped shallots*
½ *cup finely chopped onions*
2 *tablespoons minced garlic*
2 *tablespoons all-purpose flour*
1 *teaspoon salt*
1 *teaspoon white pepper*
½ *teaspoon cayenne pepper*
¾ *cup beef stock*
½ *cup dry red wine*

---

*See recipe on next page.

Melt butter in a medium-sized saucepan. Add mushrooms, ham, shallots, onions, and garlic; sauté until onions are golden. Add flour, salt, pepper, and cayenne. Brown well, about 7 to 10 minutes. Blend in stock and wine. Simmer over low heat 35 minutes.

Brennan's Hollandaise Sauce

    4 egg yolks
    2 tablespoons fresh lemon juice
    ½ pound butter, melted
    ¼ teaspoon salt
      Pepper to taste

Heat egg yolks and lemon juice in top of a double boiler over low heat, cooking very slowly and never allowing water in bottom pan to come to a boil. Add butter, a little at a time, stirring constantly with a wooden spoon. When mixture thickens, add salt and pepper.

Omelets

As noted in the introduction, there are many, many kinds of omelets—savory or sweet, plain or filled, puffy or flat, small or large. At Madame Romaine de Lyon, a restaurant in New York City that specializes in omelets, the twenty-page menu, the size of a small book, lists over 500 varieties that range from a simple cheese omelet to a costly creation filled with caviar or *foie gras* in various combinations. Here are a few international omelets.

French Plain Omelette

The classic plain *omelette*, golden on the outside and creamy moist inside, is a delectable creation that takes skill and practice to prepare. It should be properly made in an omelet pan, one with a 7- or 8-inch bottom for a 2 or 3 egg omelet, or a 10- or 12-inch bottom for a large omelet. Larger omelets are difficult to handle. The pan should be thick-bodied to respond to high heat. Good pans are made of carbon steel, copper or extra-heavy aluminum with a smooth interior, sloping sides, and a long handle. Most omelet pans should be pre-seasoned, should not be used for cooking other foods, and not washed in water.

Clean by wiping with paper toweling, or remove food spots by rubbing with salt.

   3 *large fresh eggs*
   ½ *teaspoon salt*
   1 *teaspoon cold water*
   1 *tablespoon or more unsalted butter*
      Few grindings pepper

Break eggs into a small bowl; add salt and water; mix briskly with a fork to blend whites and yolks. Heat an ungreased 7- or 8-inch omelet pan until very hot. Add 1 tablespoon butter and, when melted, tip pan so it coats bottom and sides. When butter is hot and golden, pour in all of egg mixture quickly, and let eggs set a few seconds. Then take handle in left hand and shake pan vigorously back and forth. At the same time, stir eggs quickly with a fork in the right hand. The eggs should be sliding freely and not sticking to pan. When eggs begin to thicken or set and are still creamy, smooth the top with a fork; tilt pan away from you and with a fork fold the omelet so that it rolls over on itself. Reversing hand so thumb is at top of handle, tip the pan forward and roll omelet out onto a warm plate. Top with a little butter, spreading it with a fork, if desired, and sprinkle with pepper. Serve at once. Serves one as an entrée.

Variations:

There are many possible variations of this basic recipe. Here are a few.

Herb: Add 3 tablespoons of one or more chopped fresh herbs (parsley, dill, basil, marjoram, tarragon, chives) to egg mixture before cooking.

Filled: 1. Sprinkle 3 tablespoons grated cheese (Swiss, Parmesan, Cheddar or Jack), sautéed vegetables, crisp bacon bits or chopped cooked ham over omelet just before you fold the eggs over.
   2. Put 2 to 3 tablespoons hot creamed seafood, buttered cooked spinach, sautéed mushrooms, curried chicken, smoked salmon, sour cream and red caviar, sautéed chicken livers, or creamed asparagus tips over omelet just before you fold the eggs over and top finished omelet with an additional spoonful of filling.

Omelet Bar

For a party featuring omelets, set up an omelet bar: Prepare the egg mixture beforehand, together with any of the fillings described above; set out pans, small stoves or burners, and plates on a long table. Have the host or hostess, a guest, or chef prepare the omelets, and serve with such accompaniments as grilled bacon or ham, broiled tomatoes, hot breads, and any favorite dessert.

American Puffy Omelet

This version of the omelet is made by beating the egg yolks and whites separately and then combining them before cooking on top of the stove and in the oven.

   4 *eggs, separated*
   4 *tablespoons hot water or milk*
   ½ *teaspoon salt*
   ⅛ *teaspoon pepper*
   2 *tablespoons butter or margarine*

Beat egg whites in a medium-sized bowl until stiff but not dry. Mix egg yolks in a small bowl until thick and creamy; add water or milk, salt and pepper; mix well. Gently fold egg yolk mixture into whites. Heat butter or margarine in a heavy medium-sized skillet until hot; tilt to spread on bottom and sides; add egg mixture. Cook over low heat several minutes, or until puffy on top and firm on bottom. Put in a preheated 350° F. oven; bake about 12 minutes, until top is firm to the touch of a finger, and puffed and golden. Serve at once plain or with a hot tomato, and cheese or mushroom sauce. Serves 4.

Turkish Vegetable Omelet

   6 *slices bacon, diced*
   2 *medium-sized onions, chopped*
   2 *cloves garlic, crushed*
   1 *cup diced cooked carrots*
   1 *cup cooked green peas*
   1½ *cups diced cooked peeled potatoes*
   8 *eggs*
     Dash cayenne
     Salt and pepper to taste
   3 *tablespoons chopped fresh parsley*

Fry bacon in a large skillet until crisp; remove; drain on paper toweling; set aside. Pour off all except 3 tablespoons fat. Add onions and garlic; sauté until tender. Add carrots, peas, and potatoes; sauté 1 minute. Beat eggs in a bowl; add cayenne, salt, pepper, and parsley; mix well. Add to vegetables. Cook over low heat until eggs are set and surface is dry. While cooking, slip a knife around edges and tilt pan to let wet mixture run. Sprinkle top with bacon. Cut into wedges to serve. Serves 6.

Syrian Squash Omelet

Good for a small breakfast or brunch.

  2 *small zucchini, washed, stemmed, and dried*
  ½ *cup sliced scallions, with some tops*
  2 *tablespoons olive or vegetable oil*
  3 *tablespoons butter or margarine*
  6 *large eggs*
    Salt and pepper to taste
  2 *tablespoons chopped fresh mint*

Cut zucchini lengthwise into quarters; then cut crosswise in half. Sauté with scallions in heated oil and butter or margarine in a medium-sized skillet until zucchini is fork tender. Beat eggs in a bowl; add salt, pepper, and mint; mix well. Pour over vegetables; mix well. Cook over low heat until eggs are set and surface is dry. While cooking, slip a knife around edges and tilt pan to let wet mixture run underneath. Fold over and serve at once. Serves 4.

Roman Artichoke Omelet

An elegant omelet for a small meal.

  1 *9-ounce package frozen artichoke hearts, defrosted*
  ¼ *cup olive or vegetable oil*
  1 *garlic clove, crushed*
    Salt and pepper to taste
  2 *tablespoons fresh lemon juice*
  8 *eggs*
  ¼ *cup chopped fresh parsley*

Slice artichoke hearts lengthwise. Sauté in heated oil with garlic in a small skillet until tender. Season with salt and pepper; add lemon juice. Spoon into a buttered shallow baking dish. Beat eggs in a bowl; add parsley. Pour over artichokes, and tilt dish to spread evenly. Bake in a preheated 350° F. oven about 15 minutes, or until eggs are set. Serves 4.

Egg "Pancakes"

There are several international preparations combining eggs, bits or pieces of vegetables, meat or seafood, and herbs or other seasonings, and made into pancake-like omelets that are fried quickly on both sides, and served flat instead of rolled over. They are superb for breakfasts and brunches since they are easy to make, simple to cook, inexpensive, and can be served hot or if you wish, lukewarm or cold. Here are a few recipes for some of the best known varieties.

Chinese Egg Foo Yong

You can make this well known Chinese flat omelet into individual "pancakes" or one large one.

    2 tablespoons soy sauce
    1½ tablespoons cornstarch
    1 cup beef bouillon
    1 teaspoon sugar
    ⅓ cup minced scallions
    2 tablespoons peanut or salad oil
    ¼ cup diced cooked ham
    ½ cup sliced fresh mushrooms
    ⅓ cup diced celery
    ⅓ cup sliced bamboo shoots
    ⅓ cup chopped green peppers
    6 eggs
    Pepper to taste

Heat soy sauce in a small saucepan. Mix cornstarch into bouillon and add, with sugar, to soy sauce. Mix well; heat, stirring, until thickened. Keep warm. Sauté scallions in heated oil in a large skillet.

Add ham and vegetables; sauté 1 minute. Beat eggs in a bowl; season with pepper; pour over vegetable mixture; mix well. Cook slowly until eggs are set and surface is dry. While cooking, slip a knife around edges and tilt pan to let wet mixture run underneath. Cut into wedges and serve with warm sauce. Serves 4.

Spanish Tortilla

The Spanish omelet called *tortilla* is fat and substantial, enriched with a wide variety of foods but especially vegetables and seafood. The simplest and most popular kind includes only potatoes. You can make several omelets, each with a different kind of vegetable, and serve them stacked with tomato sauce between and over them.

Spanish Potato Tortilla

1 large onion, finely chopped
1 large potato, peeled and diced
¼ cup olive oil or salad oil (approximately)
Salt and pepper to taste
4 eggs, beaten

Sauté onion and potato in heated oil in a small skillet several minutes, until soft. Do not brown. Season with salt and pepper. Pour half of beaten eggs over vegetables; tilt to spread evenly. Cook over low heat, lifting up around edges to let wet mixture run underneath. Add remaining eggs and cook until golden brown and dry on top. Slide a spatula underneath to see if bottom is golden and to loosen. Remove from heat and invert a plate over omelet; turn over. Oil skillet; return omelet to it. Cook until golden and crisp on other side. Serve hot or cold. Serves 2.

Variations: Substitute any favorite vegetable or two of them. Especially good are tomatoes, green peas, asparagus, beans, eggplant, or mushrooms.

Hangtown Fry

This egg-oyster specialty from the West Coast is prepared in several variations. Here is one of them.

  16 *small oysters*
     All-purpose flour
   7 *eggs*
   1 *tablespoon milk*
   3 *tablespoons butter or margarine (approximately)*
     Salt and pepper to taste
     Fine dry breadcrumbs

Wipe dry oysters; dust with flour; dip in 1 beaten egg mixed with milk and seasoned with salt and pepper. Roll in breadcrumbs; fry in heated butter or margarine in a large skillet until golden. Mix remaining 6 eggs in a bowl; season with salt and pepper. Pour over oysters and cook over medium heat until set. Remove from heat; top with a plate; invert. Add more butter to skillet; return omelet to skillet; cook on other side until golden. Serve with fried bacon strips and/or fried onions and green peppers, if desired. Serves 4.

Italian Frittata

The traditional Italian omelet called *frittata* can be made with a diverse selection of ingredients. It has an appealing nut-like flavor and golden crust because it is fried in olive oil, or a combination of olive oil and butter. Here is a typical recipe.

  1½ *tablespoons butter (approximately)*
  1½ *tablespoons olive oil*
   ½ *cup sliced scallions, with some tops*
   1 *or 2 garlic cloves*
   1 *cup finely chopped cooked spinach, thoroughly drained*
   ½ *teaspoon dried basil*
  ⅓ *cup grated Parmesan cheese*
   6 *large eggs, beaten*
     Salt and pepper to taste

Heat the butter and oil in a medium-sized omelet pan or skillet. Add scallions and garlic; sauté until tender. Combine remaining ingredients in a bowl; mix well and pour quickly all at once into pan, tilting it to spread evenly. Cook until eggs are set and bottom is golden and crusty. While cooking loosen edges to let uncooked egg run underneath. Remove from stove; put a large plate over pan and invert frittata onto it. Lightly grease pan, if necessary, and slide frittata into pan, cooked side up. Cook underside 1 or 2 minutes. Remove to a warm plate. Cut into wedges. Serves 4.

Iranian Kuku

In Iran a baked vegetable or meat and egg dish called a *kuku* is served hot or cold. You can vary the fillings and double or triple this basic recipe, even cook it in individual custard cups for a large breakfast or brunch.

> 3 *small zucchini (about 1 pound)*
>   *Salt (for zucchini)*
> 1 *medium-sized onion, chopped*
> 3 *tablespoons olive oil or salad oil*
> 2 *tablespoons fresh lemon juice*
> ⅛ *teaspoon ground nutmeg*
>   *Salt and pepper to taste*
> 6 *eggs, beaten*
> ¼ *cup chopped fresh parsley*
> ½ *cup chopped walnuts*
> 1 *cup plain yogurt*
> ⅓ *cup chopped fresh mint*

Remove ends from zucchini and cut into small julienne-style shreds. Put into a colander, sprinkle with salt, and let stand 15 minutes or longer; wring out all moisture in a towel and dry. Sauté zucchini and onion in heated oil until zucchini is tender but still crisp. Remove from heat; add lemon juice, nutmeg, salt, and pepper. Combine eggs with parsley and walnuts; add to zucchini mixture. Spoon into a greased round shallow baking dish. Cook in a preheated 350° F. oven about 25 minutes, until set. Let stand several minutes. Cut into wedges to serve. Top with yogurt combined with mint. Serves 4.

Soufflés

A perfect soufflé is a work of art, but is surprisingly easy to prepare. It is also inexpensive. A soufflé is based on a thick sauce with the addition of flavorings and eggs. The egg whites are the essential ingredient that provides the characteristically airy appearance.

In preparing a soufflé it is important to remember certain guidelines. Egg whites at room temperature beat better than chilled ones. They are preferably and traditionally beaten in copper bowls, because the light acidity of the metal acts as a stabilizer. Otherwise, use a stainless steel or heavy plastic bowl, but not one made of aluminum or glass. Be sure the whites are free of egg shell or yolk. To beat, use a large balloon whisk or an electric or rotary beater that is thoroughly clean. Beat the whites until they are glossy and stiff enough to hold a peak, but not dry. While a soufflé is generally cooked in the classic straight-sided white china dish that is ovenproof and comes in sizes from one to eight cups, casseroles or ovenproof bowls can also be used.

You can prepare the basic sauce several hours ahead, and then beat and add the egg whites just before baking. A soufflé should be served and eaten as soon as possible after baking so that it does not collapse and lose its airy state. Given below is the basic soufflé recipe, and some variations.

BASIC RECIPE

>   4 *whole eggs*
>   1 *egg white*
>   4 *tablespoons butter or margarine (approximately)*
>   ¼ *cup fine dry breadcrumbs or grated Parmesan cheese*
>   3 *tablespoons all-purpose flour*
>   1 *cup milk heated to boiling point*
>   *Salt, freshly ground pepper, and any other seasoning to taste*
>   1 *cup minced cooked meat, poultry or seafood or puréed cooked*
>   *vegetables*
>   *Pinch cream of tartar*

Take eggs from refrigerator one hour before using. Separate and let stand at room temperature. Grease sides and bottom of a 1½ quart soufflé or baking dish with about 1 tablespoon butter or margarine. Add crumbs or cheese and tilt dish to spread it over the sides and bottom. Shake off any excess. Melt 3 tablespoons butter or margarine in a medium-sized saucepan. Stir in flour to form a *roux*; cook, stirring, over low heat 1 or 2 minutes. Gradually add milk, stirring, and cook slowly until thick and smooth, about 5 minutes. Remove from heat and cool a little.

Beat egg yolks slightly; stir into mixture; mix well. Add seasonings and prepared meat or other food and cook over low heat, stirring, about 1 minute, until well blended. Let cool. Add a pinch of cream of tartar to egg whites in a copper or other bowl; beat with a balloon whisk or beater until shiny and stiff enough to hold a peak but not dry. Carefully fold about ⅓ of egg whites into the sauce mixture with a rubber spatula. Repeat to use all egg whites.

Spoon mixture into prepared dish and smooth over top. Make a slight indentation with tip of a finger around inside of dish. Bake, uncovered, on a rack set at the middle level of a preheated 375° F. oven 35 to 40 minutes, or until puffed and golden and set. Do not open oven door while cooking. Serve at once. Serves 4 as an entrée.

Note: To make a cheese soufflé, substitute ¾ cup grated cheese (Swiss, Cheddar, Jack, or Parmesan) for meat.

French Mushroom Soufflé

4 *whole eggs*
1 *egg white*
1 *tablespoon minced shallots or scallions*
5 *tablespoons butter or margarine*
1 *tablespoon fresh lemon juice*
1 *cup finely chopped fresh mushrooms*
  Dash freshly grated nutmeg
  Salt and pepper to taste
3 *tablespoons all-purpose flour*
1 *cup light cream or milk*
  Pinch of cream of tartar
3 *tablespoons grated Parmesan cheese*

Take eggs from refrigerator one hour before using; separate and let stand at room temperature. Sauté shallots or scallions in 1 tablespoon

114 / The Complete International Breakfast/Brunch Cookbook

butter or margarine in a small skillet until tender. Add lemon juice and mushrooms; sauté 3 minutes. Add seasonings; remove from heat. Melt 3 tablespoons butter or margarine in a medium-sized saucepan; stir in flour to form a *roux;* cook, stirring, over low heat 1 or 2 minutes. Gradually add cream or milk, stirring, and cook slowly until thick and smooth, about 5 minutes. Remove from heat and cool slightly. Beat egg yolks and stir into mixture; mix some of hot sauce with yolks and return to pan. Stir in mushroom mixture. Let cool. Add cream of tartar to egg whites; beat until shiny and stiff enough to hold a peak. Carefully fold into mushroom mixture, adding ⅓ at a time. Spoon mixture into a 1½ quart soufflé or baking dish, greased with 1 table-spoon butter or margarine and lined with cheese. Bake, uncovered, on a rack at middle level in a preheated 375° F. oven 35 to 40 minutes, until puffed and golden and set. Serve at once. Serves 4.

Cheese Soufflé in Tomatoes

This is a very attractive entrée to serve a few persons or a large group.

> 4 *large firm tomatoes*
> ¼ *cup butter or margarine*
> ¼ *cup all-purpose flour*
> ⅔ *cup milk*
> 2 *eggs, separated*
> 6 *ounces Swiss cheese, grated*
> *Salt and pepper to taste*

Slice tops from tomatoes and carefully scoop out pulp, leaving a firm shell. Drain tomatoes. Put in small soufflé dishes or large custard cups. Heat butter or margarine in a small saucepan; stir in flour; cook, stirring, 1 minute. Gradually add milk, and continue stirring while cooking over low heat until thickened. Beat in egg yolks; add cheese, salt and pepper, and mix well. Remove from heat and cool. Beat egg whites until stiff but not dry. Fold into cheese sauce. Spoon into tomato shells. Bake in a preheated 375° F. oven about 30 minutes, until puffed and golden. Serves 4.

Other Egg Dishes

Bacon and Egg Cups

This is an easy dish to serve a large group. You can cook the ingredients in individual custard or muffin cups.

12 slices thin bacon, partially cooked
12 eggs
  Salt and pepper to taste
  Chopped fresh parsley or grated Parmesan cheese
12 rounds of hot buttered toast

Coil a strip of bacon with lean portion on top around inside of a custard or muffin cup. Break an egg inside each bacon ring. Sprinkle with salt and pepper and parsley or cheese. Bake in a preheated 375° F. oven about 12 minutes, until bacon is cooked and egg is set. Carefully remove and serve on toast. Serves 12.

Note: Serve on toasted English muffins or over mounds of hot seasoned mashed potatoes, if desired.

Algerian Chakchouka

This vegetable-egg dish is a colorful entrée.

2 medium-sized onions, chopped
2 to 3 garlic cloves, crushed
1/3 cup olive oil or salad oil
4 medium-sized green peppers, cleaned and sliced
4 large tomatoes, peeled and sliced
2 small hot red peppers, cleaned and chopped, or about 1 teaspoon
  ground red pepper
  Salt and pepper to taste
12 eggs, beaten
1/3 cup chopped fresh parsley

Sauté onions and garlic in heated oil in a medium-sized skillet until tender. Add vegetables and sauté 2 or 3 minutes. Season with salt and pepper. Spoon into a fairly large shallow baking dish, 11¾ x 7½ inches. Combine eggs and parsley in a bowl; season with salt and pepper. Pour over vegetables, and tilt dish to spread evenly. Bake in a preheated 350° F. oven until set, about 25 minutes. Serves 8.

German Farmer's Breakfast

This traditional German meal-in-itself is a hearty one-dish entrée for breakfast or brunch.

12 *slices thin bacon, cut in small pieces*
2 *medium-sized onions, chopped*
6 *medium-sized potatoes, parboiled, peeled and cubed*
12 *eggs, beaten*
1/3 *cup chopped parsley*
  Salt and pepper to taste

Fry bacon in an extra-large skillet until crisp; remove from pan; drain on paper toweling; set aside. Pour off all but 1/3 cup of fat; add onions; sauté until tender. Stir in potatoes and cook over medium heat, mixing occasionally, until tender and golden brown. Meanwhile, combine cooked bacon, eggs, parsley, salt, and pepper in a medium-sized bowl; mix well. Pour over potato-onion mixture; cook over low heat until eggs are set. While cooking, slip a knife around egg mixture and tilt pan to let the liquid run underneath. When cooked, remove from heat and let set a few minutes. To serve, cut into wedges. Serves 8.

5

Easy Light Entrées

From the standpoint of casual dining at breakfasts and brunches, the entrées in this chapter are primarily designed for simple elegance and easy service.

Consider, for example, the versatility of cheese, the world's oldest man-made food, which is superb in quiches, puddings, pies, tarts, sandwiches, baked dishes, and in such specialties as Welsh Rabbit and Golden Buck.

Creative cold and hot homemade sandwiches are marvelous entrées, either for informal impromptu meals or more carefully planned occasions. You will find that some are especially good for outdoor gatherings.

Always appealing are filled baked or fried pastries and the ever popular pizza. And there are a variety of innovative dishes made with seafood, chicken, and vegetables.

The recipes that follow have been chosen to display the versatility of light entrées that are especially good for family and informal company meals.

Quiches

A savory baked custard tart called a quiche, and believed to have originated in France's province of Lorraine, is now a traditional American brunch specialty. The best known is a Quiche Lorraine, made with bits of bacon and sometimes cheese added to the custard. There are also countless other versions prepared with seafood, meat, and vegetables in various kinds of pastry. Here are four good quiches.

Quiche Lorraine

Pastry for 1 9-inch pie shell
6 *slices thin bacon*
4 *large eggs*
2 *cups heavy cream*
Dash nutmeg
Salt and pepper to taste
2 *tablespoons butter or margarine*

Line a flan ring placed on a cookie sheet, or a straight-sided cake pan, or quiche dish with pastry. Flute the edge of the shell and prick bottom with a fork. Place a piece of aluminum foil over pastry and fill it with dried beans or rice to keep pastry from shrinking while cooking. Bake in a preheated 400° F. oven 8 minutes. Take from oven; remove foil and beans or rice. Prick again with a fork; return to oven to cook about 2 minutes longer, or until done. Remove from oven and cool. Cook bacon until crisp in a small skillet; drain it on paper toweling, and crumble over bottom of pastry shell, spreading evenly. Beat eggs in a large bowl; mix in cream, nutmeg, salt, and pepper. Pour over bacon. Bake in a preheated 375° F. oven for 25 to 35 minutes, or until custard is set and knife inserted in it comes out clean. Remove from oven and let stand 2 or 3 minutes. Remove ring and slide quiche onto a warm plate. Or serve in cake pan or quiche dish. Cut into wedges. Serves 6.

Cheese Quiche

Prepare pastry as directed in the above recipe. Omit bacon. Instead, mix together 2 cups (½ pound) grated Swiss cheese and 1 tablespoon all-purpose flour, and spread evenly in pastry shell. Cover with same custard ingredients as in recipe above, or substitute light cream for heavy cream, and cook and serve the same way.

Italian Zucchini-Cheese Quiche

2 *medium-sized zucchini, about ½ pound each, washed and stemmed*
1 *medium-sized onion*
3 *tablespoons salad oil (approximately)*
1 *teaspoon dried basil*
  Salt and pepper to taste
4 *eggs*
½ *cup sour cream, at room temperature*
½ *cup grated Parmesan cheese*
1 *9-inch pastry shell, baked 10 minutes and cooled*

Wipe zucchini dry; slice thinly. Cut onion in half lengthwise and slice thinly. Sauté onion in heated oil in a medium-sized skillet until tender. Push aside; add zucchini slices, several at a time; sauté until tender, adding more oil, if needed. Remove to a bowl when cooked. Add basil, salt, and pepper; mix well. Combine eggs, sour cream, and cheese in another bowl; add to zucchini. Turn into pastry shell, spreading evenly. Bake on the middle rack of a preheated 375° F. oven about 30 minutes, until puffed and golden and a knife inserted in the center comes out clean. Let stand 2 or 3 minutes. Cut into wedges. Serves 6.

Swiss Mushroom Quiche

8 *slices bacon, cut into 1-inch pieces*
1 *9-inch pastry shell, baked 10 minutes and cooled*
1 *cup grated Swiss cheese*
½ *cup minced onion*
3 *tablespoons butter or margarine*
½ *pound fresh mushrooms, cleaned and sliced lengthwise*
1 *tablespoon all-purpose flour*
4 *eggs, beaten*
1¼ *cups light cream*
  Dash nutmeg
  Salt and pepper to taste

Cook bacon until crisp; drain; set aside. Sprinkle bacon over pastry. Top with cheese. Sauté onion in butter or margarine in a small skillet. Add mushrooms and sauté 4 minutes. Stir in flour; cook 1 minute. Remove from stove and cool. Spoon over cheese. Combine eggs, cream, nutmeg, salt, and pepper; pour over mushroom mixture. Bake in a preheated 425° F. oven 15 minutes; reduce heat to 300°; cook about 30 minutes longer, or until knife inserted in the center comes out clean. Let stand 2 or 3 minutes. Cut in wedges. Serves 6.

Other Entrées

Dutch Baked Cheese Sandwich

An easy-to-prepare sandwich for a family breakfast.

> 8 *slices firm white bread, crusts removed*
>   *Butter or margarine*
> 1 *tablespoon sharp mustard (approximately)*
> 4 *thick large slices Edam or Gouda cheese*
> 2 *eggs*
> 1 *cup milk*
>   *Salt and pepper to taste*

Spread 4 slices bread with butter or margarine and mustard. Top with cheese and remaining bread to make four sandwiches. Place in a shallow baking dish. Combine remaining ingredients; mix well, and pour over sandwiches. Dot with butter or margarine; let stand about 10 minutes. Bake in a preheated 350° F. oven 30 minutes. Serve hot. Serves 4.

Roman Skewered Bread and Cheese

This tasty Roman snack is called *spiedini*, skewered. Prepare beforehand and serve when you wish.

> 1 *long loaf Italian bread*
> 1 *pound Mozzarella cheese*
> ¾ *cup butter or margarine*
> 10 *flat anchovy fillets, drained and minced*
> 1 *tablespoon fresh lemon juice*

Cut bread into slices about ½-inch thick. Trim off crusts to form squares. Cut cheese into slices the same size as the bread and about ¼ inch thick. Thread bread and cheese, alternately, beginning and ending with bread, on small skewers. Push together. Place in a pie plate or shallow baking dish. Cook in a preheated 450° F. oven about 15 minutes, turning once, until bread is golden and cheese is melting. Meanwhile, heat butter or margarine, anchovies, and lemon juice. Spoon over hot bread and cheese. Serve at once. Serves 6.

Scotch Eggs

You can make these innovative sausage-covered eggs beforehand, cooking just before serving, and serve hot; or cook beforehand and serve cold.

  2 *pounds sausage meat*
  ¼ *cup chopped fresh parsley*
  ¼ *cup minced onion*
  ¼ *teaspoon cayenne pepper*
    Salt and pepper to taste
 12 *hard-cooked eggs, shelled*
    Flour
  2 *eggs, beaten*
    Fine dry bread crumbs
    Deep fat for frying

Combine sausage, parsley, onion, cayenne, salt, and pepper; mix well. Roll out evenly on a piece of waxed paper. Dust each egg lightly with flour. Coat each egg with sausage mixture to cover completely. Roll each egg in beaten egg and then in bread crumbs. Fry in hot deep fat (375° F. on a frying thermometer) for about 5 minutes, or until done. To serve, cut into halves. Serves 12.

New Mexican Chilies Rellenos

You may serve these cheese-filled chilies at a Southwestern or Mexican brunch.

2 *7-ounce cans whole green chilies*
1 *pound Jack or Cheddar cheese (approximately)*
1½ *cups all-purpose flour (approximately)*
8 *eggs, separated*
2 *tablespoons water*
  Salt and pepper to taste
  Oil or fat for frying

Drain chilies; rinse and cut a slit down side of eight chilies; remove seeds and membranes. Stuff each chili with a piece of cheese cut 1 inch shorter than the chili and wide and thick enough to fit into the chili; fold over edges to cover the cheese. Roll each chili in flour to coat on all sides. Beat egg whites until stiff. Mix egg yolks, previously beaten, with 8 tablespoons flour, the water and a little salt and pepper; fold into whites. Heat a well-greased extra-large skillet. Add 1 cup egg mixture to form a mound; add remaining mixture in the same way to make a total of eight mounds. Put a stuffed chili in center of each mound and cover with some of egg mixture to enclose each chili. Cook about 3 minutes, until golden, and turn to cook another 3 minutes, or until done. Serve at once plain, or with chili sauce or grated cheese, if desired. Serves 8.

Vermont Cheddar Cheese Pie

6 *slices thin bacon*
1 *unbaked 9-inch pie shell*
1½ *cups (6 ounces) grated Cheddar cheese*
3 *eggs, beaten*
1½ *cups light cream, or 1 cup evaporated milk and ½ cup milk*
½ *teaspoon dry mustard*
½ *teaspoon salt*
  Dash cayenne

Fry bacon in a small skillet until crisp; drain on paper toweling; crumble and sprinkle evenly over pie shell. Top with cheese, spreading evenly. Combine remaining ingredients in a medium-sized bowl; mix well. Turn into pie shell. Bake in a preheated 375° F. oven 45 minutes, or until tester inserted into filling comes out clean. Let set a few minutes. Cut into wedges. Serves 6.

Oysters Rockefeller

This traditional dish is always a good brunch entrée.

      36 *oysters in shells*
       2 *cups chopped cooked spinach, drained*
      ¼ *cup minced onion*
       2 *tablespoons chopped fresh parsley*
      ½ *teaspoon celery salt*
      ½ *teaspoon salt*
       6 *drops Tabasco sauce*
      ¹/₃ *cup butter or margarine*
      ½ *cup fine dry bread crumbs*

Shuck oysters; drain and put on deep half of shells; place on a cookie sheet or in a shallow baking dish. Purée spinach, onion, and parsley. Add seasonings. Cook over low heat in butter or margarine in a skillet for 5 minutes; mix in bread crumbs. Spread over oysters. Bake in a preheated 400° F. oven 10 minutes, until hot and bubbly. Serve garnished with lemon slices, if desired. Serves 6.

Russian Salmon Kulebiaka

This delectable salmon-filled pastry is a superb brunch entrée. It is well worth the time it takes to prepare it.

       1 *package dry yeast*
      ²/₃ *cup lukewarm milk*
      ¼ *cup butte or margarine melted*
       4 *eggs*
       1 *tablespoor sugar*
         Pinch salt
      3¼ *cups sifted all-purpose flour (approxim ely)*
         Salmon Filling (recipe b low)
       2 *cups cold cooked rice*
       3 *hard-cooked eggs, sliced*

Sprinkle yeast over ¹/₃-cup lukewarm milk in a large bowl; after 1 or 2 minutes, stir to dissolve. Add remaining milk, melted butter or margarine, 3 eggs, one at a time, sugar, and salt; mix well. Add 1½ cups flour; beat well. Add remaining flour, enough to make a soft dough; beat well again. Turn dough onto a lightly floured surface; knead until smooth and elastic. Form into a large ball; put in a greased large bowl; turn dough over to grease other side. Leave in a warm place, covered with a light towel, until doubled in bulk, about 1½ hours. Punch down; turn out on a lightly floured surface, and knead again.

Roll into a rectangle, 20 inches by 14 inches. Spread half the Salmon Filling lengthwise along center of the rectangle, leaving a 4-inch border on all sides. Top with layers of cooked rice, egg slices, and remaining Salmon Filling. Bring long sides of dough together and pinch. Fold two short sides over and pinch. Seal edges with water; press to close firmly. Sprinkle a greased cookie sheet lightly with flour; carefully place filled dough on it with sealed edges underneath. Make several small slashes in top of dough. Cover with a light cloth and let rise in a warm place about 30 minutes, until light and enlarged. Brush with remaining egg, beaten. Bake in a preheated 375° F. oven about 30 minutes, until dough is crisp and golden. To serve, slice crosswise. Makes 12 servings.

Salmon Filling

2 *medium-sized onions, chopped*
¼ *cup butter or margarine*
1 *cup chopped mushrooms*
2 *tablespoons fresh lemon juice*
3 *cups cooked or canned salmon, flaked*
¼ *cup chopped fresh dill*
   Salt and pepper to taste

Sauté onions in butter or margarine in a small skillet until tender. Add mushrooms and lemon juice; sauté 4 minutes. Combine with remaining ingredients in a large bowl; cool.

Italian Cheese in a Carriage

This inviting fried cheese sandwich called *mozzarella in carrozza* is a good brunch entrée.

¼ *cup butter or margarine*
¼ *cup olive or salad oil*
4 *flat anchovy fillets, drained and minced*
1 *tablespoon fresh lemon juice*
¼ *cup chopped fresh parsley*
 Pepper to taste
8 *slices firm white bread*
4 *thick slices mozzarella cheese*
2 *eggs*
3 *tablespoons milk*
 Salt and pepper to taste
 Olive oil and/or butter for frying

Heat butter or margarine and oil in a small saucepan; add anchovies, lemon juice, parsley, and pepper to blend flavors. Keep warm or reheat. Remove crusts from bread and place a slice of mozzarella on top of 4 slices. Top with remaining slices of bread to form sandwiches. Combine eggs, milk, salt, and pepper in a shallow dish. Dip the sandwiches in mixture to coat well on both sides. In heated oil or butter fry sandwiches in a large skillet on both sides until they are golden and the mozzarella begins to melt. Remove and drain on paper toweling. Serve hot with hot anchovy sauce. Serves 4.

Swiss Onion Tart

2 *thin slices bacon, chopped*
2 *large onions, thinly sliced*
3 *tablespoons butter or margarine*
2 *eggs, lightly beaten*
½ *cup heavy cream*
1 *teaspoon sugar*
 Freshly grated nutmeg to taste
¹/₃ *cup grated Swiss cheese*
 Salt and pepper to taste
1 *9-inch baked pastry shell*

Fry bacon until crisp; drain on paper toweling; set aside. Sauté onions in heated butter or margarine in a skillet until tender, being careful not to brown. Combine remaining ingredients, except pastry shell, in a bowl. Add onions, mix well, and turn into pastry shell.

Spread evenly and top with cooked bacon. Bake in a preheated 375° F. oven about 35 minutes, or until set and knife inserted into center comes out clean. Serve warm. Serves 6.

German Mushrooms on Toast

Prepare the mushroom mixture beforehand; reheat and serve on toast triangles.

>   1 *pound fresh mushrooms*
> 1/3 *cup butter or margarine*
>   *Juice of 1 lemon*
> ¼ *cup all-purpose flour*
> 1½ *cups rich brown gravy*
> ½ *cup dry white wine*
>   *Dash nutmeg*
>   *Salt and pepper to taste*
>   8 *slices toast, crusts removed*
> ¼ *cup chopped fresh parsley*

Rinse mushrooms quickly or wipe with wet paper toweling to remove any dirt; trim stem ends, and cut crosswise into thin slices. Sauté mushrooms in heated butter or margarine and lemon juice 2 minutes. Stir in flour and then half the gravy. Cook, stirring, 1 minute. Add remaining gravy, wine, nutmeg, salt, and pepper. Cook slowly, stirring, 1 or 2 minutes, until mixture is thickened. Cut toast into triangles. Top with the mushroom mixture. Sprinkle with parsley. Serves 4.

English Kedgeree

This traditional English breakfast dish originated in India where it was made with lentils, rice, eggs, and spices. This is one of many versions.

> 1/3 *cup butter or margarine*
>   1 *or 2 tablespoons curry powder*
>   2 *tablespoons fresh lemon juice*
> 2½ *cups cooked long-grain rice*
> 2½ *cups flaked cooked fish (cod, haddock, salmon, or other fish)*
>   4 *hard-cooked eggs, chopped*

  ¹/₃ *cup chopped fresh parsley*
  2 *teaspoons Worcestershire sauce*
    Salt and pepper to taste

Heat butter or margarine in a medium-sized saucepan, stir in curry powder, and cook 1 minute. Add lemon juice, rice, and fish. Cook slowly, stirring, until food is hot. Mix in remaining ingredients; leave on stove long enough to heat through. Serves 6.

Swedish Chicken Salad

An attractive entrée for a summer brunch.

  4 *cups diced cooked cold chicken*
  ¹/₃ *cup mayonnaise*
  ½ *cup dairy sour cream*
  3 *to 4 teaspoons curry powder*
    Salt and pepper to taste
    Crisp lettuce leaves, washed and dried
    Garnishes: 12 stuffed olives, 3 hard-cooked eggs quartered, 2 tablespoons capers, 6 dill pickles

Combine chicken, mayonnaise, sour cream, curry powder, salt, and pepper in a large bowl. Chill 1 hour or longer to blend flavors. Serve on lettuce leaves on a platter, or on individual plates with garnishes. Serves 6.

Baked Ham-Cheese Strata

This version of an American bread-cheese casserole can be prepared several hours beforehand and refrigerated until ready to cook.

  1 *large onion, chopped*
  2 *tablespoons butter or margarine*
  1½ *cups diced cooked ham*
  1½ *cups canned whole kernel corn, drained*
  12 *slices whole wheat or white bread, crusts removed and quartered*
  ½ *pound Swiss cheese, grated*
  8 *eggs, beaten*
  4 *cups light cream or milk*
  ¼ *teaspoon dry mustard*
    Salt and pepper to taste

Sauté onion in heated butter or margarine in a small skillet until tender. Add ham and corn; sauté 1 minute. Arrange half the bread in bottom of a greased 9- x 13-inch baking dish. Top with half the ham-corn mixture and cheese. Repeat layers. Combine remaining ingredients; mix thoroughly. Pour over top layer in pan. Store in refrigerator until shortly before cooking. Bake in a preheated 350° F. oven about 50 minutes, or until baked and puffed. Cut into large squares and serve from baking dish. Serves 8.

West Coast Seafood Casserole

A good dish for an impromptu meal.

    1 *pound fresh mushrooms*
    5 *tablespoons butter or margarine*
    3 *tablespoons all-purpose flour*
    2 *cups light cream or milk*
      Grated nutmeg, salt, pepper to taste
    1 *5-ounce can shrimp, cleaned and drained*
    1 *6½- to 7-ounce can crabmeat, cleaned*
  ⅓ *cup fine dry bread crumbs*
  ¼ *cup grated Parmesan cheese*

Rinse mushrooms quickly or wipe with wet paper toweling to remove any dirt. Trim stem ends, carefully remove stems from caps, and chop stems and set aside. Sauté caps in butter or margarine in a medium-sized skillet for 3 minutes. Remove with a slotted spoon to a plate. Add chopped stems to drippings and sauté 3 minutes. Stir in flour; blend well. Gradually add cream or milk; cook slowly, stirring, until thickened. Add nutmeg, salt, and pepper. Stir in shrimp and crabmeat; cook 1 minute to blend flavors.

Arrange mushroom caps, except five of them, in a greased shallow baking dish. Spoon seafood and sauce over them. Sprinkle top with bread crumbs and cheese. Decorate top with the five reserved mushroom caps. Put in a preheated 425° F. oven about 15 minutes, or until hot and bubbly. Serves 6.

Chinese Wor Mein

½ *pound Chinese or American thin egg noodles*
  About ⅓ cup peanut or salad oil
1 *to 2 tablespoons soy sauce*
2 *cups diced uncooked chicken*
1 *cup chopped scallions, with some tops*
2 *cups diced celery*
1 *6-ounce package frozen snow peas (green pea pods)*
⅓ *cup sliced water chestnuts*
2 *cups medium-sized shrimp, cooked and cleaned*

Cook noodles in boiling salted water until just tender; drain. Combine with 1 tablespoon oil and soy sauce; set aside. Heat 2 tablespoons oil in a large skillet or wok. Add chicken and cook a few minutes, until done. Remove with a slotted spoon to a plate. Add a little more oil, the scallions, celery, and peas. Cook, stirring, until vegetables are just tender and still crisp. Remove to a platter. Add water chestnuts, shrimp, and more oil, if needed, to skillet or wok. Cook, stirring, 1 minute. Put noodle mixture in another large skillet; fry until golden. Return chicken, vegetables, and juices to skillet. Mix with water chestnuts and shrimp; heat to warm through. Serve over noodles. Serves 4 to 6.

West Coast Monte Cristo

Serve this chicken, ham, and cheese sandwich from San Francisco as an easy entrée for brunch.

12 *slices firm white bread*
 6 *tablespoons butter or margarine, softened*
 4 *thin slices cooked white meat of chicken*
 4 *teaspoons sharp prepared mustard*
 4 *thin slices boiled or baked ham*
 4 *thin slices Swiss cheese*
 3 *eggs, slightly beaten*
⅓ *cup milk*
¼ *teaspoon salt*
⅓ *cup salad oil for frying*

Spread four slices of bread with a thin layer of butter or margarine.

Top with a slice of chicken. Spread four more slices of bread with butter or margarine on one side and mustard on the other. Place, buttered sides down, over chicken. Cover with slices of ham and cheese. Butter remaining slices of bread and put, buttered side down, over cheese. Press lightly with fingers and secure at corners with toothpicks. Using a sharp knife, trim crusts and filling to make edges even. Cut each sandwich diagonally into quarters. Combine eggs, milk, and salt in a shallow dish. Dip sandwich quarters on all sides into mixture. Fry in heated oil in a skillet until golden on all sides. Remove toothpicks and serve at once. Serves 4.

Derby Chicken Sandwich

This hearty hot sandwich, a specialty of Louisville's Brown Hotel, is traditionally served at Kentucky Derby breakfasts.

> ¼ *cup butter or margarine*
> 2 *tablespoons all-purpose flour*
> 2 *cups light cream or milk*
> ¼ *teaspoon grated nutmeg*
>   *Dash cayenne*
>   *Salt and pepper to taste*
> 1½ *cups grated American cheese*
> 8 *slices firm white bread, toasted*
> 8 *slices cooked white meat of chicken, about ¼" thick*
> 16 *slices bacon, fried crisp and drained*
> ½ *cup grated Parmesan cheese*

Heat butter or margarine in a medium-sized saucepan; blend in flour; cook 1 or 2 minutes. Gradually stir in cream or milk, and cook slowly, still stirring, until thickened and smooth. Mix in nutmeg, cayenne, salt, pepper, and cheese. Cook slowly until cheese melts. Put each toast slice in a small ovenproof dish, or place them all on a cookie sheet. Top each with a slice of chicken and ⅛ of the sauce. Top each with 2 slices bacon and 1 tablespoon grated cheese. Put under preheated broiler about 5 minutes, until bubbly hot. Serves 8.

Easy Ham and Egg Sandwich

½ cup minced onions
½ cup butter or margarine
1 cup diced cooked ham
2 pounds fresh mushrooms, cleaned and sliced
12 eggs, lightly beaten
¼ cup chopped fresh parsley
   Salt and pepper to taste
16 slices white bread

Sauté onions in heated butter or margarine in a large skillet until tender. Add ham and mushrooms; sauté 4 minutes. Combine eggs, parsley, salt, and pepper in a bowl; mix well. Turn into skillet. Cook slowly until mixture is set and dry on top. While cooking, tilt pan to let wet mixture run underneath. Cut into 8 portions. Arrange each portion on a slice of bread. Top with another slice of bread. Spread top with butter or margarine. Insert toothpicks to hold sandwich together. Put under a preheated broiler until golden. Turn over; butter other side; broil. Serve garnished with a cherry tomato and small whole mushroom on a toothpick, if desired. Serves 8.

South American Cheese Empanadas

These traditional cheese turnovers can be made beforehand and frozen, if desired.

2 tablespoons butter or margarine
2 tablespoons all-purpose flour
1 cup milk
½ pound sharp Cheddar or American cheese, diced
   Paprika, salt, pepper to taste
2½ cups all-purpose flour
¼ cup melted shortening
1 cup lukewarm water (approximately)
   Fat for deep frying

Heat butter or margarine in a small saucepan; blend in flour; cook 1 minute. Stir in milk and cook slowly, still stirring, until thickened and smooth. Add cheese, paprika, salt, and pepper. Cook slowly until cheese melts. Remove from stove and cool. Combine flour, shortening, 1 teaspoon salt, and enough water to make a soft dough in a large bowl. Turn out on a lightly floured surface and roll out very thin. Cut into 4-inch rounds. Place 1 tablespoon cool cheese mixture on side of each round of dough. Fold over; press edges together, crimping with a fork to seal and enclose cheese. Fry in hot deep fat (375° F. on a frying thermometer) a few minutes, until cooked and golden. Serve hot. Makes about 2½ dozen.

Italian Pizza

You can prepare these delicious homemade pizzas in any quantity you wish, and serve them for a small family breakfast or brunch or a large get-together.

> 1 *package active dry yeast*
>   *Pinch sugar*
> 1⅓ *cups very warm water*
> 4 *cups all-purpose flour*
> 1½ *teaspoons salt*
> 2 *tablespoons salad oil*
>   *Pizza Topping (recipe below)*

Sprinkle yeast and sugar over ⅓-cup warm water (120° F.) in a small bowl. Let stand 2 or 3 minutes; stir to dissolve. Sift flour and salt into a large bowl. Make a well in center; pour in yeast mixture, 1 cup warm water, and the oil. Mix to form a ball and turn out onto a floured surface. Knead about 10 minutes, or until dough is smooth and elastic. Put into a greased large bowl, cover with a light towel, and let rise in a warm place until doubled in bulk, about 2 hours. Punch dough down and divide into two halves. Knead each half 1 or 2 minutes. Flatten with palms of hands and stretch dough by pulling to form a circle. Roll with a rolling pin on both sides to develop a circle with a diameter of 14 to 15 inches. While kneading and rolling add a little more flour if dough is at all sticky. Put each circle of dough on an oiled 12-inch pizza pan and push with fingers until it is stretched to fit the pan. Crimp edges to form a rim. Let rest 10 minutes. Top with Pizza Topping. Bake in a preheated 425° F. oven about 25 minutes, until the crust is golden and the topping is bubbly hot. Each pizza serves 4 to 6.

Pizza Topping

    4 *cups coarsely chopped tomatoes or prepared pizza sauce*
    1 *pound mozzarella cheese, shredded*
   24 *flat anchovy fillets, drained*
    1 *teaspoon dried oregano*
    1 *teaspoon dried basil*
      Pepper to taste
    3 *tablespoons olive oil*

Spread each pizza with half the tomatoes or sauce. Sprinkle with half the cheese, and top with half the anchovy fillets, oregano, basil, and pepper. Sprinkle with half the oil. Bake as directed above.

Welsh Rabbit

A traditional British savory dish, made basically with cheese, often mixed with ale or beer, and served on toast, is called rabbit or rarebit from the original "rare-bit." You can serve it from a chafing dish at the table or from a double boiler in the kitchen.

    ¼ *cup butter or margarine*
    2 *pounds sharp Cheddar cheese, grated*
    2 *teaspoons dry mustard*
    1 *teaspoon salt*
    ¼ *teaspoon cayenne pepper*
   1½ *to 2 cups beer, ale, or milk*
    4 *egg yolks, slightly beaten*
    2 *teaspoons Worcestershire sauce*
   16 *slices toast*

In top of a large double boiler or chafing dish, melt butter or margarine. Add cheese, mustard, salt, and cayenne; stir over bubbling water with a wooden spoon in one direction until cheese melts. Gradually stir in beer, ale or milk. When well blended remove from heat and mix in egg yolks. Cook again over low heat until smooth. Add Worcestershire sauce. Serve at once over hot toast. Serves 8.

Golden Buck

Serve Welsh Rabbit spooned over toast. Top each serving with a poached egg. Garnish with 2 crossed anchovy fillets and a sprinkling of chopped fresh parsley.

Mexican Tostadas

You can prepare the beef mixture for the topping beforehand and assemble the tostadas just before serving. A good entrée for a Mexican brunch.

2 *pounds ground beef*
2 *cups minced onions*
2 *7½-ounce cans green chili sauce*
2 *6-ounce cans tomato paste*
2 *cups water*
12 *tostada shells*
2 *1-pound, 4 ounce-cans refried beans, heated*
4 *cups shredded lettuce*
4 *cups shredded Cheddar cheese*
2 *large tomatoes, peeled and chopped*
2 *cups chopped black olives*

Fry beef and onions in a large skillet until redness disappears. Spoon off any excess fat. Add chili sauce, tomato paste, and water. Cook slowly, uncovered, about 15 minutes, stirring occasionally. When ready to serve, heat tostada shells in a preheated 350° F. oven 8 minutes, or until crisp and golden. To assemble tostadas, spread each with a layer of hot refried beans and the beef mixture. Sprinkle each with lettuce and cheese. Top with tomatoes and olives. Serves 12.

Commander's Palace Crabmeat Imperial

Commander's Palace in the Garden District of New Orleans has gracious dining rooms, a handsome patio, and an extensive menu that includes some of Brennan's breakfast specialties. It is great fun to visit the restaurant for the week-end jazz brunches. Here is one of their special dishes.

2 *tablespoons butter*
¼ *cup minced onions*
2 *tablespoons minced green pepper*
2 *tablespoons minced celery*
¼ *cup scallions, tops only, minced*
½ *teaspoon freshly ground black pepper*
1 *teaspoon powdered garlic*

1 cup mayonnaise
½ cup minced pimento, drained
¼ cup Creole mustard
1 tablespoon Worcestershire sauce
1 tablespoon Tabasco sauce
2 tablespoons chopped parsley
2 pounds cooked fresh lump crabmeat, cleaned
Topping: 8 tablespoons mayonnaise, paprika

Melt butter in a large skillet; add onions, green pepper, celery, scallions, and seasonings; sauté 15 minutes. Remove from heat. Add mayonnaise, pimento, mustard, Worcestershire and Tabasco sauces, and parsley; mix well. Let cool 20 minutes. Place crabmeat in a large bowl; ladle sauce over crabmeat and mix carefully to coat the crabmeat without breaking up the lumps. Using the hands, fill individual casserole dishes, ramekins, or large flat shells, using ¾ cup for each. Coat each dish with 1 tablespoon mayonnaise. Sprinkle top with paprika. Cook in a preheated 350° F. oven 8 to 10 minutes, until bubbly hot. Serves 8.

6

Hearty Main Dishes

The forerunners of today's breakfasts and brunches were substantial meals featuring a few or several hearty main dishes made with many different kinds of food. Prized for their versatility and convenience, these specialties are particularly appropriate for contemporary dining.

As noted in the introduction, northern Europeans have long been accustomed to sitting down in the morning to a variety of wholesome fare. The British are still devoted to their essential ham and bacon (rashers of "streaky" or "middle back" indicating the amount of fat) served with fried eggs, fried bread, and grilled tomatoes or fried mushrooms.

Both the Scots and English believed in beginning the day with some spirits and food of substance such as game and meat pies, smoked and salt fish, deviled kidneys, potted meats, sprats, bloaters, fried cod's roe, sausage, meat loaves, cold roast meats or beefsteak. The lines of an old ballad say

> Elizabeth Tudor her breakfast
>   would make
> On a pot of strong beer and a pound
>   of beefsteak

Early American breakfasts were patterned after those of northern Europe, especially the British Isles. Southern plantation morning meals were noted for their lavishness and featured hot and cold seafood, country hams, puddings, curries, country-fried chicken with gravy, creamed dishes, croquettes, fried fish, and game.

New Englanders dined on hashes, codfish balls and cakes, salt pork, stewed oysters, lobsters, baked beans, and brown bread or, as the saying goes, foods that are "a-nourishing" and stick to the ribs. The Pennsylvania Dutch relished pork dishes, scrapple, creamed specialties, and meat pies.

Westerners required good strong meats for breakfast. Country hands ate grizzly bear steak or broiled venison while city folk served lamb chops or cutlets, veal scallops, beef fillets, grilled salmon, or baked trout.

Americans are still fond of bacon, ham, and sausage for breakfast and brunch. Standard dishes are also steak and eggs with potatoes and hamburgers with all sorts of toppings. Here are hearty main dishes that are popular in America and many other countries.

HASHES

Corned Beef Hash

Corned beef hash has been a treasured American breakfast dish since Colonial times. In most homes it provided warmth and nourishment and was easily made with a few basic ingredients. Now the hash, prepared in several variations, is also a favorite brunch dish. Here are two good recipes for it.

1 medium-sized onion, chopped
4 cups, or 2 12-ounce cans corned beef, chopped
4 cups diced peeled boiled potatoes
½ teaspoon dried thyme or oregano
¼ cup chopped fresh parsley
Salt and pepper to taste
2 to 3 tablespoons butter or margarine
½ cup heavy cream or milk
8 poached eggs
Warm chili sauce or ketchup

Combine onion, corned beef, potatoes, and seasonings in a large bowl; mix well. When ready to cook, heat 2 tablespoons butter or margarine in a medium-sized skillet. Add hash mixture; press down firmly with a spatula. Cook over medium heat until a crust forms on the bottom. Turn with a spatula so that some of the crust is brought to the top. Add cream or milk and continue cooking until a final crust forms. Serve in portions with each helping topped with a poached egg and a little chili sauce or ketchup. Serves 8.

Note: The hash can be partially cooked beforehand and reheated. For a larger amount, flatten the hash on a flat surface to about a 1-inch thickness. Cut into large circles and fry in a large skillet or on a griddle.

Wayne's Baked Corned Beef Hash

This is my husband's favorite brunch hash. It can be prepared for a small family meal, or in greater quantity for a large get-together. Serve with buttered toasted English muffins.

   ¾ cup finely chopped onions
   ¾ cup finely chopped celery
   1 medium-sized green pepper, cleaned and minced
   2 cups seasoned mashed potatoes
   2 cups or 1 12-ounce can corned beef, coarsely chopped
      Pepper to taste
   ¼ cup grated Parmesan cheese
   2 teaspoons butter or margarine (approximately)

Combine onions, celery, green pepper, potatoes, corned beef, and pepper in a large bowl; mix well. Spoon into a greased 10-inch pie plate or shallow baking dish, spreading evenly. Sprinkle top with cheese and dot with butter or margarine. Bake in a preheated 375° F. oven 25 minutes, or until bubbly hot. Slide under heated broiler 2 or 3 minutes, until top is golden. Serves 4.

INTERNATIONAL HAMBURGERS

Chopped or ground meat, shaped into patties or other forms and cooked in various ways, is an ancient specialty that probably originated in India or the Middle East. Although the name for this creation, hamburger, is believed to have derived from Germany's port city of

Hamburg, a broiled or fried ground beef patty served on a bun made its debut at the St. Louis World's Fair of 1904. Since then the all-American favorite has become known around the world and is made in a hundred variations called Big Mac, Whopper, Mighty Mo, or burgers with other fancy appellations.

Many restaurants feature hamburgers on their brunch menus and serve them on several kinds of rolls or bread with all sorts of toppings. At H.A. Winston & Co. in the Philadelphia area and Washington, D.C., you can order 20 kinds with "Gourmet Toppings" ranging from British (sautéed onions and Cheddar cheese) to Tijuana (chili peppers and Monterey Jack Cheese). At Mr. Smith's in Georgetown, the "famous hamburger" list even includes a Nudeburger ("dressed only in a slice of cheese and reclining on a bed of fresh greens—for the very skinny or those who want to be").

Here is a basic recipe which you can embellish with a variety of garnishes.

1½ pounds lean ground beef
Salt
1 tablespoon butter or margarine
Pepper to taste
3 split toasted hamburger buns, French rolls, pita bread or 6 slices toast

Shape the beef, preferably freshly ground, into six patties. Sprinkle a large heavy skillet with a layer of salt and heat. Add patties and sear on one side; turn with a spatula; reduce heat and continue cooking until done, several minutes. Or, omit salt, heat butter or margarine in a skillet and cook, turning once. Do not pat or press with a spatula during the cooking. Or, cook under a preheated broiler, turning once. Season with salt and pepper and serve on buns, rolls, or bread with ketchup or any of the garnishes suggested below. Serves 6.

Chinese: Hot sautéed chopped scallions with bean sprouts and chopped green peppers moistened with soy sauce.

French: Hot sautéed herbed mushrooms and clams in wine sauce.

German: Hot sauerkraut flavored with capers and chopped fresh parsley or dill.

Hawaiian: Grilled pineapple slice topped with chopped almonds and coconut.

Indian: Sautéed chopped onions in curry-flavored butter or margarine with chutney and chopped peanuts.

Italian: Top hamburger with a slize of mozzarella cheese and broil. Top with hot marinara or herbed tomato sauce.

Mexican: A grilled tomato slice sprinkled with shredded lettuce, Jack cheese, and dried oregano.

Russian: Sour cream and red or black caviar, or sautéed dill-flavored chopped mushrooms.

Scandinavian: A wedge of blue cheese, dill-sprinkled and vinegar-marinated cucumber slice, and red onion ring.

Spanish: A slice of pimento, stuffed olives and chopped lettuce.

Western Barbecued Burgers

This is a good entrée for an outdoor brunch. Make the sauce ahead and refrigerate. Serve with hamburgers prepared as directed above.

½ cup minced onion
1 tablespoon salad oil
2 cloves garlic, crushed
1 teaspoon dried oregano
2 teaspoons sugar
2 tablespoons wine vinegar
2 teaspoons Worcestershire sauce
2 or 3 dashes hot sauce
2 8-ounce cans tomato sauce

Sauté onion in oil in a medium-sized saucepan until tender. Add remaining ingredients; mix well. Cook slowly, uncovered, stirring occasionally, for 30 minutes. Makes about 2 cups.

BACON

There are many good and different ways to serve America's favorite breakfast and brunch meat, bacon. Here are a few suggestions.

Baked Bacon: This is an easy way to cook a quantity of bacon at one time. Lay strips, with fat edges overlapping the lean of the next slices, on rack in a shallow baking dish. Bake in a 400° F. oven 12 to 15 minutes, or until desired crispness. Do not turn or drain.

Broiled Bacon: Place bacon strips on rack of a broiler pan; put pan under pre-heated broiler about 3 inches below heat. Broil about 2 minutes on each side, turning quickly.

Pan-Fried Bacon: Put bacon strips on a cold griddle or skillet. Cook slowly over low heat, turning occasionally, 6 to 8 minutes, or until evenly crisp. Pour off fat as it accumulates. Drain and serve.

Bacon Curls: Slowly pan-fry bacon strips. When half cooked but still limp, put fork in center of each strip and turn over and over, wrapping strip around it. Carefully remove fork; complete frying.

Breaded Bacon: Coat bacon slices with yellow or white cornmeal or packaged cracker meal; sauté or broil until crisp and brown.

CANADIAN BACON

Canadian bacon is boned pork loin, with tenderloin removed, sugar-cured and smoked like ham. It is very lean and more expensive than regular bacon. It can be bought by the pound in one piece and baked; or sliced for pan-frying or broiling.

Pan-Fried Canadian Bacon: Put slices into a lightly greased skillet and cook over low heat, turning frequently, for 5 to 10 minutes, depending on thickness of slices. Serve with a tart fruit sauce.

Fruit-Glazed Canadian Bacon

1½ pounds Canadian bacon, in one piece
½ cup brown sugar
¼ teaspoon ground ginger
⅛ teaspoon dry mustard
   Salt and pepper to taste
1 tablespoon corn syrup
1 tablespoon fruit syrup
6 thick apple slices
6 canned peach halves or pineapple slices

Remove casing from bacon and score fat side. Bake in a preheated 350° F. oven 1 hour. Combine sugar, ginger, mustart, salt, and pepper; mix with syrups. Remove bacon from oven; spread with glaze. Bake in a 400° F. oven 10 minutes. Add fruit to pan; baste with drippings. Cook another 10 minutes. Serve slices of bacon with pan sauce and fruit. Serves 6.

HAM

Cured and smoked ham, imported specialty hams, and American country-style ham have long been traditional breakfast and brunch fare in many countries. Here are some suggestions for cooking and serving it.

Broiled Ham Slices: Slash fat edges of a fully cooked ham slice, ½- to 1-inch thick. Arrange on broiler pan, set about 3-inches below broiler and broil 6 to 10 minutes on each side, turning once. Serve with a tart fruit sauce or broiled fruit.

Pan-Fried Ham Slices: Trim fat from fully cooked ham slice, ¼-to ½-inch thick, and rub fat over heated skillet. Slash edges in several places. Put in skillet and panfry until browned on each side, 1½ to 2 minutes.

With Fruit: Serve with canned pineapple slices or peach halves, apple or banana slices, sprinkled with brown sugar and sautéed in ham fat.

Home-Fried Ham and Eggs: Pan-fry ham slices, allowing 2 per person, in a little butter or margarine, until golden. Remove to a warm dish and keep warm. Add more butter in skillet if necessary, and slip in 2 eggs per serving; cook gently, basting with juices, until whites are solid white; turn over, if desired. Sprinkle with salt and pepper, and perhaps a little chopped fresh parsley. Or remove eggs and add a little cream to drippings, heat, and spoon over ham.

Austrian Asparagus-Ham Bundles

This is a marvelous spring brunch dish.

    2½ pounds fresh asparagus, cleaned and cooked
    6 large thin slices cooked ham
    2 tablespoons butter or margarine
    2 tablespoons all-purpose flour
    1½ cups light cream or milk

½ *cup grated Parmesan cheese*
Dash grated nutmeg
Salt and pepper to taste

Drain asparagus and divide spears into 6 bundles of equal size, with tips in same direction. Wrap each bundle in a slice of ham; arrange bundles in a large rectangular heatproof baking dish. Meanwhile, heat butter or margarine in a medium-sized saucepan; stir in flour; cook 1 minute. Gradually add cream or milk; cook slowly, stirring, until smooth and thickened. Add ⅓ cup cheese, nutmeg, salt, and pepper; cook 1 or 2 minutes. Spoon warm sauce over bundles; sprinkle with remaining cheese. Put under heated broiler a few minutes, until bubbly hot. Serves 6.

French Creamed Ham

This is a good dish to serve with white or green noodles.

4 *medium-sized onions, peeled and minced*
½ *cup butter or margarine*
½ *cup all-purpose flour*
3 *cups light cream*
1½ *cups milk*
6 *tablespoons tomato purée*
Salt and pepper to taste
4 *pounds ham steak, trimmed of fat*

Sauté onions in heated butter or margarine in a heavy saucepan until tender. Stir in flour; cook 1 minute. Slowly add cream, still stirring, and cook slowly until thickened and smooth. Stir in tomato purée and wine. Season with salt and pepper. Cook over low heat about 10 minutes. Meanwhile, cut ham crosswise into ¼-inch strips and heat in a skillet. Put ham into a serving dish. Cover with sauce. Serves 10.

SAUSAGES

There are numerous ways of serving the wide variety of fresh and smoked sausages for breakfasts and brunches. Try some of these ideas.

Baked Pork Sausage Links or Patties: This is a good way to cook a large quantity of sausages. Spread sausages in a shallow baking dish. Bake in a preheated 400° F. oven about 25 minutes, turning with tongs or a spatula or until browned evenly.

Pan-Fried Pork Sausage Links: Allowing 2 to 3 per person, put sausages into a skillet with about ¼ cup water. Simmer, covered, 5 minutes. Drain off water and cook slowly, uncovered, several minutes, turning once or twice, until browned evenly.

Pan-Fried Pork Sausage Patties: Shape sausage meat into 2½- or 3-inch patties about ½ inch thick. Put into unheated skillet, and cook over low heat about 15 minutes, or until thoroughly cooked and well browned. Pour off fat as it accumulates.

German Bratwurst with Apples

>   3 *large apples, peeled, cored, and quartered*
>   1 *teaspoon ground cinnamon*
>   3 *tablespoons brown sugar*
>   8 *bratwurst*
>   2 *tablespoons butter or margarine*

Put apples into a medium-sized bowl; sprinkle with cinnamon and sugar. Mix well, and let stand 2 to 3 hours. Fry bratwurst in heated butter or margarine in a medium-sized skillet 3 to 4 minutes. Add apple mixture and cook slowly, covered, about 25 minutes, or until tender. Serves 4.

Swedish Herbed Sausage Patties on Tomatoes

A good winter entrée for a breakfast or brunch.

>   2 *pounds pork sausage meat*
>   2 *tablespoons grated onion*
>   2 *teaspoons dried thyme*
>   1 *tablespoon parsley flakes*
>   *Salt and pepper to taste*
>   8 *broiled thick tomato slices*
>   8 *toasted English muffin halves*

Combine sausage, onion, thyme, parsley, salt, and pepper in a large bowl. Shape into 8 large patties. Put into an unheated skillet; cook over low heat 15 minutes, or until thoroughly cooked and well browned. Pour off fat as it accumulates. To serve, put a tomato slice over an English muffin half and top with a sausage patty. Serves 8.

English Mixed Grill

This is an attractive one-dish meal for a small winter brunch.

    6 *lamb chops, 1 inch thick*
   12 *pork sausage links*
   12 *slices bacon*
    6 *thick tomato slices*
    6 *large mushroom caps*
    2 *tablespoons (approximately) butter or margarine, melted*
      Salt and pepper to taste

Arrange lamb chops, sausage, and bacon on a broiler pan. Broil under a preheated broiler about 7 minutes. Turn meats. Add tomato slices and mushroom caps; brush with butter or margarine. Season with salt and pepper. Return to broiler; broil until meats are cooked, about 6 minutes. Serve with fried potatoes, if desired. Serves 6.

OTHER HEARTY ENTRÉES

Scottish Finnan Haddie

Smoked haddock, a Scottish national dish, derived its name from the village of Findon in Scotland, and is popularly called by a corruption of the name, finnan haddie. This is a favorite British breakfast dish.

   ¼ *cup butter or margarine*
    2 *pounds smoked haddock or finnan haddie, skinned and cut into small pieces*
      Pepper to taste
    4 *teaspoons cornstarch*
    2 *cups milk*
    8 *hot poached eggs*

Heat butter or margarine in a large skillet. Add haddock or finnan haddie. Sprinkle with pepper. Cook over low heat 5 minutes. Combine cornstarch with a little of the milk; add to fish. Pour in remaining milk; cook another 5 minutes. Serve with the eggs over the fish. Serves 8.

Russian Beef Stroganoff

This well-known Russian dish is a favorite brunch entrée.

> 4 *pounds beef sirloin or tenderloin*
> ²/₃ *cup butter or margarine (approximately)*
> 2 *medium-sized onions, chopped*
> 1 *pound fresh mushrooms, sliced*
> ¹/₃ *cup tomato paste*
> 2 *tablespoons prepared mustard*
> 2 *cups beef bouillon*
> ½ *teaspoon sugar*
>   *Salt and pepper to taste*
> 4 *teaspoons all-purpose flour*
> 2 *cups sour cream at room temperature*

Cut any fat off the beef; cut the beef crosswise into strips about ½ inch thick and 3 inches long. Heat ¼ cup butter or margarine in a large skillet; add some of beef and brown quickly; remove to a platter. Add remaining beef and more butter or margarine and continue browning. Then add onions to drippings; sauté until tender. Add mushrooms and more butter or margarine; sauté until just tender. Stir in tomato paste and mustard. Add bouillon, sugar, salt, and pepper. Bring to a boil. Lower heat and cook slowly, covered, 10 minutes. Add beef and cook about 5 minutes longer. Lastly stir in flour combined with sour cream. Leave on the stove over low heat 3 to 5 minutes. Serves 8.

Brunch Chicken Livers

> 2 *pounds chicken livers*
> ¹/₃ *cup all-purpose flour*
>   *Dash paprika*
>   *Salt and pepper to taste*
> ½ *cup butter or margarine*

1 *cup chicken broth*
½ *cup dry white wine*
2 *8-ounce cans sliced mushrooms, drained*
2 *cups dairy sour cream, at room temperature*

Dredge chicken livers in the flour seasoned with paprika, salt, and pepper. Heat butter or margarine in a large skillet. Add chicken livers; sauté 4 minutes. Stir in broth, wine, and mushrooms; cook slowly about 3 minutes. Mix in sour cream and heat through. Serve over toast points. Serves 8.

Old-Fashioned Creamed Chipped Beef

This old favorite is a good entrée for an impromptu breakfast or brunch.

½ *cup butter or margarine*
½ *cup all-purpose flour*
4 *cups light cream or milk*
 Pepper to taste
2 *5-ounce jars dried beef, shredded*
4 *hard-cooked eggs*
8 *slices toast or English muffins*

Heat butter or margarine in a large saucepan; mix in flour; cook 1 or 2 minutes. Gradually stir in cream or milk, and cook over low heat until thickened and smooth. Season with pepper. Mix in beef and cook slowly about 5 minutes. Meanwhile, cut eggs into halves; remove yolks; chop whites; add whites to beef mixture. Sieve yolks. Serve beef over toast with sieved yolks sprinkled on top. Serves 8.

Cuban Piccadillo

This flavorful ground beef dish is served over hot white rice. It is a superb brunch entrée.

¼ *cup salad oil*
2 *medium-sized onions, chopped*
3 *to 4 garlic cloves, crushed*
4 *large tomatoes, peeled and chopped*
2 *pounds lean ground beef*
  Salt and pepper to taste
2 *large green peppers, diced*
1 *cup seedless raisins, previously plumped in hot water*
3 *tablespoons drained capers or sliced green olives*
6 *cups hot cooked white rice*

Heat oil in a large skillet. Add onions and garlic; sauté until tender. Mix in tomatoes; cook 1 minute. Add beef and continue cooking, stirring with a fork, until the redness disappears. Season with salt and pepper. Cook, uncovered, stirring occasionally, 20 minutes. Add green peppers and cook 5 minutes longer. Stir in raisins and capers or olives just before serving. Serve over hot rice. Serves 8.

Here are three excellent entrées that can be made with fresh or frozen trout.

Colorado Baked Mountain Trout

6 *slices thin bacon*
6 *fresh or thawed quick-frozen trout*
  Salt and pepper to taste
¼ *cup chopped fresh parsley*
¼ *cup chopped chives*
2 *tablespoons all-purpose flour*
3 *tablespoons butter or margarine*
½ *cup fine dry bread crumbs*

Arrange 3 slices bacon in a shallow baking dish. Wash trout and wipe dry. Sprinkle with salt and pepper. Combine parsley and chives; sprinkle over bacon. Place trout over them. Blend flour with butter or margarine; spread over trout. Sprinkle with crumbs. Arrange remaining 3 slices bacon over trout. Bake, uncovered, in a preheated 400° F. oven about 15 minutes, until trout flakes but is still moist. Serves 6.

Poached Rainbow Trout

2 *rainbow trout, fresh or frozen and defrosted*
3 *cups water*
2 *tablespoons fresh lemon juice*
1 *teaspoon salt*

Wash trout. Put into a large skillet. Bring water, lemon juice, and salt to a boil in a saucepan; pour over fish to barely cover. Simmer, covered, 4 to 6 minutes, until fish flakes easily with a fork. Serve with butter or Hollandaise sauce. Serves 2.

Scottish Trout Fried In Oatmeal

This is a favorite breakfast dish in Scotland.

Wash and dry cleaned trout, allowing 1 per person. Dip each in milk and dredge on both sides with oatmeal. Season with salt and pepper. Fry quickly in heated lard or other fat until fish is golden on both sides and flesh is fork tender. Serve at once, garnished with a cube of butter and a lemon wedge.

London Broil With Mushroom Sauce

An exceptional entrée for a small sit-down brunch.

1 *flank steak, about 1½ pounds*
⅓ *cup peanut or salad oil*
3 *tablespoons soy sauce*
¼ *cup dry red wine*
2 *tablespoons minced shallots or scallions*
1 *garlic clove, crushed*
  Pepper to taste
3 *tablespoons butter or margarine*
½ *pound fresh mushrooms, thickly sliced*
3 *tablespoons all-purpose flour*
1½ *cups beef bouillon*
  Salt
  Freshly grated nutmeg

Cut any fat and membrane from steak. Put steak into a shallow dish, and cover with the oil, soy sauce, wine, shallots or scallions, garlic, and pepper. Marinate 3 hours or longer, turning occasionally. Broil for 5 minutes each side, or until desired degree of doneness. Remove to a serving dish and keep warm. Spoon steak drippings into a small skillet. Add butter or margarine and heat; add prepared mushrooms and sauté 4 minutes. Mix in flour. Gradually add bouillon and cook slowly, stirring, until gravy thickens. Season with salt, pepper, and nutmeg. To serve, slice steak very thin, cutting diagonally across the grain. Spoon sauce over steak slices. Serves 4.

South American Empanadas

You can make these beef-filled turnovers and freeze to serve when you wish.

> 1 *pound lean ground beef*
> 1 *cup minced onion*
> 1 *tablespoon paprika*
> 1 *teaspoon salt*
> 1 *teaspoon ground cumin*
> 4 *cups unsifted all-purpose flour*
> 2 *tablespoons sugar*
> ½ *teaspoon salt*
> ¾ *cup shortening*
> 1 *cup milk*
> ¼ *cup seedless raisins*
> ¼ *cup chopped ripe olives*
> 2 *hard-cooked eggs, sliced*
> 1 *egg white*

Cook beef in a medium-sized skillet until redness disappears, stirring occasionally with a fork. Drain off any fat. Add onion, paprika, salt, and cumin; mix well. Cook 5 minutes. Cool and refrigerate until mixture is so cold that no liquid is left. Meanwhile, combine flour, sugar, and salt in a large bowl. Cut in shortening with two knives or a pastry blender. Add milk; mix well. Turn out on a lightly floured surface; divide into twelve portions. Roll each into a circle 6 inches in diameter. Place 3 tablespoons filling on half of each circle. Top with a few raisins, chopped olives, and a slice or two of hard-cooked egg.

Fold over the other half of dough. Pinch edges together firmly, turning them upward. Brush with egg white. Bake in a hot oven (400° F.) 25 to 30 minutes. Makes 12.

Italian Eggplant Parmigiana

Make one casserole for a small brunch, or two for a larger get-together.

> 2 *eggplants, about 1¼ pounds each, washed and stemmed*
> *Salt*
> 1 *large onion, peeled and chopped*
> 1 *cup olive or salad oil (approximately)*
> 1 *6-ounce can tomato paste*
> 2½ *cups water*
> 1 *teaspoon dried basil*
> ½ *teaspoon dried oregano*
> ¼ *teaspoon pepper*
> 1 *cup all-purpose flour (approximately)*
> 2 to 3 *eggs, beaten*
> ¾ *pound Mozzarella cheese, sliced*
> 1 *cup grated Parmesan cheese*

Cut eggplants crosswise into slices about ¼-inch thick; put into a colander, and sprinkle with salt. Allow to drain 30 minutes, then wipe with paper toweling. Sauté onion in 2 tablespoons hot oil in a large skillet until tender. Mix in tomato paste, water, basil, oregano, 1 teaspoon salt, and pepper. Cook slowly, uncovered, 20 minutes, stirring occasionally. Remove from heat. Dust each eggplant slice with flour; dip in beaten egg. Fry on both sides in hot oil in another skillet until soft and golden, adding more oil as needed. Drain on paper toweling. Line a shallow baking dish, about 2½ quarts, with a little of the tomato sauce. Arrange a layer of eggplant slices over it. Cover with a layer of Mozzarella slices, more sauce, and a sprinkling of grated cheese. Repeat layers to use all ingredients. Bake in a preheated 350° F. oven 30 minutes, or until tender, and golden on top. Serves 6.

Breakfast Braised Quail

This is an elegant entrée for a special-occasion breakfast.

    4 quail, cleaned
    ½ cup butter or margarine (approximately)
    1 pound fresh mushrooms, thickly sliced
    1½ cups dry white wine
    ½ teaspoon dried rosemary
      Salt and pepper to taste
    4 rounds buttered white bread

Brown quail on all sides in heated butter or margarine in a large skillet. Remove with a slotted spoon to a warm platter: Add mushrooms to drippings, adding more butter or margarine, if needed; sauté 4 minutes. Remove and set aside. Return quail to skillet. Add wine, rosemary, salt, and pepper; cook slowly, covered, about 30 minutes, until tender. Return mushrooms to skillet 5 minutes before cooking is finished. Remove quail and mushrooms to a warm platter. Fry bread rounds in warm drippings. Serve each quail over a fried round of bread. Spoon any remaining gravy over the quail. Serves 4.

Down-East Codfish Cakes

    1 pound salt codfish
    3 cups sliced potatoes
    2 tablespoons butter or margarine
    2 eggs, slightly beaten
    ¼ cup milk
      Dash grated nutmeg
      Pepper to taste
      Fat for frying

Soak codfish in cold water to cover several hours. Drain well; shred. Put codfish and potatoes into a medium-sized saucepan; cover with boiling water. Cook, covered, about 30 minutes, or until fish and potatoes are tender. Drain and mash. Add butter or margarine, eggs, milk, nutmeg, and pepper. Chill until ready to cook. Shape into six patties. Fry in heated fat in a skillet on both sides until golden. Serves 6.

Mexican Enchiladas

These baked beef-filled enchiladas are topped with sour cream. They are colorful entrées for a Mexican brunch.

1 *medium-sized onion, chopped*
1 *or 2 garlic cloves, crushed*
⅔ *cup salad oil (approximately)*
1 *pound lean ground beef*
2 *to 3 teaspoons chili powder*
1 *teaspoon dried oregano*
   Salt and pepper to taste
3 *cups canned Enchilada or tomato sauce*
16 *prepared or canned corn tortillas*
¾ *cup chopped scallions, with some tops*
1½ *cups shredded Monterey Jack or Cheddar cheese*
1 *pint dairy sour cream*

Sauté onion and garlic in 1 tablespoon heated oil in a medium-sized skillet until tender. Add beef and fry, separating with a fork, until redness disappears. Add chili powder, oregano, salt, pepper, and ½ cup sauce; mix well. Cook slowly, uncovered, 15 minutes, stirring occasionally. Meanwhile, heat oil in a skillet and fry tortillas, one at a time, on both sides. As soon as tortilla is limp, dip into heated sauce; then spoon about 3 tablespoons beef sauce along center of each tortilla, and sprinkle with about 2 teaspoons scallions. Roll up around filling. Arrange, seam side down, next to each other in a shallow baking dish. Top with remaining sauce and sprinkle with cheese. Bake, uncovered, in a preheated 350° F. oven 25 minutes, or until bubbly hot. Pass sour cream to be used as a topping with enchiladas. Serves 8.

Old-Fashioned Turkey Hash

Here's a good breakfast or brunch entrée for a large group.

½ *cup butter or margarine*
2 *medium-sized onions, chopped*
2 *cups chopped celery*
6 *cups chopped cooked turkey*
6 *cups chopped peeled cooked potatoes*
1 *cup light cream, milk, or gravy (approximately)*
  Salt and pepper to taste
2 *large green peppers, chopped*

Heat butter or margarine in a large skillet. Add onions and sauté until tender. Add remaining ingredients, except green peppers. Cook over medium heat until brown on underside. Press with a spatula while cooking. Turn hash over and cook until brown on other side. Mix in peppers for last 2 minutes of cooking. Serves 12 to 14.

South African Curried Meat Casserole

This colorful traditional dish called *babotie* can be prepared beforehand and baked just before serving.

2 *slices white bread*
2 *cups milk*
2 *pounds ground beef or lamb*
4 *eggs*
2 *large tart apples, peeled, cored, and minced*
⅔ *cup chopped seedless raisins*
2 *medium-sized onions, chopped*
2 *tablespoons butter or margarine*
2 *to 3 tablespoons curry powder*
4 *teaspoons sugar*
2 *teaspoons salt*
½ *teaspoon pepper*
¼ *cup fresh lemon juice*
24 *blanched almond slivers*

Put bread into a small bowl. Cover with milk. Let soak until soft. Squeeze bread dry. Reserve drained milk. Put bread into a large bowl, and add beef or lamb, 2 eggs, apples, and raisins; mix well. Sauté onions in heated butter or margarine in a small skillet until tender. Add curry powder, sugar, salt, pepper, and lemon juice. Cook 1 minute. Add to meat mixture; mix well. Spoon into two 10-inch pie plates or a large shallow baking dish, smoothing top with a spatula to flatten evenly. Dot with almonds. Combine reserved milk and remaining eggs; beat with a wire whisk. Slowly pour over meat mixture. Bake in a preheated 350° F. oven 45 minutes, or until meat is cooked and custard is set. Serves 8.

Easy Creamed Chicken

This is an easy entrée for a Christmas or New Year's breakfast or brunch that can be made beforehand.

2 *medium-sized onions, finely chopped*
½ *cup butter or margarine*
¼ *cup all-purpose flour*
4 *cups light cream or milk*
6 *cups diced cooked white meat of chicken*
2 *7-ounce cans pimento, drained and chopped*
  Dash paprika
  Salt and pepper to taste
3 *tablespoons chopped chives*

Sauté onions in heated butter or margarine in a large saucepan until tender. Stir in flour; cook 1 minute. Gradually add cream or milk and cook slowly, stirring, until smooth and thickened. Add chicken and pimento, and heat through over low heat. Season with paprika, salt, and pepper. Serve, garnished with chives, over warm waffles or toast. Serves 12.

Kippers

Kippers are herring that are split open, mildly salted and smoked. They have an appealing golden-brown color, and a delicate smoky taste. In Britain kippers, grilled, fried, baked, or poached, are traditional breakfast fare. Generally they are served with scrambled or poached eggs and oat cakes or toast.

To grill: Brush washed and cleaned kippers with melted butter and put on a rack a few inches below heat. Grill about 3 minutes on each side. Season with pepper.

To fry: Fry washed and cleaned kippers in heated butter about 3 minutes on each side. Season with pepper. Serve with pan juices.

7

Vegetables and Salads

Flavorful and nutritious vegetables, cooked individually or in combination with other foods, are excellent for breakfasts and brunches. You can serve them as appealing accompaniments to eggs, meats, or other main dishes, or with light entrées. Some vegetable creations also make attractive garnishes.

In Mediterranean and Oriental countries a typical breakfast for many might be a few raw vegetables with bread or rice. Crisp raw vegetables such as paper-thin cucumber slices, carrot strips, small artichokes, tomato slices, broccoli or cauliflower flowerets, red or green pepper wedges, sliced zucchini, radishes, or celery, with or without an accompanying sauce or dressing, are always good for morning or midday meals.

In countries where the potato is grown it has long been a staple for early day dining. Hash browns, home fries, and French fries are still American favorites in homes and restaurants, and in northern Europe you find an imaginative repertoire of potato dishes.

Other starchy vegetables such as beans or other legumes, corn, squash, pumpkin, and chayote are commonplace morning fare in countries where potatoes are less popular.

Over the years the vogue for certain vegetables has fluctuated remarkably. For some time, however, tomatoes and mushrooms, once considered "forbidden foods," have appeared prominently on breakfast tables, particularly as garnishes for meats.

Salads made with one or more greens or lettuces, and sometimes including other foods, as well as those made with vegetables, fruits, and grains, are delectable and attractive for brunches.

Here's a round-the-world sampler of tasty vegetable and salad accompaniments.

Hash-Brown Potatoes

This classic American side dish is a simple potato mixture served in omelet form. Here is the basic recipe.

5 tablespoons (approximately) bacon drippings or other fat
5 medium-sized waxy potatoes, peeled and coarsely chopped
¼ cup minced onion
Salt and pepper to taste

Heat 3 or 4 tablespoons drippings or fat in a medium-sized skillet. Add potatoes, onion, salt, and pepper. Press with a spatula. Cook over medium heat, shaking skillet from time to time, until bottom is browned and potatoes are almost tender. Invert onto a plate. Add more drippings or fat to skillet. Return potatoes to skillet, unbrowned side down, and cook until browned on other side. Remove with a spatula to plates. Serves 6.

Home-Fried Potatoes

4 medium-sized potatoes, boiled, peeled, and cut in ⅛-inch slices
3 to 4 tablespoons butter or margarine
Salt and pepper to taste
1 tablespoon chopped fresh parsley (optional)

Fry potatoes in heated butter or margarine in a medium-sized skillet until brown on underside. Shake pan gently 2 or 3 times. Turn over with a spatula and brown on other side. Serves 4.

O'Brien Potatoes

This dish was created at Jack's, a fashionable New York restaurant, in the early 1900s.

1 *medium-sized onion, finely chopped*
4 *tablespoons butter or other fat*
4 *medium-sized potatoes, peeled, cooked, and sliced or diced*
¼ *cup minced green pepper*
½ *cup diced canned pimento*
    Salt and pepper to taste
2 *tablespoons chopped fresh parsley*

Sauté onion in heated butter or fat in a medium-sized skillet until tender. Add potatoes and fry until brown. Mix in green pepper and pimento. Cook 1 or 2 minutes, stirring once or twice. Season with salt and pepper. Serve sprinkled with parsley. Serves 4.

Danish Sugar-Browned Potatoes

8 *small potatoes, peeled*
    Salt
5 *tablespoons sugar*
½ *cup butter or margarine*

Cook potatoes in salted water until just tender. Drain and cool slightly. Heat sugar in a medium-sized skillet until it begins to brown. Stir in butter or margarine and cook until it melts. Add potatoes and cook, shaking the pan often, until they are golden and well glazed with the sugar and butter. Serves 8.

Swiss Rösti

This national dish of Switzerland can include grated cheese instead of the onion, if desired.

6 *medium-sized potatoes, washed*
1 *small onion, finely chopped*
    Salt to taste
¼ *cup (approximately) butter or margarine*

Cook unpeeled potatoes in boiling salted water until just tender. Drain and cool. Remove skins and grate potatoes. Mix with onion and salt. Heat 2 tablespoons butter or margarine in a medium-sized skillet. Add potato mixture and flatten with a spatula. Cook over moderate heat until a golden crust forms on the bottom. Shake pan occasionally while cooking. Loosen around edges. Invert onto a plate. Add more butter or margarine to pan. Return potato cake to pan. Cook until golden brown on other side. Serves 4 to 6.

German Heaven and Earth

This potato-apple dish is eaten with fried sausages in Germany.

6 *medium-sized potatoes, peeled*
6 *medium-sized apples, cored and peeled*
  Pinch sugar
  Salt and pepper to taste
¼ *pound bacon, chopped and fried*

Cook potatoes in salted boiling water until tender; drain and mash. Cook apples in water to cover until soft; drain and purée. Combine potatoes and apples while they are still hot. Add sugar, salt, and pepper. Serve topped with cooked bacon. Serves 6.

Pennsylvania Dutch Potato Pancakes

2 *cups seasoned mashed potatoes*
2 *eggs, separated*
¼ *cup all-purpose flour*
2 *teaspoons baking powder*
  Salt and pepper to taste
1 *cup milk*
1 *small onion, finely chopped (optional)*
  Fat for frying

Combine potatoes, egg yolks, flour, baking powder, salt, and pepper in a large bowl. Add milk and onion; mix until smooth. Beat egg whites until stiff and fold into potato mixture. Drop by tablespoons into a well-greased large skillet. Brown on both sides, adding more fat as needed. Serve at once. Serves 6.

Jewish Potato Latkes

3 medium-sized potatoes, peeled and grated
1 egg
1 small onion, grated
  Salt and pepper to taste
½ cup (approximately) matzo meal or flour
  Peanut oil or shortening

Wrap potatoes in cheesecloth and squeeze tightly to press out all water. Put into a bowl. Add egg, onion, salt, pepper, and matzo meal or flour, using enough to make a firm mixture; mix well. Drop by tablespoons into a well-greased large skillet. Brown on both sides and serve at once. Serve with hot applesauce, cream cheese, or sour cream, if desired. Serves 6.

Nevada Basque Potatoes

3 large potatoes, peeled and thinly sliced
1 medium-sized onion, finely chopped
1 garlic clove, crushed
3 tablespoons olive or salad oil
1 cup chopped pimentos
1 cup chicken broth
2 tablespoons chopped fresh parsley
  Salt and pepper to taste

Fry potatoes, onion, and garlic in oil in a medium-sized skillet until potatoes are browned. Add other ingredients and simmer until potatoes are tender, about 10 minutes. Serves 4 to 6.

Southern Candied Sweet Potatoes

6 medium-sized sweet potatoes
  Salt
¾ cup brown sugar
¹/₃ cup butter or margarine

Scrub potatoes and cook in boiling salted water until just tender, about 30 minutes. Cool, peel, and slice. Arrange in layers in a buttered shallow baking dish, sprinkling each layer with salt, brown sugar, and bits of butter. Bake in a preheated 375° F. oven 30 minutes, turning potatoes when half baked. Serves 6.

Note: Another version uses canned potatoes, honey, and orange juice.

Swedish Jansson's Temptation

This is a piquant potato dish, flavored with onions and anchovies. Prepare beforehand and serve for a brunch.

    1 2-ounce can flat anchovy fillets
    2 medium-sized onions, thinly sliced
    4 tablespoons butter or margarine (approximately)
    6 medium-sized potatoes, peeled, and cut into small strips
      Pepper
    1½ to 2 cups light cream or milk
    ⅛ cup buttered fine dry bread crumbs (optional)

Drain anchovies, reserving liquid, and chop into small pieces. Sauté onions in 3 tablespoons heated butter or margarine in a small skillet until tender. Arrange potatoes and onions in layers in a greased shallow baking dish, sprinkling with chopped anchovies and pepper and dotting with butter or margarine. Slowly pour cream or milk over ingredients, using enough to cover them. Also pour in the reserved anchovy liquid. Sprinkle top with buttered crumbs or dot with butter or margarine. Bake, covered, in a 400° F. oven 30 minutes. Uncover and continue to cook several minutes longer, until potatoes are tender and top is golden brown. Serves 6 to 8.

Broiled Tomatoes

Use this recipe for a large get-together.

Cut out stem ends from 12 firm large tomatoes. Cut each into halves crosswise. Sprinkle cut surfaces with crumbled dried basil, salt, and pepper. Dot with butter. Arrange in broiler pan and cook under broiler 3 to 5 minutes. Or bake in a preheated 350° F. oven for 15 minutes. Serves 24.

French Herbed Tomatoes

4 *large tomatoes*
4 *scallions, with some tops, minced*
¼ *cup butter or margarine*
¼ *teaspoon dried basil or oregano*
  Salt and pepper to taste
1 *cup fine dry bread crumbs*
1 *tablespoon chopped fresh parsley*

Cut out stem ends from tomatoes. Cut each into halves crosswise. Place cut sides up in a shallow baking dish. Sauté scallions in heated butter or margarine in a small skillet until tender. Add remaining ingredients; mix well. Spoon over tomato halves. Bake in a preheated 350° F. oven 15 minutes. Serves 8.

Old-Fashioned Scalloped Tomatoes

This is an easy side dish to prepare beforehand.

3 *cups cooked fresh or canned tomatoes, drained*
1 *teaspoon sugar*
1 *small onion, finely chopped*
  Salt and pepper to taste
2 *cups soft breadcubes*
1 *tablespoon butter or margarine (approximately)*

Combine tomatoes, sugar, onion, salt, and pepper in a medium-sized bowl. Arrange in layers with bread cubes in a shallow baking dish, and top with bread cubes. Dot top with bits of butter or margarine. Bake in a preheated 400° F. oven for 20 minutes, or until golden and crisp on top. Serves 4.

Italian Broiled Tomatoes

6 *large firm tomatoes*
4 *tablespoons grated Parmesan cheese*
4 *tablespoons chopped fresh parsley*
  Dried basil
  Salt and pepper to taste
4 *tablespoons melted butter or margarine, or olive oil*

Cut out stem ends from tomatoes, and cut each into halves crosswise. Place cut sides up in a broiler pan. Top each with 1 teaspoon cheese and parsley, a little basil, salt, and pepper. Drizzle top with butter, margarine, or oil. Broil under preheated broiler 3 to 5 minutes. Serves 12.

Southern Fried Tomatoes

4 *large tomatoes*
 All-purpose flour
½ *cup bacon drippings or butter (approximately)*
½ *cup brown sugar*
2 *cups milk*
 Salt and pepper to taste

Cut tomatoes into ½-inch thick slices. Dredge each with flour. Fry in drippings or butter until golden on both sides. Remove to a plate and keep warm. Sprinkle with brown sugar. Add ¼ cup flour to pan drippings; mix well. Add more drippings or butter, if needed. Gradually add milk and cook slowly, stirring, until thickened. Season with salt and pepper. Spoon gravy over fried tomatoes and serve at once. Serves 8.

Broiled Mushrooms

Broiled mushrooms are an excellent garnish or accompaniment for such meats as steaks or hamburgers as well as other entrées. Here are some suggestions:

Rinse large fresh mushrooms quickly or wipe with wet paper toweling to remove any dirt. Pull off stems. Rub caps inside and out with butter, margarine, or oil. Place, hollow sides down, in a shallow baking dish. Cook under heated broiler 2 or 3 minutes. Remove from heat and turn over caps. In each cap put a little butter, margarine, or oil, a little lemon juice, salt, and pepper. Just before serving, return to broiler for 2 or 3 minutes.

Variations:

1. Add fresh or dried herbs such as basil, oregano, marjoram, or parsley to butter.

2. Spoon chopped garlic and shallots or scallions into caps.

Baked Mushroom Caps

Rinse fresh mushrooms quickly or wipe with wet paper toweling to remove any dirt. Pull off stems and trim ends. Chop stems. Sauté caps in hot oil or butter for 2 or 3 minutes. Remove with a slotted spoon to a buttered shallow baking dish. Sauté chopped stems in drippings; spoon into caps. Sprinkle with fresh lemon juice, salt, and pepper. Bake in a preheated 350° F. oven 25 to 30 minutes.

Variations:

1. Add fine dry breadcrumbs and minced scallions to chopped stems; sprinkle with oil before baking.

2. Add chopped garlic, tomatoes, and dried oregano to stems.

3. Sprinkle caps with dry white wine and chopped fresh parsley before baking.

Creole Eggplant

    2 medium-sized eggplants, about 1 pound each
    1½ cups olive oil or salad oil
    1½ cups chopped onion
    3 or 4 garlic cloves, crushed
    2 cups chopped green pepper
    2 1-pound cans tomatoes
    1 cup tomato sauce
    1 teaspoon dried oregano
      Salt and pepper to taste
    ¼ cup chopped fresh parsley

Wash eggplants; cut off stems. Cut into large cubes. Heat ⅔ cup oil in a large skillet; add onion and garlic and sauté until tender. Add eggplant cubes, several at a time, and sauté 1 minute. Add more oil as needed. Mix in remaining ingredients, except parsley; cook slowly, covered, about 30 minutes, or until eggplant is cooked. Stir in parsley. Serves 8. Prepare beforehand and reheat, if desired.

Mexican Refried Beans

This well-known specialty called *frijoles refritos* goes well with Southwestern or Mexican dishes.

²⁄₃ *cup bacon drippings or fat*
8 *cups cooked or canned pinto or red beans*
½ *cup chopped onions*
½ *cup diced Jack or Cheddar cheese*

Heat drippings or fat in a large skillet. Add beans, a few at a time, mashing well as they are added. Moisten with a little bean liquid, enough to make them mushy. Cook over fairly high heat until crisp on the bottom and the fat is absorbed. Serve sprinkled with onions and cheese. Serves 8.

Grecian Zucchini

4 *small zucchini, about 2 pounds, washed*
1 *large onion, chopped*
1 *or 2 garlic cloves, crushed*
¹⁄₃ *cup olive oil or salad oil*
3 *medium-sized tomatoes, peeled and chopped*
 Juice of 1 lemon
½ *teaspoon dried oregano*
 Salt and pepper to taste
¹⁄₃ *cup chopped fresh parsley*

Remove stems from zucchini; cut lengthwise into quarters, then cut across in half. Sauté onion and garlic in heated oil until tender. Add zucchini and remaining ingredients, except parsley, and cook slowly, stirring occasionally, about 10 minutes, until zucchini is just tender. Stir in parsley. Serves 6.

Asparagus Polonaise

An attractive vegetable dish for a small brunch.

1 *pound fresh asparagus, cooked*
 Salt and pepper to taste
3 *tablespoons butter or margarine*
¹⁄₃ *cup fine dry bread crumbs*
1 *tablespoon fresh lemon juice*
1 *hard-boiled egg, chopped*
1 *tablespoon chopped fresh parsley (optional)*

Arrange hot asparagus on a warm serving plate. Season with salt and pepper. While cooking asparagus, heat butter or margarine in a small skillet until golden brown. Mix in breadcrumbs and toss. Add lemon juice, egg and parsley; toss. Spoon over asparagus. Serve at once. Serves 4.

Oriental Peas and Mushrooms

1 *pound fresh mushrooms*
2 *tablespoons peanut or salad oil*
2 *10-ounce packages frozen green peas*
2 *5-ounce cans sliced bamboo shoots*
3 *to 4 teaspoons soy sauce*
1 *cup bouillon or broth*
¹/₃ *cup cornstarch*
²/₃ *cup cold water*
   Slivered almonds (optional)

Rinse mushrooms under running water or wipe with wet paper toweling to remove any dirt. Slice lengthwise. Heat oil in a medium-sized skillet. Add peas and break apart with a fork. Add bamboo shoots, mushrooms, soy sauce, bouillon or broth. Cook, stirring frequently, 5 minutes. Mix cornstarch with cold water; stir into vegetables. Cook, stirring, until thick and peas are just tender. Serve sprinkled with almonds. Serves 8.

Jewish Vegetable Casserole (Tsimmis)

3 *cups sliced cooked carrots*
4 *cups sliced cooked or canned sweet potatoes*
4 *medium-sized tart apples, peeled, cored, and sliced*
½ *cup honey or brown sugar*
½ *cup hot water*
2 *tablespoons fresh lemon juice*
2 *teaspoons grated lemon rind*
   Salt and pepper to taste

Arrange carrots, potatoes, and apples in layers, sprinkling each layer with a little honey or sugar, water, lemon juice and rind, salt, and pepper, in a greased shallow baking dish. Bake, covered, in a preheated 350° F. oven 30 minutes, until bubbly hot. Serves 8.

Scalloped Corn

You can easily make a larger quantity of this dish for a breakfast or brunch.

1 *small onion, minced*
½ *cup minced green pepper*
5 *tablespoons butter or margarine*
2 *tablespoons all-purpose flour*
  Dash cayenne pepper
  Salt and pepper to taste
½ *cup milk*
1 *egg, beaten*
2 *cups whole-kernel corn, fresh, canned, or frozen, defrosted and*
  drained
½ *cup fine dry breadcrumbs*
⅔ *cup stale bread, cubed*

Sauté onion and pepper in 2 tablespoons butter or margarine in a medium-size saucepan until tender. Mix in flour and seasonings. Gradually add milk and cook slowly, stirring, until thickened and smooth. Mix in egg and corn. Remove from heat. Sauté breadcrumbs in 1 tablespoon butter or margarine in a small skillet; stir into corn mixture. Turn into a greased shallow baking dish. Sauté bread cubes in remaining butter or margarine and sprinkle over top of dish. Bake in a preheated 400° oven 12 minutes, or until golden on top. Serves 6.

Turkish Vegetable Stew

You can prepare this dish beforehand and reheat.

1 *medium-sized eggplant, about 1 pound*
  Salt
1 *bunch scallions, sliced, with some tops*
3 *tablespoons olive or salad oil*
2 *tablespoons butter or margarine*
3 *small zucchini, washed, sliced*
2 *large green peppers, chopped*
¼ *cup tomato paste*
½ *cup water*
1 *teaspoon dried basil or oregano*
  Pepper to taste
¼ *cup chopped fresh parsley*

Wash eggplant and cut off stem. Cut into 1-inch cubes. Put into a colander, sprinkle with salt, and let drain 30 minutes. Dry with paper toweling. Sauté scallions in oil and butter or margarine in a large saucepan until tender. Add eggplant cubes and sauté 1 minute. Then add remaining ingredients, except parsley; mix well. Cook slowly, covered, about 35 minutes, or until vegetables are tender. Mix in parsley. Serves 6.

Broiled Apple Rings

Wash and core large firm red or green apples; cut into ¼-inch slices. Place on a broiler rack; brush with melted butter or margarine and sprinkle with lemon juice. Broil about 4 minutes, or until slices begin to soften. Turn with a spatula. Brush other side with butter and lemon juice; sprinkle with sugar and ground cinnamon. Broil about 4 minutes, or until golden brown.

Fried Apple Rings

Wash and core large firm cooking apples; cut into ½- to ¾-inch slices. Sauté in heated butter or margarine on both sides until tender. Sprinkle with white or brown sugar while cooking, if desired.

Glazed Apple Rings

Wash and core large firm red or green apples; cut into 1-inch slices. Arrange in a shallow baking dish. Dust with ground cinnamon and nutmeg. Drizzle with maple syrup or honey. Put a little water in the dish. Bake in a preheated 325° F. oven 20 minutes.

Baked Onions

Peel small whole onions or medium-sized onions. Cut the latter in half crosswise. Boil 10 minutes; drain; place into a greased shallow baking dish. Sprinkle with brown sugar, salt, and pepper; dot with butter. Bake, covered, in a preheated 425° F. oven 15 minutes. Uncover and bake 15 minutes longer.

French Fried Onion Rings

3 *large sweet onions*
⅓ *cup milk*
⅓ *cup all-purpose flour*
   Salt
   Fat or salad oil for frying

Slice onions ¼-inch thick; separate into rings. Dip into milk and then flour, seasoned with salt. Fry onion rings, a few at a time, in hot deep fat (375° F. on frying thermometer) until golden brown. Drain on paper toweling. Serves 4.

Norwegian Lettuce Salad

2 *small heads lettuce (Boston, or similar)*
1 *cup dairy sour cream*
2 *teaspoons sugar*
4 *teaspoons vinegar*
½ *teaspoon prepared mustard*
   Salt and pepper to taste
2 *hard-boiled eggs, cut into wedges*

Wash lettuce; drain and dry thoroughly; tear into bite-size pieces; refrigerate. Combine remaining ingredients, except eggs; mix well; refrigerate. When ready to serve, put lettuce into a salad bowl. Add sour cream mixture; toss. Serve garnished with egg wedges. Serves 8.

Belgian Hot Vegetable Salad

1½ *pounds fresh green beans*
 6 *medium-sized potatoes*
 2 *thin slices bacon, chopped*
⅓ *cup vinegar*
 2 *medium-sized onions, finely chopped*
   Salt and pepper to taste

Remove stems from beans; break into 1-inch pieces. Cook in lightly salted boiling water 20 minutes, or until tender. Drain. Meanwhile, peel and cube potatoes; cook in lightly salted boiling water 12 minutes, or until just tender. Drain. Just before serving, cook bacon in a large skillet. Add vinegar; heat; add beans, potatoes, and onions.

Cook a few minutes, long enough to heat through. Season with salt and pepper. Serve hot. Serves 6 to 8.

French Cold Rice-Vegetable Salad

4 *cups cold cooked long-grain rice*
1 *cup cooked green peas*
½ *cup cooked diced carrots*
¼ *cup each of green pepper, tomato, and parsley, all chopped*
6 *scallions, with some tops, chopped*
½ *cup olive oil or salad oil*
3 *tablespoons white vinegar*
  Salt and pepper to taste

Combine ingredients in a large bowl or serving dish. Refrigerate 3 hours or longer to blend flavors. Serves 8.

Old-Fashioned Potato Salad

A good salad for a large summer outdoor brunch.

12 *medium-sized waxy potatoes*
  Juice of 4 lemons
 2 *cups diced celery*
1½ *cups diced seeded cucumber*
 2 *medium-sized onions, diced*
⅔ *cup diced green pepper*
 1 *cup chopped fresh parsley*
  Salt and pepper to taste
1½ *cups mayonnaise (approximately)*

Cook potatoes in their jackets in lightly salted boiling water 25 minutes, or until tender. Drain well; peel, and while still warm, cube into a large bowl. Add lemon juice and leave at room temperature to marinate 30 minutes. Add vegetables, parsley, salt, and pepper; mix well. Add mayonnaise, enough to bind ingredients. Cool at room temperature 1 hour or longer to blend flavors. Serve or refrigerate. Serves 12.

Moroccan Orange Salad

 4 *large navel oranges, peeled and sliced crosswise*
12 *red radishes, sliced*
 1/3 *cup olive oil or salad oil*
 2 *tablespoons fresh lemon juice*
 1 *teaspoon sugar*
 1 *tablespoon orange-flower water (optional)*
   Salt and pepper to taste
   Romaine leaves, washed, dried, and chilled

Prepare oranges and radishes; chill. Combine remaining ingredients, except romaine, and chill. When ready to serve, arrange a bed of romaine leaves in a salad bowl or serving dish. Top with oranges and radishes. Pour dressing over salad. Serves 6.

Austrian Cucumber Salad

2 *medium-sized cucumbers*
  Salt
3 *tablespoons white vinegar*
3 *tablespoons salad oil*
1 *teaspoon sugar*
  Freshly ground white pepper
2 *tablespoons minced chives, fresh dill, or parsley*

Peel cucumbers, cut off ends, score lengthwise with a fork, and slice thinly. Put into a colander and sprinkle with salt. Allow to stand 30 minutes; drain well. Turn into a serving dish. Add vinegar, oil, and sugar. Season with salt and pepper. Refrigerate 2 hours or longer. Serve garnished with chives, dill, or parsley. Serves 6.

California Romaine-Avocado Salad

2 *large ripe avocados*
2 *tablespoons fresh lemon juice*
2 *small heads romaine, washed, broken up, and chilled*
¾ *cup (approximately) French or Italian dressing*

Cut avocados in halves lengthwise. Remove pits; peel. Cut into slices; sprinkle with lemon juice. To serve, combine with romaine and add enough dressing to coat greens. Serves 8.

German Dilled Coleslaw

6 *cups finely shredded green cabbage*
2 *tablespoons cider vinegar or lemon juice*
2 *tablespoons grated onion*
1 *cup mayonnaise, or ½ cup mayonnaise and ½ cup sour cream*
4 *or 5 teaspoons sugar*
2 *tablespoons chopped fresh dill or 2 teaspoons dillweed*

Combine ingredients in a bowl; refrigerate, covered, 2 hours or longer. Toss before serving. Serves 8.

8

Cereals and Pasta

Edible seeds of the grass family, more commonly known as cereals or grains, have been man's most important food since prehistoric times. Dishes made with barley, corn, millet, oats, rice, wild rice, rye, or wheat have always had a prominent place at breakfast tables and brunch get-togethers.

After wild grasses began being cultivated as crops, they provided foods that became such important staples of life that once-nomadic tribes started settling in permanent locations. The history of civilization became intertwined with the quest for rich grain-bearing land and the crops it yielded. Those who lived in the Middle East and near Rome depended on wheat and millet. Northern and Eastern Europeans relied on oats, barley, and buckwheat. The ancient cultures of Asia were based on the growing of rice; whereas the early Central, South, and North American civilizations relied primarily on maize, what is now called corn.

One of the earliest grain dishes was a kind of gruel or mush later called porridge; it was made by boiling grains or meal with water or another liquid. This nourishing, inexpensive mixture was a morning staple in Europe for centuries. Many variations developed around the world. Africans eat mealie, a millet porridge. Italians and Romans favor a cornmeal mush. A staple in Russia is *kasha,* made with buck-wheat groats. Poles are accustomed to barley porridge, and in Finland there are rye, semolina, and barley porridges. Asians have long eaten boiled rice in the morning. The word porridge is now associated with oatmeal and is claimed by the Scots who treasure it as their national breakfast dish.

Early Americans relished oatmeal porridge and similar dishes made with corn products. In every household a bowl of hot cereal for breakfast was traditional. Over the years, however, Americans came to prefer ready-to-eat cereals first developed in 1893 and now made in over 100 varieties. We still have excellent uncooked cereals, too. Some are "instant." Others take only a few minutes to cook. The processing of breakfast cereals is a tremendous enterprise in the United States and these are now exported throughout the world.

Cereals and grains are a major part of our daily diet. Wheat and rye, for example, are milled into flour which is essential to the making of breads, baked goods, and many everyday dishes. The hard durum wheat is important to the preparation of pasta products. Corn is processed into meal and grits, oil and syrup, as well as into the popular corn flakes and convenience foods.

Whole grains provide valuable nutrients, being rich in the B-vitamins, in protein, starch, iron, and phosphorous. The grains which contain the whole kernel—the bran, germ, and endosperm—are con-sidered more healthful, but the refined products are also nutritious.

Grocery stores and supermarkets offer a wide variety of cereals and pasta in many forms. The buyer can select from a number of rices, noodles, macaronis, oats, barleys, and corn products. Specialty food stores and some supermarkets carry less well known but nutritious products which have long been appreciated in foreign countries, such as *bulgur, cous cous,* buckwheat groats, millet, and sorghum.

You'll want to try some of these inviting international recipes for cereals and pasta.

HOT CEREALS

Cooked cereals are of two types, quick-cooking and those requiring a cooking period of one hour or more. The latter can be prepared beforehand and reheated. The more natural the form in which you buy the cereals, the more you save in cost and nutritional value. Oats, sold as either rolled oats or oatmeal, provide the best protein, followed by buckwheat, whole wheat, rye, corn, brown rice, and barley. Cook cereals according to package directions and serve hot with milk, cream, butter or margarine, white or brown sugar, syrup, or honey. Add raisins, dates, prunes, figs, or fresh fruit, if desired.

Put any leftover cooked cereal into a shallow baking dish, spreading evenly about 1-inch thick. Refrigerate overnight. In the morning, cut into squares, dust with flour or dip in bread crumbs, fry on both sides until golden brown in hot butter, margarine, or bacon fat. Serve hot with cooked bacon or sausage.

Scotch Oatmeal Porridge

A traditional Scottish breakfast dish called porridge is usually made with sweet and nutty flavored Highland oats. Sometimes the dish is made with bere meal, a kind of barley. The porridge was once called "stirabout," because it was stirred clockwise with a straight wooden spoon called a spurtle or theevil. The proper way of eating it was to ladle the porridge into wooden bowls and to serve with individual dishes of cold cream or milk. Each person used a horn spoon and dipped a spoonful of hot porridge into the cream or milk before eating.

2½ cups water
½ cup Scotch rolled oats or oatmeal
½ teaspoon salt

Bring water to a boil in a medium-sized saucepan. Add oatmeal in a steady stream, stirring while adding. Reduce heat. Cook slowly, covered, 10 minutes. Stir in salt. Continue cooking about 15 minutes longer, or until cooked. Serve piping hot with cold cream or milk. Serves 6.

Russian Kasha

Kasha, a dry porridge made with a grain, usually buckwheat groats, is a staple dish in Russia. It is eaten with milk for breakfast and is used as an accompaniment to meats and poultry. Leftover kasha can be fried and eaten with melted butter and/or sour cream. In the United States, buckwheat groats are packaged and sold as kasha.

1 cup medium kasha (buckwheat groats)
1 egg, slightly beaten
1 teaspoon salt
2 cups boiling water
1 or 2 tablespoons butter or margarine

Combine kasha and egg in a bowl. Put into an ungreased skillet or saucepan and cook, uncovered, stirring constantly, until grains are toasted and separate. Add salt and boiling water and cook slowly, tightly covered, about 30 minutes, or until grains are tender and liquid is absorbed. Stir in butter or margarine. Serves 6.

Middle-Eastern Pilaf

There are many versions of this superb rice dish. This is a basic recipe to which other foods can be added, if desired.

8 tablespoons butter or margarine
4 cups rich chicken broth
2 cups long-grain rice
  Salt and pepper to taste

Melt 4 tablespoons butter or margarine in a large saucepan. Add broth and bring to a boil. Stir in rice. Season with salt and pepper. Reduce heat and cook slowly, covered, about 25 minutes, or until liquid is absorbed and grains are tender. Do not stir while cooking. Place a light clean cloth over the pan; top with the cover. Leave in a warm place 15 minutes. Stir in remaining butter or margarine. Serves 8.

Tomato Pilaf: Add 2 peeled and chopped large tomatoes or 4 tablespoons tomato paste to butter or margarine before adding the chicken broth.

Other Pilafs: After adding rice to the chicken broth, stir in pine nuts, currants, fresh herbs or spices, and cook with the rice. Or, after the pilaf is cooked, add cut-up cooked chicken, meat, seafood or vegetables.

Indian Khichri

This ancient rice-lentil dish is very nutritious.

1 *medium-sized onion, chopped*
2 *garlic cloves, crushed*
3 *tablespoons butter or margarine*
1 *teaspoon ground turmeric*
½ *teaspoon paprika*
¼ *teaspoon ground cloves*
¼ *teaspoon ground cinnamon*
¼ *teaspoon ground coriander*
½ *teaspoon black pepper*
  Salt to taste
1 *cup long-grain rice*
1 *cup dried lentils, washed*
4½ *cups water*

Sauté onion and garlic in heated butter or margarine in a large saucepan until onion is tender. Add spices and cook over low heat 3 or 4 minutes, stirring often. Add rice and lentils; mix well. Pour in water; mix. Bring to a boil. Lower heat and cook slowly, covered, about 25 minutes, until rice and lentils are tender and liquid has been absorbed. Serves 8.

Romanian Baked Mamaliga with Tomato Sauce

The national dish of Romania is a cornmeal porridge or mush called *mamaliga* with many variations. This is one good one.

1 *cup yellow cornmeal*
1 *cup cold water*
1 *teaspoon salt*
3 *cups boiling water*
1 *cup farmer's or cottage cheese, drained and crumbled*
¾ *cup grated Parmesan cheese (approximately)*
1 *cup tomato sauce*
2 *tablespoons fine dry bread crumbs*
1 *tablespoon melted butter or margarine*

Combine cornmeal, cold water, and salt in a small bowl; mix to form a thick paste. Turn cornmeal paste all at once into boiling water (making sure that the boiling doesn't stop) and stir constantly with a wooden spoon to keep the mixture smooth. Reduce the heat to low and simmer, covered, about 12 minutes, or until cornmeal is very thick and all the liquid has been absorbed.

Turn ⅓ of mixture into a buttered 1½-quart casserole. Top with ⅓ cup farmer's or cottage cheese, ¼ cup grated Parmesan, and ⅓ cup tomato sauce. Repeat layers. Sprinkle top with bread crumbs and melted butter or margarine. Bake in a preheated 350° F. oven 30 minutes, or until bubbly hot and golden on top. Serves 6.

Portuguese Rice with Vegetables

This dish is a good accompaniment for seafood or poultry.

    2 *medium-sized onions, finely chopped*
    2 *garlic cloves, crushed*
    6 *tablespoons salad oil*
    1 *cup diced cooked ham*
    3 *large tomatoes, peeled and chopped*
    5 *cups water or chicken broth*
    2 *cups long-grain rice*
    2 *cups fresh or frozen green peas, or other chopped green vegetable*
    ⅓ *cup chopped fresh parsley*
      Salt and pepper to taste

Sauté onions and garlic in heated oil in a large saucepan until tender. Add ham; sauté 1 minute. Stir in tomatoes; sauté 5 minutes. Add water or broth and bring to a boil. Stir in rice. Reduce heat and cook slowly, covered, about 25 minutes, or until rice is tender and the liquid has been absorbed. Add peas or vegetable 10 minutes before cooking is finished. Add parsley, salt, and pepper before serving. Serves 8 to 10.

Polish Barley-Mushroom Pot

This is an inexpensive, nutritious accompaniment for a winter brunch.

    ¼ *cup butter or margarine*
    2 *medium-sized onions, chopped*
    ½ *pound fresh mushrooms, sliced*
    2 *cups pearl barley*
    8 *cups beef bouillon*
    3 *tablespoons chopped fresh dill or parsley*
      Salt and pepper to taste

Heat butter or margarine in a large saucepan. Add onions; sauté until tender. Add mushrooms; sauté 2 minutes. Stir in barley. Add bouillon. Cook over low heat, tightly covered, about 1 hour, until barley is tender. Add dill or parsley. Season with salt and pepper. Serve with sour cream, if desired. Serves 8 to 10.

Italian Cheese Gnocchi

Gnocchi, small and delicate dumplings made from several farinaceous foods and in a number of forms, are one of Italy's most interesting and least known pastas. This version can be prepared beforehand, and cooked just before serving.

> 3 *cups milk*
> 1 *teaspoon salt*
>   *Few grindings black pepper*
>   *Pinch ground nutmeg*
> ¾ *cup semolina, farina, or cream of wheat*
> 2 *eggs, beaten*
> ⅔ *cup grated Parmesan cheese*
> ¼ *cup melted butter or margarine*

Put milk, salt, pepper, and nutmeg into a medium-sized saucepan. Bring to a boil. Add semolina, farina, or cream of wheat in a steady stream, stirring constantly with a wooden spoon. Cook over moderate heat so milk is still bubbling, stirring constantly and vigorously and scraping sides and bottom of pan, until mixture is so thick that the spoon will stand upright in it. This will take several minutes. Remove from heat. Add eggs and ⅓ cup Parmesan; mix well. Turn mixture onto a greased cookie sheet and spread evenly about ¼-inch thick. Refrigerate 1 hour or longer, until firm. Cut into 1½- or 2-inch circles and arrange, overlapping each other, in a buttered large shallow baking dish. Sprinkle top with melted butter or margarine and remaining Parmesan. Bake, uncovered, in a preheated 400° F. oven about 15 minutes, or until golden crisp. Serve at once from baking dish. Serves 6 to 8.

Jewish Noodle Kugel (Lohkshin Kugel)

This sweet noodle pudding is a good accompaniment for poultry.

> 1 8-ounce package medium egg noodles
> 2 tablespoons butter or margarine
> 2 eggs, slightly beaten
> 1 cup sour cream, at room temperature
> ¼ to ⅓ cup brown sugar
> ½ cup golden raisins
> ⅓ cup chopped nuts
> 1 teaspoon grated orange peel

Cook noodles in lightly salted boiling water in a large saucepan until tender. Drain. While still warm, turn into a large bowl. Add butter or margarine. Mix eggs and sour cream and toss with noodles. Stir in remaining ingredients. Spoon into a greased shallow rectangular baking dish. Bake in a preheated 350° F. oven about 35 minutes, or until cooked. Serve cut into squares. Serves 6.

Carolina Corn Pie

You can easily make one or several of these pies that are good for outdoor meals.

> 2 eggs, slightly beaten
> 1 or 2 teaspoons sugar
> 1 tablespoon yellow cornmeal
> 1 tablespoon melted butter or margarine
> 1 cup milk
> 2 cups canned whole kernel corn, drained
> Salt and pepper to taste

Combine eggs, sugar, and cornmeal in a medium-sized bowl; mix well. Add remaining ingredients and mix. Turn into a buttered 9- or 10-inch pie plate. Bake in a preheated 375° F. oven for 40 minutes, or until filling is set and a knife inserted into the center comes out clean. Serves 4.

Japanese Noodles with Mushrooms

You can make this noodle dish beforehand, and reheat just before serving.

> 1 pound Japanese udon noodles, or spaghetti
> 8 cups dashi or chicken broth

2 *tablespoons sake or dry sherry*
¼ *cup soy sauce*
1 *tablespoon sugar*
8 *scallions, with some tops, chopped*
8 *medium-sized fresh mushrooms, sliced*
12 *cubes bean curd (tofu)*

Cook noodles in lightly salted boiling water until soft, about 5 minutes. Drain. Heat *dashi* or broth in a large saucepan. Add remaining ingredients and noodles and heat through over medium heat. Serves 8.

Southern Baked Grits

Coarsely ground hulled kernels of white or yellow corn, called grits or hominy grits, have long been traditional breakfast fare in many parts of the South. Boiled grits are served simply with butter or, as in Charleston, S.C., garnished with a flavorful shrimp paste. They can also be mixed with eggs and scrambled, or combined with milk and eggs and baked. Leftover cooked grits are good fried in bacon fat or butter. Grits are a good accompaniment for bacon and eggs or fried fish cakes. Cook fine, medium, or coarse grits according to the package directions and serve as desired. Here's a good easy recipe for a casserole.

3 *cups milk*
2 *cups water*
1 *teaspoon salt*
2 *cups hominy grits*
2 *tablespoons butter or margarine*
4 *eggs, separated*
½ *cup grated Parmesan cheese*

Put 2 cups milk and the water into a large saucepan and bring just to a boil. Add salt. Slowly add hominy grits, stirring. Reduce heat and cook very slowly, stirring, until thick. Add 1 cup milk and the butter or margarine, and continue to stir. Remove from heat and mix in egg yolks. Beat egg whites until stiff and fold into mixture. Turn into a greased large baking dish and cook in a preheated 350° F. oven 30 minutes, or until cooked and set. Serves 8.

Southwestern Hominy

This is a good dish for an outdoor meal.

2 *medium-sized onions, chopped*
2 *garlic cloves, crushed*
4 *tablespoons bacon drippings or salad oil*
2 *teaspoons chili powder*
1 *cup minced green pepper*
2 *1-pound cans tomatoes*
1 *teaspoon dried oregano*
  Salt and pepper to taste
4 *cups cooked or canned hominy*

Sauté onions and garlic in heated drippings or oil in a large saucepan. Add chili powder and cook 1 minute. Stir in green pepper and tomatoes, breaking them up with a spoon. Mix in oregano, salt, and pepper. Cook slowly, uncovered, 10 minutes. Mix in hominy and cook slowly, covered, 15 minutes. Serves 8.

Armenian Cracked Wheat Pilaf

Cracked wheat, or bulgur, consists of small brown kernels, which are actually the hulled and pounded wheat. It has an appealing nutty flavor.

6 *tablespoons butter or margarine*
2 *medium-sized onions, chopped*
3 *large tomatoes, peeled and chopped*
2 *cups medium cracked wheat (bulgur)*
5 *cups beef bouillon*
  Salt and pepper to taste

Heat butter or margarine in a large saucepan. Add onions and sauté until tender. Add tomatoes and cook 2 to 3 minutes. Stir in cracked wheat and cook, stirring constantly, 3 minutes. Add bouillon, salt, and pepper. Bring to a boil. Reduce heat and cook slowly, covered, about 30 minutes, until cracked wheat is tender. Serves 8.

South Seas Brown Rice with Fruit

1 *medium-sized onion, finely chopped*
1 *garlic clove, crushed*
3 *tablespoons peanut oil or salad oil*
1 *cup water*
2 *cups pineapple or orange juice*
1 *cup natural brown rice*
½ *teaspoon ground ginger*
  Salt and pepper to taste
1 *cup pineapple or orange chunks*
½ *cup chopped nuts*
1 *cup plain yogurt, at room temperature*

Sauté onion and garlic in heated oil in a large saucepan until tender. Add water and juice; bring to a boil. Stir in rice, ginger, salt, and pepper. Reduce heat and cook slowly, covered, 50 minutes, or until rice is tender and liquid has been absorbed. Stir in pineapple or orange chunks, nuts, and yogurt, and keep over burner until mixture is heated through. Serves 6.

Venetian Risoto with Zucchini

In Venice, traditional rice dishes called *risotos* are made with just about every kind of vegetable. This is one such dish.

3 *small zucchini, about 1 pound in all*
5 *tablespoons butter or margarine*
½ *cup minced onion*
1 *or 2 garlic cloves, crushed*
1 *cup short or medium-grain rice*
4 *cups hot chicken broth or water*
1 *cup chopped fresh parsley*
  Salt and pepper to taste
¼ *cup grated Parmesan cheese*

Cut stems from zucchini; wipe dry and slice thinly. Sauté in 2 tablespoons heated butter or margarine in a large skillet 2 or 3 minutes, until golden. Remove zucchini with a slotted spoon and set aside. Add 2 more tablespoons butter or margarine to the skillet. Add onion and garlic; sauté until tender. Add rice and sauté until grains become golden. Add 2 cups broth and cook over medium heat, uncovered, stirring occasionally, 10 minutes. Add 1 more cup broth, the zucchini, parsley, salt, and pepper, and continue cooking until almost all liquid is absorbed. Add 1 more cup broth and continue cooking a little longer, until rice is just tender. Stir in remaining 1 tablespoon butter or margarine and cheese. Serve while still moist and creamy. Serves 6.

Minnesota Wild Rice

A good dish for a holiday or special occasion brunch.

1/3 cup butter or margarine
½ cup sliced scallions, with some tops
1 cup sliced fresh mushrooms
1¼ cups wild rice
1 10½-ounce can condensed consommé
1½ cups boiling water
½ teaspoon dried basil, thyme, or marjoram
Salt and pepper to taste
½ cup dry sherry

Heat butter or margarine in a large saucepan. Add scallions and mushrooms; sauté 3 minutes. Mix in rice, consommé and water. Bring to a boil. Add herb, salt, and pepper. Reduce heat and cook slowly, covered, 40 minutes, or until rice is tender and the liquid has been absorbed. Add sherry; mix well. Serves 6.

Elegant Macaroni and Cheese

This version of a favorite American casserole, macaroni and cheese, includes bacon, tomatoes, and sour cream.

4 cups macaroni, bows, shells, or twists
8 thin slices bacon, diced
1 cup minced onion
2 cups canned tomatoes, with liquid
1 teaspoon dried oregano
Salt and pepper to taste
2 cups sour cream, at room temperature
2 cups diced American cheese
1/3 cup grated Parmesan cheese
1 tablespoon butter or margarine

Cook macaroni in lightly salted boiling water in a large saucepan until tender; drain. Meanwhile, cook bacon in a skillet until tender; drain off all but 6 tablespoons fat. Add onion and sauté until tender. Add tomatoes and their liquid, oregano, salt, and pepper. Cook slowly 10 minutes. Combine with cooked macaroni, sour cream, and American cheese. Spoon into a large greased casserole. Sprinkle the top with Parmesan cheese; dot with butter or margarine. Bake in a preheated 350° F. oven 25 minutes, or until hot and the top is golden. Serves 8.

Indonesian Spicy Rice

2 *medium-sized onions, finely chopped*
2 *garlic cloves, crushed*
6 *tablespoons peanut oil or salad oil*
2 *tablespoons ground turmeric*
1 *teaspoon ground ginger*
1 *teaspoon ground coriander*
½ *teaspoon paprika*
2 *cups long-grain rice*
2 *cups milk*
2 *cups plain yogurt, at room temperature*
   Salt and pepper to taste

Sauté onions and garlic in heated oil in a large saucepan until tender. Stir in spices; cook 1 minute. Add rice and sauté about 2 minutes. Pour in milk; add yogurt. Season with salt and pepper. Cook slowly, covered, 30 minutes, or until rice is tender. Serve garnished with fried onion flakes, made by frying chopped onions in butter or margarine until golden, if desired. Serves 8.

Italian Cornmeal

You can make a basic Italian cornmeal dish called *polenta* before-hand and serve it any number of ways. When cooked it can be served hot, with butter and grated cheese. Cold slices of polenta that have become firm can be fried in oil, grilled or baked and served with sauces, especially those made with tomatoes or cheese. An excellent casserole can be made with thick cold polenta slices spread with a creamy mushroom sauce and grated Parmesan cheese which, when baked, is cut into squares.

> 6 *cups water*
> 1½ *teaspoons salt*
> 1½ *cups finely ground Italian* polenta, *or yellow cornmeal*

Put water and salt into a large saucepan; bring to a boil. Slowly pour the polenta or cornmeal into the boiling water, stirring as it is added to prevent lumping. Be sure the water continues to boil. When smooth, reduce the heat and cook, uncovered, stirring frequently, 30 minutes, or until thick. A good test is to see if a wooden spoon will stand in the center of the mush without falling. Serve warm or spoon into a shallow buttered round or rectangle baking dish, and chill 1 hour or longer, until very firm. Slice or cut into pieces. Fry, bake, or grill and serve with butter and grated cheese or a warm sauce. Serves 4 to 6.

North African Cous Cous with Vegetables

The staple grain of North Africa is *cous cous,* made in the form of small dough pellets from hard durum semolina or millet and water. They are generally served with a stew-like topping of vegetables in season. Packaged cous cous is sold in American specialty food stores and in supermarkets.

> 1 *package (500 grams, about 17 ounces)* cous cous
> ½ *cup water*
> 2 *large onions, sliced*
> ¼ *cup olive oil or salad oil*
> 1 *tablespoon crushed red pepper*
> ½ *teaspoon ground cumin*
>   *Salt and pepper to taste*
> 1 *1-pound, 12-ounce can tomatoes*
> 3 *medium zucchini, about 1½ pounds, washed and sliced*
> 2 *small turnips, peeled and cubed*
> 2 *large green peppers, cleaned and cut into strips*
> 1 *1-pound, 4-ounce can chick-peas, drained*
> 1½ *cups plain yogurt*
> ⅓ *cup chopped fresh parsley or coriander*

Spread the cous cous over a tray, sprinkle with water, and mix with the fingers. When ready to cook, put into a colander lined with cheese cloth or in the top of a cous cous steamer. Sauté onions until soft in hot oil in a large kettle, or in the bottom of the cous cous steamer. Add red pepper, cumin, salt, and pepper; cook about 1 minute. Stir in tomatoes; cook 1 or 2 minutes and break up with a spoon. Add zucchini, turnips, green peppers, and a little water. Put colander or steamer with the cous cous over the vegetables. Cook, covered, about 30 minutes, or until the cous cous and vegetables are cooked. Add chick-peas 10 minutes before cooking is finished. Stir in the yogurt and parsley, or coriander. To serve, spoon the cous cous onto a large platter and arrange the vegetables and liquid over and around it. Serves 6.

Note: Check the liquid during cooking, and add more water, if needed. There must be a fair amount of liquid because the cous cous cooking above the vegetables absorbs the liquid from them.

Yugoslavian Rice with Vegetables

A good dish to serve with grilled sausages or hamburgers.

    1 large onion, chopped
    2 garlic cloves, crushed
    ½ cup bacon drippings or salad oil
    1½ cups long-grain rice
    3 cups beef bouillon
    1 cup uncooked green peas
    1 cup diced zucchini or other squash
    1 teaspoon paprika
      Salt and pepper to taste
    2 tablespoons chopped fresh parsley
    3 tablespoons chopped fresh dill

Sauté onion and garlic in heated drippings or oil in a large saucepan until tender. Add rice; sauté about 2 minutes. Add bouillon, peas, squash, and paprika. Season with salt and pepper. Cook slowly, covered, about 30 minutes, or until rice is tender and liquid has been absorbed. Stir in parsley and dill. Serves 6.

Continental Baked Green Noodles

12 *ounces green, or spinach, noodles*
²/₃ *cup sliced scallions, with some tops*
10 *tablespoons butter or margarine*
 6 *tablespoons all-purpose flour*
 4 *cups light cream*
 2 *teaspoons Worcestershire sauce*
   Salt and pepper to taste
 2 *cups sliced fresh mushrooms*
   Juice of 1 large lemon
¼ *teaspoon ground nutmeg*
 2 *cups shredded Swiss cheese*
¹/₃ *cup fine dry bread crumbs (approximately)*

Cook noodles in lightly salted boiling water in a kettle until just tender; drain. Sauté scallions in 6 tablespoons heated butter or margarine in a medium-sized saucepan until tender. Stir in flour; cook 1 minute. Gradually add cream and cook slowly, stirring, until sauce is thickened and smooth. Add Worcestershire sauce. Season with salt and pepper. Remove from heat. Sauté mushrooms in 2 tablespoons butter or margarine in a small skillet for 2 minutes. Add lemon juice and nutmeg. Arrange half the cooked noodles in a buttered shallow baking dish. Put half the sautéed mushrooms and drippings and half the shredded cheese over the noodles. Repeat the layers. Pour cream sauce over ingredients. Sprinkle top with bread crumbs. Dot with remaining 2 tablespoons butter or margarine. Bake in a preheated 375° F. oven for 25 minutes, or until bubbly hot and golden on top. Serves 6.

9

Pancakes and Waffles

The pancake, one of the most ancient and versatile forms of bread, was originally a humble mixture of meal and water cooked on hot stones. Over the centuries the popularity of the round, flat creation grew until it became an international favorite prepared in many sizes and shapes, and served with a diverse selection of foods. Pancakes and waffles have long been breakfast favorites and are superb brunch fare.

In Europe the traditional basic pancake, prepared with flour, eggs, milk, and butter, became important in each cuisine. Many nationalities have interesting variations, such as the French *crêpe*, Hungarian *palacsinta*, Russian *blini*, German *Pfannkuchen*, Polish nalesniki, Swedish *plättar*, Italian *cannelloni*, and the Dutch *flensje*.

In early Christian days, when Lent involved a strict abstinence from dairy foods, pancakes were made to celebrate the last day before Lent, Shrove Tuesday. In England it became customary on this day to have a colorful community event called a Pancake Race, which is still an annual competition. The French relished pancakes on the same day, which they called Fat Tuesday, or Mardi Gras.

Pancakes appear in an unbelievable number of international versions. There are the Jewish *blintz*, Mexican corn *tortilla*, Chinese egg

189

roll and doily, Indian *chapati*, Scottish scone, and the Ethiopian millet *injera*, to name only a few.

While pancakes are often made from wheat, there are also those prepared from rice, wild rice, corn, buckwheat groats, oatmeal, potatoes, squash, or pumpkin. They can be leavened or unleavened; prepared flat, rolled, or folded; plain or stacked; filled or unfilled; sweetened or unsweetened; and served as appetizers, entrées or desserts.

In early America pancakes were a staple, a dish that could be easily made and cooked just about anywhere. Rural households and pioneer wagons moving across the country kept an earthenware pancake jar with a starter that could be replenished as it was used.

Americans became devotees of stacks of hot steaming white, buckwheat, sourdough, or corn pancakes served with syrup or other toppings. These were variously called griddle cakes, hot cakes, hoe cakes, wheat cakes, flannel cakes, slapjacks, flapjacks, or stack o'wheats. The variety and quantity of pancakes still eaten in the United States is almost limitless. There are many kinds of batters, thick or thin, and they can be made in every imaginable variation from apple and beer to yogurt and zucchini.

One crisp, light golden bread, a type of pancake, is made with a smooth batter that is poured and cooked on a special iron or mold of two metal parts hinged together. It is, of course, the waffle.

No one knows for certain where and when the waffle originated. Thin cake-like breads called wafers, cooked on special long-handled irons in two parts, have been made in England since the twelfth century. Usually round but sometimes square, the wafers were stamped by the irons with designs, pictures, symbols, or letters and sold in the streets, particularly near church doors at religious festivals.

The wafers were first called *gaufres* in England from the French *gofer*, to crisp or flute. In French the waffle is still called *gaufre*. The English name, however, comes from an ancient German word meaning honeycomb, which resembles the pattern of the modern waffle iron. In Dutch the food is called *wafle*.

Waffles have long been popular in Belgium and Holland as well as in England and France. Dutch settlers are credited with bringing the waffle to America.

George Washington's favorite breakfast was rice waffles, served with a combination of honey and maple syrup. Thomas Jefferson became fond of waffles while minister to France, and he purchased an iron for making them in Holland. Later, as president, he introduced waffles at the White House and thereafter they became traditional presidential favorites.

With the invention of the electric waffle iron, waffles became very fashionable, and in most American households they were prepared daily to serve not only for breakfast but also for light meals and desserts.

American cooks created many kinds of waffles, leavened with yeast or baking powder, made with flour, white or yellow cornmeal, buckwheat, sweet potatoes or yams. The batter could be spiced, enriched with grains, sour milk or cream. In the South crisp sweet potato waffles are still served with fried chicken or ham and a rich gravy. A Kentucky Derby breakfast specialty is a cornmeal waffle topped with turkey hash; whereas a traditional holiday delicacy is a spicy gingerbread waffle topped with honey butter, hard sauce, brandy sauce, or mock Devonshire cream.

Waffles may be savory or sweet. You can serve them plain with butter, syrup, honey, molasses, sour or sweet cream, or various preserves. They are good accompaniments to scrambled eggs, sausage, ham, or bacon; they make an excellent base for creamed dishes or hash; and they are delicious topped with fruits, sauces, whipped cream or ice cream. You can serve them like a shortcake with various toppings, or as sandwiches with any kind of filling.

Waffles should be cooked on electric waffle irons according to the manufacturer's instructions. Correct use of the baker is important since you should have the right temperature, the right amount of batter, follow the correct baking procedure, and take proper care of the baker after using.

Try some of the delicious American and international pancake and waffle recipes below.

PANCAKES

American Pancakes

Here is a basic recipe for American pancakes and suggested variations.

> 1½ *cups all-purpose flour*
> 2 *teaspoons baking powder*
> ½ *teaspoon salt*
> 1¼ *cups milk*
> 1 *egg, beaten*
> 3 *tablespoons melted butter or margarine, slightly cooled*

Sift flour, baking powder, and salt into a medium-sized bowl. Combine milk, egg, and butter or margarine; add to dry ingredients, and stir quickly to moisten. Do not beat. Pour about 2 tablespoons batter for each pancake onto a greased hot griddle or into a skillet. Cook until bubbles appear on surface and pancake is golden brown underneath; turn with a spatula and cook on other side until golden brown and done. Keep warm in a preheated 250° F. oven after cooking, if desired. Serve hot with butter or margarine, syrup, honey, or preserves. Makes about 12.

Note: For a thicker pancake, use 1 cup milk. For a thinner pancake, use 1½ cups milk.

Variations:

Apple: Fold 1 cup finely chopped, peeled apple, 2 tablespoons sugar, and ⅛ teaspoon ground cinnamon into batter before cooking.

Blueberry: Combine 1 cup washed and dried blueberries and 2 to 3 tablespoons sugar. Fold into batter before cooking.

Corn: Fold 1 cup drained cooked or canned corn and ⅛ teaspoon dried oregano or thyme into batter before cooking.

Ham: Fold 1 cup minced cooked ham into batter before cooking. Batter can be refrigerated in a covered container for several days; but because the batter thickens after standing, thin with 1 or 2 tablespoons milk before cooking.

New England Buttermilk Griddlecakes

These are very light pancakes.

2 *cups all-purpose flour*
2 *teaspoons baking powder*
½ *teaspoon baking soda*
½ *teaspoon salt*
2 *tablespoons sugar*
2 *cups buttermilk*
2 *tablespoons melted butter or margarine, slightly cooled*
2 *eggs, separated*

Combine flour, baking powder, soda, salt, and sugar in a medium-sized bowl. Stir in buttermilk, butter or margarine, and egg yolks. Beat egg whites until stiff but not dry. Fold into flour mixture. Pour 1 to 2 tablespoons batter for each pancake onto a greased hot griddle or into a hot skillet. Cook until bubbles appear on surface and pancake is golden underneath; turn and cook on other side until golden and done. Serve hot with syrup. Makes about 20.

Note: Keep warm in a preheated 250° F. oven after cooking, if desired.

Old-Fashioned Buckwheat Cakes

Buckwheat, an ancient grain native to Central Asia, has long been a staple food in Russia and was brought to America by early European settlers. The grain was treasured as an inexpensive and nutritious flour grain, and when ground fine it was widely used for making pancakes. Buckwheats, as the standby was affectionately called, were consumed in steaming stacks in tremendous quantities. In Pennsylvania they were so popular that a native of the state was dubbed "a buckwheat." Stephen Foster (a native Pennsylvanian) increased their fame by writing:

> De buckwheat cake was in her mouth,
> De tear was in her eye;
> Says I "I'm coming from de South,
> Susanna don't you cry.

In recent years buckwheat has regained some of its fo mer stature, since it is now particularly valued for its high vitamin B content and abundant protein. Buckwheat flour is used in combination with white flour for better color and texture. You can prepare the pancake batter at night and cook them the next morning.

1 package active dry yeast
2 cups lukewarm (110-115° F.) milk
1 teaspoon salt
1 cup all-purpose flour
1 cup buckwheat flour
2 tablespoons molasses
¼ teaspoon baking soda
2 tablespoons lukewarm water
2 tablespoons melted shortening, butter or margarine

Sprinkle yeast over lukewarm milk in a large bowl; leave 1 or 2 minutes; stir to dissolve. Add salt and flours; mix well until smooth. Let rise, covered with a light cloth, in a warm place overnight or several hours. Punch down batter; add molasses, baking soda dissolved in lukewarm water, and shortening, butter or margarine. Spoon onto a hot greased griddle or skillet. When bubbles form on top and the underside is cooked, turn over and cook on the other side. Keep warm while cooking others. Makes about 1½ dozen. Serve warm with butter, syrup or honey.

Southern Cornmeal Pancakes

You can serve these appealing pancakes with a topping of creamed chicken or turkey for brunch, or with a simpler topping for breakfast.

1½ cups yellow cornmeal
⅓ cup all-purpose flour
¾ teaspoon salt
2 teaspoons baking powder
2 teaspoons sugar
1 egg
1½ cups milk
2 tablespoons melted butter or margarine

Combine cornmeal, flour, salt, baking powder, and sugar in a medium-sized bowl; mix well. Add remaining ingredients. Stir quickly to moisten dry ingredients. Let stand 15 minutes or longer.

Pour about 1½ tablespoons batter for each pancake onto a greased hot griddle or skillet. Cook until bubbles appear on the surface and the underside is golden; turn with a spatula and cook on other side until golden and done. Keep warm in a preheated 250° F. oven while cooking the other pancakes. Serve hot with butter or margarine, syrup, orange marmalade, or another topping. Makes about two dozen.

Swedish Bacon Pancakes

These attractive pancakes are traditionally served with lingonberries, but cranberries are a good substitute.

  4 slices thin bacon, chopped
  ¾ cup all-purpose flour
  ¼ teaspoon salt
  1 teaspoon sugar
  2 eggs
  1½ cups milk

Fry bacon until crisp; drain, reserving 2 tablespoons of the fat. Combine flour, salt, sugar, eggs, and ¾ cup milk in a medium-sized bowl; mix until smooth. Add remaining ¾ cup milk, the reserved 2 tablespoons of fat, and bacon; mix until smooth.

Heat a lightly greased 6- or 7-inch crepe pan or small skillet. Pour in 2 tablespoons batter. Lift and tilt pan at once to spread batter evenly. Fry until golden on underside; turn over and cook on other side until golden and done. Remove to a plate. Keep warm in a preheated 250° F. oven. Repeat with remaining batter, greasing pan as necessary, to make about 16 pancakes. Serve warm with lingonberries or cranberries.

Polish Mushroom-Filled Pancakes

Delectable Polish pancakes called *nalesniki* are filled with savory and sweet mixtures. This is one of the best.

Pancakes

> 1 *cup milk*
> 2 *eggs*
> 1 *cup all-purpose flour*
> ¼ *teaspoon salt*
>   *Mushroom Filling (recipe below)*
> 1 *cup sour cream, at room temperature*

Combine milk and eggs in a medium-sized bowl; mix well. Stir in flour and salt; mix until smooth. Let stand 1 hour or longer. Heat a lightly greased 6- or 7-inch crepe pan or small skillet. Pour in 3 tablespoons batter. Lift and tilt pan at once to spread batter evenly. Fry until golden on underside; turn over with a spatula and cook on other side. Remove to a plate. Keep warm in a preheated 250° F. oven while cooking other pancakes. Repeat with remaining batter, greasing pan as necessary, to make 12 pancakes. Put a large spoonful of Mushroom Filling along center of each pancake. Fold over two sides and roll up. Serve at once topped with a spoonful of sour cream. Serves 6.

Mushroom Filling

> 1 *pound fresh mushrooms*
> 6 *scallions, with some tops, minced*
> 3 *to 4 tablespoons butter or margarine*
> ½ *cup sour cream, at room temperature*
> 1 *tablespoon all-purpose flour*
> 2 *tablespoons chopped fresh dill or parsley*
>   *Salt and pepper to taste*

Clean mushrooms by rinsing quickly or wiping with wet paper toweling. Sauté scallions in heated butter or margarine in a medium-sized skillet until tender. Add mushrooms; sauté 4 minutes. Stir in remaining ingredients and cook 2 or 3 minutes.

Note: You can make the pancakes and filling beforehand and assemble them just before serving.

Scotch Dropped Potato Scones

Prepare these scones beforehand and cook just before serving.

1 cup warm mashed potatoes
1 tablespoon melted butter or margarine
½ teaspoon salt
1 egg
2 tablespoons buttermilk
⅛ teaspoon baking soda
½ cup all-purpose flour (approximately)

Combine all ingredients in a medium-sized bowl. Use as much flour as the potatoes will take without becoming too dry. The amount varies with the type of potato used. Drop by tablespoons onto a lightly greased hot griddle or heavy skillet. Cook about 5 minutes on each side, until golden and done. Makes about 10.

Romanian Beef-Spinach Pancakes

This is a great entrée for a small brunch. Stacked pancakes are spread with a beef-spinach mixture, tomatoes, and cheese.

1 cup all-purpose flour
¼ teaspoon salt
2 eggs
1 cup milk
6 tablespoons (approximately) melted butter or margarine
1 large onion, finely chopped
2 tablespoons salad oil
1 pound lean ground beef
2 teaspoons paprika
⅓ cup chopped fresh parsley
    Salt and pepper to taste
1½ cups chopped cooked spinach, drained
½ cup light cream
2 cups minced peeled tomatoes
1 cup grated Parmesan cheese
⅓ cup chopped fresh dill

Combine flour, salt, and eggs in a medium-sized bowl. Add ½ cup milk; mix well. Add remaining ½ cup milk and 2 tablespoons melted butter or margarine; mix until smooth. Heat a lightly greased 6- or 7-inch crepe pan or small skillet. Pour in about 2 tablespoons batter. Lift and tilt pan at once to spread batter evenly. Fry until golden on underside; turn over with a spatula and cook on other side. Remove to a plate. Repeat with remaining batter, greasing pan as necessary, to make 12 pancakes.

Sauté onion in heated oil in a medium-sized skillet until tender. Add beef; cook, separating with a fork, until redness disappears. Stir in paprika and parsley. Season with salt and pepper. Cook 1 minute. Spoon into a medium-sized bowl; add spinach and cream; mix well.

Place one pancake on a buttered pie plate. Spread with a layer of the beef-spinach mixture; top with some tomatoes; sprinkle with cheese. Top with four other pancakes and spread with the same ingredients. Then top the stack with another pancake; spread it with about 2 tablespoons melted butter or margarine. Sprinkle with dill.

Repeat the same procedure to make another stack with the remaining six pancakes and ingredients. Cook the two stacks in a preheated 350° F. oven 30 minutes. Cut each stack into three wedges and serve hot. Serves 6.

Russian Buckwheat Yeast Pancakes

These plump pancakes called *blini* are usually eaten as appetizers but they can be superb as an entrée for a brunch.

> *1 package dry yeast*
> *1 cup lukewarm water*
> *1 cup all-purpose flour*
> *1 cup buckwheat flour*
> *1 teaspoon sugar*
> *½ teaspoon salt*
> *1 cup milk*
> *3 eggs, separated*
> *1 tablespoon melted butter or margarine*
> *Garnishes: melted butter or margarine, sour cream, chopped hard-cooked egg whites and yolks; pickled herring, sliced smoked salmon or other fish, red or black caviar, cottage cheese or sautéed mushrooms.*

Sprinkle yeast over lukewarm water in a large bowl; let stand 1 or 2 minutes; stir to dissolve. Add flours, sugar and salt; mix well. Add milk and egg yolks, previously beaten; mix until smooth. Set in a warm place about 1½ hours, or until bubbles form on top and mixture has risen. Beat egg whites until stiff but not dry. Add them with butter or margarine to pancake mixture.

To cook, drop ¼ cup batter on a greased hot griddle or skillet to form a puffy round. Cook 2 or 3 minutes on each side. Remove to a platter and keep warm. Serve pancakes with any of the garnishes set out in small bowls for each diner to spoon over pancakes. Makes about 32 pancakes.

German Apple Pancakes

You can serve these inviting pancakes with ham or sausage or as a dessert.

1 cup all-purpose flour
¼ teaspoon salt
4 tablespoons sugar
2 eggs
1 cup milk
2 tablespoons melted butter or margarine
3 apples, cored, peeled, and sliced thinly
1 teaspoon grated lemon rind
1 teaspoon ground cinnamon

Combine flour, salt, 1 tablespoon sugar, eggs, and ½ cup milk in a medium-sized bowl; mix until smooth. Add remaining ½ cup milk and butter or margarine; mix until smooth. Let stand 30 minutes or longer. Mix in apple slices and lemon rind. Heat a greased large skillet. Pour in 3 tablespoons batter and some apple slices for each pancake; fry until golden brown on underside. Turn with a spatula and cook on other side until done. Remove to a plate and keep warm in a preheated 250° F. oven while cooking remaining pancakes. Serve hot sprinkled with remaining 3 tablespoons sugar and cinnamon, mixed together. Makes about 12.

Jewish Cheese Blintzes

The Jewish pancake, *blintz*, which originated in Eastern Europe, is served all over the world as an entrée at brunch. Blintz purists insist on filling the pancakes with a sweet cottage cheese mixture and topping them with sour cream. But you can fill or top blintzes with sweetened fruits such as apples, blueberries, or cherries.

Batter

> 1 cup all-purpose flour
> ½ teaspoon salt
> 3 eggs
> 1 cup milk
> ¼ cup butter

Combine flour, salt, eggs, and ½ cup milk in a medium-sized bowl; mix smooth. Add remaining ½ cup milk; mix until smooth. Heat a lightly greased 6- or 7-inch crepe pan or small skillet. Pour in 2 tablespoons batter. Lift and tilt pan at once to spread batter evenly. Fry until golden on underside. Remove with a spatula and place bottom side up on a large plate or clean towel. Repeat with remaining batter, greasing pan as necessary, to make about 18 pancakes.

Place 1½ tablespoons cheese filling on each pancake and roll up to completely encase filling. Fry several at a time in hot butter in a skillet until golden brown and hot. Serve garnished with sour cream, a dab of fruit preserves, or a spoonful of blueberry or cherry sauce, if desired. Makes about 18.

Cheese Filling

> 2 cups cottage cheese
> 1 egg, beaten
> 1 tablespoon sugar
> 1 teaspoon grated lemon rind

Combine ingredients in a medium-sized bowl.

FRENCH CRÊPES

The delicate thin pancakes that the French call *crêpes* were extremely fashionable throughout America on the culinary circuit in the late 1960s. *Crêperies,* restaurants with menus based entirely on crepe preparations made in every conceivable combination, sprang up across the country. Cookware departments and stores were deluged with displays of crepe-making pans and gadgets. Crepe cookbooks flourished and making crepes became the chic thing to do.

The French have long enjoyed a great variety of crepes, particularly during *Carnival*, from Epiphany on January 6 to Ash Wednesday, and less frequently during the rest of the year. There are superb savory and sweet kinds. Certainly, the sophisticated crepes Suzette, doused with brandy and an orange liqueur and flambéed, is one of the world's most famous and delectable desserts.

In Brittany, the picturesque westernmost tip of France, crepes are a specialty which Bretons have enjoyed in their homes for centuries. In *crêperies* (pancake shops) you can dine on just about any kind of traditional or modern variation, made with both white and buckwheat flours. Ladies in traditional costume cook large crepes on griddles before the diners, and the fragrance of the cooking wafts through the villages.

Although the crepe mania has subsided somewhat in America, it is still pleasurable to have them for brunch. Serving crepes turns a simple meal into an occasion. They are also inexpensive to make and, depending on the filling, can be an economical dish for entertaining.

Making a good crepe is not difficult, and once you've mastered the technique you can produce many magnificent standard crepes and serve them plain with butter, powdered sugar, or preserves; filled with cheese, seafood, or poultry mixtures; sauced and glazed; or flambéed. They can be served flat, rolled, folded in half or into quarters, or stacked in layers. Crepes are extremely versatile.

There are many kinds of modern crepe-making utensils such as the upside-down griddle pan, but the old-fashioned standard pan, used traditionally in France, is still a reliable standby. You can make small crepes (6 or 7 inches in diameter) or large ones (10 to 12 inches in diameter) in a heavy 6-, 7-, 8- or 10-inch pan (bottom measurement) with sloping sides and a sturdy handle. It should be used only for making crepes.

If possible, it is best to make the crepe batter at least one hour beforehand: the flour will become thoroughly absorbed, and you'll have a more tender pancake. You can prepare the batter more than an hour ahead and even store in the refrigerator several days, if you wish. Because the batter generally thickens as it stands, it may require thinning with the addition of a little more milk or water.

A crepe batter differs from that of a pancake in that it contains less flour and more eggs for the amount of milk used. This results in a thin light crepe. The exception is when it must hold a substantial amount of filling, so you can make a slightly thicker one by using a little more batter. Besides lightly greasing a very hot pan, preferably with butter, it is important to pour the batter onto it all at once and to tilt the pan, quickly rotating it so the bottom is evenly and thinly covered with the batter. The crepe can be turned with a spatula rather than tossing or flipping it into the air as is done in France.

There are many recipes for making crepes as the proportions of flour, eggs, and milk vary with individual cooks. Here are two good basic crepe recipes together with other recipes for using crepes.

Basic Crêpes I

¾ cup all-purpose flour
¼ teaspoon salt
3 eggs
1 cup milk, or ⅔ cup milk and ⅓ cup water
2 tablespoons melted butter or margarine

Combine flour, salt, eggs, and ½ cup liquid in a medium-sized bowl. Mix with a whisk or rotary beater until smooth. Add butter or margarine and remaining ½ cup liquid; beat until smooth.

To cook crepes, mix batter again. Heat a lightly greased 6- or 7-inch crepe pan. Pour in 2 tablespoons batter from a ladle or a small glass or cup. Lift and tilt pan at once to spread batter evenly. Fry until golden on underside; turn over with a spatula and cook on other side. Remove to a plate or flat surface. Repeat with remaining batter, greasing pan as necessary. Makes about 16 or 18 6-inch crepes.

Basic Crêpes II

1 cup all-purpose flour
¼ teaspoon salt
2 eggs
1½ cups milk
1 tablespoon salad oil

Combine flour, salt, eggs, and ¾ cup milk in a medium-sized bowl. Mix with a whisk or rotary beater until smooth. Add remaining ¾ cup milk and oil; beat until smooth. Cook as directed in above recipe. Makes about 16 6-inch crepes, using 2 tablespoons batter for each crepe.

Note: To make sweet crepes, add 2 tablespoons sugar to either of the above batters.

To Freeze: To freeze unfilled crepes, place a piece of foil or plastic wrap between each cooled crepe (to make it easier to separate), and wrap in foil or in a moisture-proof freezer bag. Keep up to three months. Remove crepes as needed and thaw completely before trying to separate.

To freeze filled crepes, put them on a cookie sheet and freeze uncovered. Remove and seal in a moisture-proof freezer bag. Return to freezer. Keep up to two months. Thaw completely before heating.

Serving Crêpes

You can serve and use crepes in many ways. Serve flat or folded with butter, jam, jelly, puréed fruit, syrup, honey, sour cream, or yogurt. Leftover cooked meat, vegetables, poultry, or seafood can be diced, bound with a sauce, and used as a filling for rolled crepes. Or you can top the crepes with such foods as sliced cheese, meat, chicken, turkey, shredded lettuce, chopped tomatoes, and a dressing, and serve as open-faced sandwiches.

For a large get-together, put prepared crepes on a warming tray or over a portable burner accompanied by dishes of prepared fillings, sauces, and chopped foods, and let guests choose their own selections for fillings and toppings.

An attractive way of serving crepes is as cups. To make them, grease the outsides of custard cups. Place a prepared crepe over each one and press to fit the cup firmly. Bake in a preheated 375° F. oven until golden and crisp. Fill with any kind of filling.

Provencal Ratatouille-Filled Crêpes

Here's a colorful crepe entrée that you can make in any quantity beforehand and store in the refrigerator or freezer.

> 3½ cups diced peeled eggplant
> 1 cup diced zucchini
>   Salt
> 1 cup minced onions
> 2 cloves garlic, crushed
> 4 tablespoons olive oil or salad oil
> 1 cup diced green pepper
> 1 16-ounce can tomatoes, drained and chopped
> 1 teaspoon dried basil
> ½ teaspoon dried thyme or oregano
> 1 teaspoon salt
> ½ teaspoon pepper
> 3 tablespoons chopped fresh parsley
> 12 prepared 6- or 7-inch crepes
> ½ cup grated Parmesan cheese

Put eggplant and zucchini into a colander; sprinkle with salt. Leave to drain 30 minutes. Pour off all liquid. Wipe dry with paper toweling. Sauté onions and garlic in heated oil in a large skillet until tender. Add eggplant and zucchini; sauté 5 minutes. Stir in green pepper, tomatoes, basil, thyme or oregano, salt, and pepper. Cook slowly, uncovered, 25 minutes, or until vegetables are cooked, stirring occasionally. Mix in parsley.

To fill crepes, spoon a portion (about ¼ cup) of ratatouille along center of each crepe. Fold over two sides and place, seam side down, in a greased shallow baking dish. Top with any leftover ratatouille mixture. Sprinkle with cheese. Bake in a preheated 375° F. oven 25 minutes, or until bubbly hot. Serves 6.

Curried Chicken-Filled Crêpes

These attractive crêpes are filled with chicken and vegetables and topped with tomato sauce.

> 2 pounds chicken breasts (6 halves)
> 3 cups water
> 1 teaspoon dried thyme
> 1½ teaspoons salt
> ¼ teaspoon pepper
> 4 tablespoons butter or margarine

 4 *tablespoons all-purpose flour*
 2 *teaspoons curry powder*
 1 *2½-ounce jar sliced mushrooms, drained*
 1 *10-ounce package frozen peas, cooked and drained*
18 *prepared 6- or 7-inch crepes*
 1 *8-ounce can tomato sauce*
 ¼ *cup chopped fresh parsley*
 ¼ *cup grated Parmesan cheese*

Put chicken breasts, water, thyme, salt, and pepper into a large saucepan. Bring to a boil; reduce heat; cook slowly 35 minutes, or until tender. Remove chicken from broth; remove meat from bones and dice. Reduce broth to 1½ cups and strain.

Heat butter or margarine in a large saucepan; add flour and curry powder; cook 1 minute. Gradually add chicken broth and cook slowly, stirring, until thickened and smooth. Add mushrooms and peas; cook 1 or 2 minutes.

To fill crepes, spoon a portion of curried filling (about ¼ cup) along center of each crepe. Fold over two sides and place, seam side down, in a lightly greased large baking dish. Top with tomato sauce and parsley. Sprinkle with cheese. Bake in a preheated 375° F. oven 25 minutes, or until bubbly hot. Serves 6 to 8.

Sausage-Filled Crêpes

These are easy to prepare crepes.

12 *sausage links*
12 *prepared 6- or 7-inch crepes*
 1 *1-pound can sauerkraut, drained*
1½ *cups dairy sour cream*
 ½ *cup minced green pepper*

Fry sausage links until brown; strain. Place a sausage in center of each crepe; top with some sauerkraut. Fold over two sides and place, seam side down, in a greased shallow baking dish. Top with sour cream and minced peppers. Bake in a preheated 375° F. oven 25 minutes, or until bubbly hot. Serves 6.

WAFFLES

Basic Waffle Recipe

2 *cups all-purpose flour*
2 *teaspoons baking powder*
1 *teaspoon salt*
2 *tablespoons sugar*
2 *eggs, separated*
1½ *cups milk*
6 *tablespoons melted shortening or butter*

Sift dry ingredients into a medium-sized bowl. Beat egg yolks in a small bowl; add milk and shortening or butter; add to dry ingredients and stir to moisten. Beat egg whites until stiff but not dry. Fold into mixture. Cook waffles according to directions for the waffle iron. Serve hot. Serves 6.

To freeze: Cool; wrap each waffle in foil. Keep frozen up to 2 weeks.

To reheat: put in toaster and heat.

Variations:

Bacon: After pouring batter on waffle iron, top each waffle section with a half of a thin strip of bacon. Cook until crisp and brown.

Blueberry: Add 1 cup well-drained, washed blueberries, sweetened to taste, to waffle batter before cooking.

Cheese: Add ¾ cup grated Parmesan, Swiss, or Cheddar cheese to batter before cooking. Serve topped with creamed ham or mushrooms.

Ham: Add ¾ cup ground or minced cooked ham to batter before cooking.

Orange: Substitute ½ cup orange juice for ½ cup milk. Add 2 teaspoons grated orange rind to batter before cooking. Serve with syrup or powdered sugar.

Pecan: Add ¾ cup chopped pecans to batter before cooking. Serve with a sweet sauce or ice cream.

Rice: Add 1 cup cold cooked rice to batter before cooking. Serve with syrup or honey.

Spice: Sift 1 teaspoon ground cinnamon, ½ teaspoon allspice, and ½ teaspoon nutmeg with dry ingredients. Serve with an orange or lemon sauce, or with orange marmalade.

Virginia Rice Waffles

President George Washington described these waffles as his favorite breakfast dish.

    1 cup all-purpose flour
    2 teaspoons baking powder
    1 tablespoon sugar
    ½ teaspoon salt
    2 eggs, separated
    1 cup milk
    1 cup cold cooked rice
    4 tablespoons melted butter or margarine

Sift flour, baking powder, sugar, and salt into a medium-sized bowl. Add egg yolks and milk, mixed together. Mix until smooth. Add rice and butter or margarine. Beat egg whites until stiff but not dry; fold into batter. Cook waffles according to directions for the waffle iron. Serve hot. Makes about 6.

Belgian Beer Waffles

You can serve these light waffles with ham or sausage, or as a dessert.

    2 cups all-purpose flour
    4 eggs, separated
    1 teaspoons sugar
    5 tablespoons melted butter or margarine
    ¼ teaspoon salt
    ½ teaspoon vanilla extract
    ½ cup light beer
    ⅔ cup milk
      Powdered sugar

Combine flour, egg yolks, sugar, butter or margarine, and salt in a medium-sized bowl; mix. Add vanilla, beer, and milk; mix again. Beat egg whites until stiff but not dry; fold into batter. Cook waffles according to directions for the waffle iron. Serve hot with powdered sugar. Makes about 8.

Moravian Waffles

These flavorful waffles are from the Moravian Old Salem community in North Carolina.

> 1 *cup all-purpose flour*
> 2 *teaspoons baking powder*
> 1½ *teaspoons arrowroot or 1 tablespoon flour*
> ½ *teaspoon salt*
> 2 *teaspoons sugar*
>   *Dash nutmeg*
> 2 *eggs, separated*
> 1 *cup evaporated milk or milk*
> 2 *tablespoons melted butter or margarine*

Sift flour, baking powder, arrowroot or flour, salt, sugar, and nutmeg into a medium-sized bowl. Add egg yolks and milk, mixed together; blend. Beat egg whites until stiff but not dry; fold into batter. Cook waffles according to directions for the waffle iron. Serve hot with melted butter or margarine and a sprinkling of ground cinnamon and sugar. Makes about 6.

10

Breads

Bread is a universal food made of flour or meal mixed with a liquid and usually a leavening agent. Formed into various shapes and baked, it comes in hundreds of varieties. Bread is a treasured staple for breakfast and brunch.

The first breads made in ancient times were unleavened, shaped like flat cakes and cooked on hot rocks. A similar flat bread, called pita or Arab bread, is still a basic food in the Middle East.

The technique of leavening bread is believed to have been discovered in Egypt. As the legend goes, a forgetful cook noted that some dough, left out overnight, had doubled in bulk. Although initially upset by his mistake, the cook baked the bread anyway and was elated with the result. So were others, and since then leavened bread, molded, twisted, and shaped in various forms, has become standard fare in many cuisines. Sweetened breads were created by combining honey, fruits, and nuts with the dough, which was baked in such shapes as animals and birds.

In ancient Greece bakeries were so popular that crafty owners painted grotesque masks on the ovens to prevent curious customers from opening doors and ruining their creations. Little wonder, for among them were gingerbreads and cheesecakes!

The early Romans further developed the technique of making bread. A tour of the ruins of Pompeii affords ample proof of the glories of their assemblages of baking utensils and stoves. Bakers were esteemed members of the staffs of wealthy households and were highly paid for their artistic creations.

In the Middle Ages, millers and bakers were respected, and every European cuisine became noted for its whole- or coarse-grained dark breads. French chefs created superb white breads.

Bread has indeed been "the staff of life" and has played a significant role in history, religion, and literature. In many cultures "breaking bread together" binds friendship. Bread grievances touched off the French Revolution. In times of need and war the poor form "bread lines" to obtain free food. Christians regard consecrated bread as the symbol of Christ's body, and we all remember Omar Khayyam's version of paradise: "Here with a Loaf of Bread beneath the Bough, A Flask of Wine, A Book of Verse—and Thou . . ."

Over the centuries, breads have been made not only with grains but also with such other food as ground nuts, and "fashions" in breads, as in all foods, have changed remarkably. Around the world we find dark and white breads, the French *baguettes*, Scottish oatcakes, Irish soda bread, Jewish challah, Alaskan sourdough bread, American cornbread, German sour rye bread and pumpernickel, and Caribbean cassava bread, among many others.

In the United States many old-world breads became staple foods. In the mid-1800s, however, a roller mill was developed to crush grain more quickly and economically, and an era of the processed light snowy white breads began. Yet the nutritious outer cover and germ of the grain had been removed, and consequently it was necessary to have flours enriched.

While American stores and bakeries sell every conceivable kind of bread, it has again become popular and wise to prepare these foods in the home. The time spent making them is well worth the effort.

You'll be glad you tried some of these recipes for many good non-sweet and sweet yeast breads, quick breads, rolls, muffins, popovers, coffeecakes, biscuits, and toasts from around the world.

French Brioche

A favorite breakfast bread in France is a buttery, egg-rich, yeast-leavened dough called *brioche* that is customarily served with *café au lait,* coffee and warm milk.

Brioche is made from a classic recipe that comes from Brie, an area of France famous for its cheese. Perhaps the cheese was once used in the dough.

Various breads can be made from the basic dough. They vary only in their shape. You can have the popular *Petites Brioches* (small rolls formed to resemble "a popover with a beret"), the *Brioche à Tête* (a large round with a topknot) or *Brioche Couronne* (crown brioche).

Brioche is a marvelous airy, delicate bread, which can be served hot with butter and/or jelly or jam for breakfast or brunch. You can also hollow it out and fill the center with warm scrambled eggs or a creamed seafood, poultry, or meat mixture, or a sweet filling such as liqueur-flavored sliced strawberries.

Here is a good basic recipe that can be prepared beforehand and kept in the refrigerator for several hours or overnight.

> 1 *package active dry yeast*
> ¼ *cup lukewarm water*
> 1 *tablespoon sugar*
> ½ *teaspoon salt*
> 2 *cups all-purpose flour*
> 3 *eggs*
> ¾ *cup butter, softened*
> 1 *egg yolk*
> 1 *tablespoon water*

Sprinkle yeast on lukewarm water (110-115° F.) in a large bowl; let stand one or two minutes; stir to dissolve. Add sugar, salt, and ½ cup flour. Beat to combine thoroughly. Add eggs, one at a time, beating after each addition until smooth. Then add remaining flour and work in the butter, a little at a time, mixing thoroughly and until butter is absorbed into the dough. Do not knead. Put dough into a large greased bowl. Let rise, covered with a light cloth, in a warm place until double in bulk, about 2 hours. Refrigerate, covered with plastic wrap, several hours or overnight. Prepare as directed below.

Brioche Ring

When ready to shape, butter a 6- or 6½-cup ring mold. With floured hands, flatten dough into a large flat round. Make a large hole in the center and work dough into a doughnut-like shape large enough to fit into the mold. Put dough into mold and pat so it is even on top. Let rise, covered with a light cloth, until dough reaches top of mold, about 2 hours. With a sharp knife make triangular gashes in several places on top of dough. Brush top with egg yolk and water mixed together. Bake in middle level of a preheated 425° F. oven for 30 minutes. Let stand a few minutes. Remove from pan and slice or serve as suggested above. Makes 1 brioche to serve about 12.

Brioche Crown

Prepare in a buttered brioche pan (9¾-inch wide and 3-inch deep) or on a buttered baking sheet. Using a sharp knife, cut off about one-quarter of dough for the topknot or cap. On a lightly floured surface, shape into a smooth ball. Set aside. Turn remaining dough out onto a lightly floured surface. Shape into a ball and put in mold or on baking sheet. With a moistened finger make a hole about 2 inches deep in center of dough. Insert smaller ball in hole. Let rise, covered with a light cloth, in a warm place until dough reaches top of mold or enlarges on sheet. Prepare and bake as directed in recipe above.

Small Brioches

Prepare small brioche as in brioche crown, making small ones with topknots. Bake in buttered small fluted brioche molds, muffin pans, or custard cups in a preheated 425° F. oven 15 to 20 minutes, or until golden brown and easily unmolded. Makes about 16.

Note: Dough can be easily made in a food processor, if desired. Brioche can be frozen for future use. Wrap in aluminum foil. Defrost and let stand at room temperature. Serve cold or reheat and serve hot.

Toasted Breads

Sliced bread, put under the broiler or in an electric toaster and browned on both sides, is always good for breakfast and brunch. Here are some suggestions for making various kinds of toast.

Use white, whole wheat, or raisin bread at least one day old. Thickly sliced bread remains soft and moist in the center when toasted; thinly sliced bread becomes crisp and dry.

Bacon and Cheese Toast: Toast bread on one side in broiler; butter untoasted side lightly. Cover with a slice of Muenster or American cheese. Top with a slice of bacon. Put under broiler until cheese melts and bacon is cooked.

Butterscotch Toast: Toast bread on one side in broiler; spread untoasted side with a mixture of creamed butter or margarine and brown sugar. Put under broiler until bubbly hot. Sprinkle with ground cinnamon or nutmeg.

Cheese Toast: Toast bread on one side; butter untoasted side lightly. Cover with grated Swiss, Cheddar, or American cheese. Sprinkle with paprika, or with a little fresh or dried parsley or dill. Put under broiler until bubbly hot.

Cinnamon Toast: Toast bread on one side in broiler; spread untoasted side with a mixture of sugar and ground cinnamon (about 3 tablespoons sugar and ½ to 1 teaspoon cinnamon). Toast in a pre-heated 375° F. oven or under broiler until sugar melts.

Orange Toast: Toast bread on one side in broiler; spread untoasted side with butter or margarine and orange marmalade. Put under broiler until bubbly hot.

Toast Cups: Trim crusts from white or whole wheat bread. Press gently into a greased muffin tin. Brush surface with melted butter or margarine; bake in a preheated 400° F. oven about 12 minutes, or until toasted and golden. Fill with scrambled eggs, or with a creamed seafood or meat mixture.

French Toast

You can serve this old stand-by in several ways for a small breakfast or large company brunch.

Basic Recipe

2 *eggs, slightly beaten*
½ *cup milk*
1 *to 2 teaspoons sugar*
   Pinch salt
1 *tablespoon salad oil*
1 *to 2 tablespoons butter or margarine*
6 *slices day-old bread, white, whole-grain, French, Italian, brioche or challah*

Combine eggs, milk, sugar, and salt in a shallow dish. Heat oil and butter or margarine in a large skillet or griddle. Dip bread in egg mixture and fry on both sides until golden brown. Serve sprinkled with powdered sugar, cinnamon and sugar, or with syrup, honey, jelly, or apple sauce. Or top with fruit ambrosia, sweetened crushed strawberries, berry preserves, creamed fish, meat, or vegetables. Or serve with broiled or fried ham, bacon, or sausage.

Variations:

1. Substitute honey for sugar and add ⅛ teaspoon vanilla extract.
2. Add ⅓ cup grated Swiss or Cheddar cheese, and ⅛ teaspoon ground nutmeg to egg mixture.
3. Cut bread into thin fingers about 1-inch wide and 3-inches long.
4. For fluffy French toast, separate eggs, combine yolks with milk, sugar, and salt; beat egg whites until stiff but not dry; fold into milk mixture; fry as in above recipe.

Note: For a large group, put bread, dipped in egg-milk mixture, on broiler pan rack; broil on each side about 5 minutes, or until golden brown.

Or put bread on a rack over a cookie sheet and bake in a preheated 450° F. oven 10 minutes. Turn and bake about 6 minutes, or until golden brown.

Swiss Onion-Cheese Bread

> 1 *package active dry yeast*
> ¼ *cup lukewarm water*
> 1½ *cups skim milk*
> 2 *tablespoons shortening or margarine*
> 2 *tablespoons sugar*
> 1½ *teaspoons salt*
> 2 *cups shredded Swiss cheese*
> ¾ *cup minced onion*
> 5 *cups sifted all-purpose flour (approximately)*

Sprinkle yeast into lukewarm water (110-115° F.) in a large bowl. Let stand a few minutes. Stir to dissolve. Combine milk, shortening or margarine, sugar, salt, and cheese in a small saucepan; heat to lukewarm. Pour over yeast; mix well. Add onion and 2 cups flour; mix well. Add enough flour to make a stiff dough, one that will not stick to sides of bowl. Turn out onto a floured surface and knead several minutes, until smooth and elastic. Form into a large ball; put into a greased warm bowl; turn over. Cover with a light cloth and let rise until doubled in bulk, about 1½ hours. Punch down and turn out on a floured board. Shape into two loaves and put each into a greased 9″ x 5″ x 3″ loaf pan. Let rise, covered with a light cloth, in a warm place until dough reaches top of pan, about 40 minutes. Bake in a preheated 375° F. oven 45 minutes, or until golden on top and cooked. Turn out on racks and cool. Makes 2 loaves.

Cape Cod Cranberry-Nut Bread

¼ *cup softened butter or margarine*
1 *cup sugar*
1 *egg, beaten*
2 *cups all-purpose flour*
1½ *teaspoons baking powder*
½ *teaspoon baking soda*
½ *teaspoon salt*
½ *cup orange juice*
1 *tablespoon grated orange rind*
½ *cup chopped walnuts*
1 *cup fresh cranberries, coarsely chopped*

Cream butter or margarine in a large bowl. Add sugar and beat until light and creamy. Add egg; beat again. Sift in flour, baking powder, soda, and salt, adding alternately with orange juice; mix well. Add orange rind, walnuts, and cranberries; mix well. Turn into a greased 9″ x 5″ x 3″ loaf pan. Bake in a preheated 350° F. oven 1 hour or until tester inserted into center of bread comes out clean. Let stand 5 minutes. Turn out onto a rack and cool. Store overnight before cutting. Makes 1 loaf.

Midwestern Black Walnut Bread

¼ cup butter or margarine
¾ cup light brown sugar
2 eggs
2 cups all-purpose flour
3 teaspoons baking powder
1 teaspoon salt
1 cup milk
1 cup chopped black walnuts

Cream butter or margarine in a large bowl; add sugar and beat until light and creamy. Add eggs; beat again. Sift in dry ingredients, adding alternately with milk; mix well. Stir in walnuts. Turn into a greased 9" x 5" x 3" loaf pan. Bake in a preheated 350° F. oven 1 hour, or until tester inserted into center of bread comes out clean. Let stand 5 minutes. Turn out onto a rack and cool. Makes 1 loaf.

Old-Fashioned Herbed Bread

1 package active dry yeast
¼ cup lukewarm water
2 cups lukewarm tomato juice
2 tablespoons sugar
2 teaspoons salt
1 tablespoon mixed dry herbs (basil, rosemary, thyme, marjoram, and
*   parsley)*
5 tablespoons melted shortening (approximately)
5½ cups sifted whole wheat flour (approximately)

Sprinkle yeast into lukewarm (110-115° F.) in a large bowl. Let stand a few minutes. Stir to dissolve. Add tomato juice, sugar, salt, herbs, and 2 tablespoons shortening; mix well. Add 2 cups flour; beat. Mix in remaining flour, enough to make a stiff dough; mix well. Turn out onto a floured surface and knead several minutes, until smooth and elastic. Form dough into a large ball, and put into a greased warm bowl. Brush with melted shortening. Cover with a light cloth and let rise until double in bulk, about 1½ hours. Punch down and turn out on a floured surface. Shape into two loaves. Put each into a greased 9" x 5" x 3" loaf pan. Brush tops with melted shortening. Let rise, covered with a light cloth, in a warm place until dough reaches top of pan, about 40 minutes. Bake in a preheated 375° F. oven 45 minutes, or until golden on top and cooked. Turn out on racks and cool. Makes 2 loaves.

New England Pumpkin-Walnut Bread

2 *cups all-purpose flour*
2 *teaspoons baking powder*
½ *teaspoon baking soda*
½ *teaspoon ground nutmeg*
1 *teaspoon ground cinnamon*
1 *teaspoon salt*
2 *eggs, well beaten*
½ *cup milk*
1 *cup sugar*
1 *cup canned or cooked pumpkin*
¼ *cup melted butter or margarine*
1 *cup chopped walnuts*

Sift flour, baking powder, soda, nutmeg, cinnamon, and salt into a medium-sized bowl. Combine eggs, milk, sugar, pumpkin, and butter or margarine in a large bowl. Add sifted dry ingredients; mix well. Fold in walnuts. Turn into a greased 9" x 5" x 3" loaf pan. Bake in a preheated 350° F. oven 55 minutes, or until tester inserted into center of bread comes out clean. Remove from oven and let stand 5 minutes. Turn out onto a rack and cool. Makes 1 loaf.

Banana Bread

1¾ *cups all-purpose flour*
1¼ *teaspoons baking powder*
½ *teaspoon baking soda*
½ *teaspoon salt*
⅓ *cup shortening*
⅔ *cup sugar*
2 *eggs*
1 *cup mashed ripe bananas, 2 to 3 medium-sized*

Sift dry ingredients into a medium-sized bowl. Cream shortening in a large bowl. Add sugar and beat until light and creamy. Add eggs; mix well. Add dry ingredients alternately with bananas; mix well. Do not beat. Turn into a greased 9″ x 5″ x 3″ loaf pan. Bake in a preheated 350° F. oven 1 hour, or until tester inserted into bread comes out clean. Remove from oven and let stand 5 minutes. Turn out onto a rack and cool. Makes 1 loaf.

Hawaiian Pineapple Muffins

   1¾ *cups all-purpose flour*
   2 *teaspoons baking powder*
   ¼ *cup sugar*
   ¾ *teaspoon salt*
   2 *eggs, slightly beaten*
   2 *tablespoons melted butter or margarine*
   ¾ *cup milk*
   ½ *cup crushed pineapple, drained*

Sift flour, baking powder, sugar, and salt into a large bowl. Combine eggs, melted butter or margarine, and milk; add to dry ingredients; mix well. Stir in pineapple. Do not beat. Spoon into 12 greased muffin tins, filling ⅔ full. Bake in a preheated 425° F. oven 20 minutes, or until tester inserted into muffins comes out clean. Makes 12.

Canadian Bran-Honey Muffins

   1½ *cups all-purpose flour*
   4½ *teaspoons baking powder*
   1 *teaspoon salt*
   1¼ *cups milk*
   ¼ *cup honey*
   1½ *cups bran*
   1 *egg, slightly beaten*
   3 *tablespoons melted shortening*

Sift flour, baking powder, and salt into a large bowl. Combine milk, honey, and bran; let stand until liquid is absorbed by bran; add egg and shortening (slightly cooled); mix well. Stir into dry ingredients; stir to combine. Do not beat. Spoon into greased muffin tins, filling ⅔ full. Bake in a preheated 400° F. oven about 25 minutes, or until tester inserted into center comes out clean. Makes about 16.

Maine Blueberry Muffins

2 *cups sifted all-purpose flour*
4 *teaspoons baking powder*
½ *teaspoon salt*
¼ *cup sugar*
¾ *cup milk*
1 *egg, beaten*
1 *cup blueberries, cleaned, washed and dried*
4 *tablespoons melted butter or margarine*

Sift flour, baking powder, salt, and sugar into a large bowl, reserving 2 tablespoons of flour to mix with blueberries. Combine milk and egg; add to dry ingredients. Coat berries with reserved flour; fold into batter. Add butter or margarine (slightly cooled); mix well. Do not beat. Spoon into 12 greased muffin tins, filling ⅔ full. Bake in a preheated 400° F. oven 25 minutes, or until tester inserted into center comes out clean. Makes 12.

Scotch Oatcakes

1½ *cups old-fashioned rolled oats*
1½ *cups all-purpose flour*
½ *cup sugar*
½ *teaspoon baking soda*
1 *teaspoon salt*
¾ *cup shortening*
⅓ *cup cold water (approximately)*
   Additional rolled oats

Combine oats, flour, sugar, baking soda, and salt in a large bowl. Cut in shortening with a pastry blender or two knives. Add enough water to make a stiff dough. Separate into two balls. Roll each to ⅛-inch thickness on a floured surface. Dust surface with rolled oats, and press down into dough with a rolling pin. Cut into small squares and put on a greased cookie sheet. Bake in a preheated 350° F. oven 15 minutes, or until done. Makes about 42.

Caribbean Banana Fritters

1 *cup all-purpose flour*
2 *teaspoons baking powder*
1 *teaspoon salt*
¼ *cup sugar*
1 *egg*
¹/₃ *cup milk*
2 *teaspoons melted shortening*
3 *ripe bananas*
   Flour for coating
   Shortening or salad oil for frying

Sift flour, baking powder, salt, and sugar into a large bowl. Combine egg, milk, and shortening; add to dry ingredients. Mix well. Peel bananas and remove "strings"; cut each into six diagonal pieces. Roll in flour; shake off any excess. Dip into batter to coat completely. Fry in deep hot fat (375° F. on frying thermometer) until golden, turning once or twice, about 4 minutes. Serve at once, dusted with powdered sugar, if desired. Serves 4 to 6.

Southern Sweet Potato Rolls

¾ *cup scalded milk*
¼ *cup butter or margarine*
¼ *cup light brown sugar*
½ *teaspoon salt*
¾ *cup mashed cooked sweet potatoes*
1 *package active dry yeast*
¼ *cup lukewarm water*
3¹/₃ *cups (approximately) sifted all-purpose flour*

Combine milk, butter or margarine, sugar, salt, and sweet potatoes in a large bowl. Let stand until lukewarm. Sprinkle yeast into lukewarm water (110-115° F.) in a small bowl. Leave a minute or two, then stir to dissolve and add to sweet potato mixture. Mix in enough flour to make a soft dough. Stir to combine thoroughly. Form into a ball and put in a greased warm large bowl; turn over. Let rise, covered with a light cloth, in a warm place until double in bulk, about 1½ hours. Punch down and let rise again until double in bulk. Turn out onto a floured surface and form dough into small balls. Place 3 balls in each section of a greased muffin tin. Let rise until dough reaches top of tin. Bake in a preheated 425° F. oven 12 minutes, or until a tester inserted into muffins comes out clean. Makes about 3 dozen.

Nova Scotian Bannock

½ *cup butter or margarine*
½ *cup brown sugar*
1 *egg*
2 *cups all-purpose flour*
½ *teaspoon baking soda*
3 *teaspoons baking powder*
1½ *teaspoons salt*
1 *cup rolled oats*
1 *cup milk*

Cream butter or margarine in a large bowl. Add sugar and beat until light and creamy. Add egg; beat again. Sift in flour, baking soda, baking powder, and salt; mix well. Stir in oats and milk. Spoon into a greased 13" x 9" baking dish. Cook in a preheated 400° F. oven 35 minutes, or until cooked. To serve, cut into squares and serve warm. Makes 24 pieces.

North Carolina Spider Cornbread

2 ⅔ *cups yellow or white cornmeal*
⅔ *cup all-purpose flour*
2 *teaspoons baking powder*
1 *teaspoon salt*
3 *to 4 tablespoons sugar*
2 *eggs, beaten*
3 *cups milk*
¼ *cup butter or margarine*

Put cornmeal into a large bowl. Sift in flour, baking powder, salt, and sugar; mix well. Combine eggs and 2 cups milk; add to dry ingredients. Melt butter or margarine in a medium-sized skillet or round baking dish. Pour in batter, and tilt pan to spread it evenly. Pour remaining 1 cup milk over the top. Do not stir. Bake at once in a preheated 375° F. oven 25 minutes, or until cooked. To serve, cut into wedges. Top each with a pat of butter or margarine. Serves about 12.

Scottish Whole Wheat Scones

2 *cups whole wheat flour*
2½ *teaspoons baking powder*
¼ *teaspoon baking soda*
½ *teaspoon salt*
1 *tablespoon sugar*
¹/₃ *cup shortening*
1 *egg*
²/₃ *cup buttermilk*

Sift flour, baking powder and soda, salt, and sugar into a large bowl. Cut in shortening with a pastry blender or two knives until mixture is crumbly. Combine egg and buttermilk; add to dry ingredients. Mix to form a soft dough, but do not overmix. Turn onto a floured board and shape into two rounds, each about 6 inches in diameter and ½-inch thick. Cut each round into 6 triangles. Place on a lightly greased cookie sheet and bake in a preheated 400° F. oven 15 minutes, or until done. Serve warm with butter or margarine and marmalade. Makes 12.

Rhode Island Cornmeal Bread

½ *cup fine yellow cornmeal*
1 *cup all-purpose flour*
¼ *cup sugar*
½ *teaspoon salt*
1 *teaspoon cream of tartar*
½ *teaspoon baking soda*
1 *cup milk*
1 *egg, beaten*
2 *tablespoons melted butter or margarine*

Combine cornmeal, flour, sugar, salt, cream of tartar, and baking soda in a large bowl. Combine remaining ingredients; mix well; add to dry ingredients. Turn into a greased 8" x 8" x 2" baking dish. Bake in a preheated 425° F. oven 20 minutes, or until tester inserted into bread comes out clean. Cut into squares. Serve hot with butter and honey, if desired. Makes 9 squares.

Swedish Coffeecake

⅔ *cup butter or margarine*
½ *cup sugar*
½ *cup strawberry or raspberry jam*
2 *teaspoons grated lemon rind*
1 *package active dry yeast*
¼ *cup lukewarm water*
2 *eggs, slightly beaten*
¼ *cup scalded milk*
2 *cups all-purpose flour*
½ *teaspoon salt*
2 *tablespoons melted butter or margarine*

Combine ⅓ cup butter or margarine, ¼ cup sugar, the jam, and lemon rind in a small saucepan. Heat and cook slowly 5 minutes. Set aside to cool. Sprinkle yeast into lukewarm water (110-115° F.) in a small dish. Leave one or two minutes; stir to dissolve. Cream remaining ⅓ cup butter or margarine in a large bowl. Add remaining ¼ cup sugar; beat until light and creamy. Combine eggs and milk; add, alternately with flour and salt, to creamed mixture. Stir in yeast; mix well to form a soft dough. Shape into a large ball. Put into a greased large bowl; turn over and let rise, covered with a light cloth, until double in bulk, about 1½ hours. Punch down dough. Turn out onto a floured surface; roll out into a rectangle about ¼-inch thick; brush with melted butter or margarine. Spread with jam mixture. Roll up lengthwise and form into a circle on a baking sheet. Divide into ¾-inch slices, cutting almost through with scissors. Turn each slice partly on its side. Let rise, covered with a clean cloth, in a warm place until almost double in bulk. Bake in a preheated 350° F. oven 25 minutes, or until tester inserted into cake comes out clean. Makes 24 slices.

Virginia Spoon Bread

3 *cups milk*
1 *cup water-ground cornmeal*
1 *teaspoon salt*
2 *tablespoons butter or margarine*
3 *eggs, beaten*
2 *teaspoons baking powder*

Combine 2 cups milk, cornmeal, and salt in a medium-sized saucepan. Heat, stirring almost constantly, until mixture comes to a boil and thickens. Remove from heat; mix in remaining 1 cup milk, butter or margarine, eggs, and baking powder; mix well. Turn into a greased round baking dish, about 1½-quart size. Bake in a preheated 375° F. oven 45 minutes, or until cooked and golden on top. Serves 6.

English Gingerbread

½ *cup butter or margarine*
½ *cup sugar*
1 *egg, beaten*
2½ *cups all-purpose flour*
1½ *teaspoons baking soda*
1 *teaspoon ground cinnamon*
1 *teaspoon ground ginger*
½ *teaspoon ground cloves*
½ *teaspoon salt*
1 *cup dark molasses*
1 *cup hot water*

Cream butter or margarine in a large bowl. Add sugar and beat until light and creamy. Add egg; mix well. Sift in flour, soda, spices, and salt, adding alternately with molasses and hot water, mixed together; mix well. Spoon into a greased 9″ x 9″ x 2″ baking dish. Bake in a preheated 350° F. oven 40 minutes, or until tester inserted into bread comes out clean. Serve plain, warm with melted butter or margarine, or cold with whipped cream. Serves about 14.

Spanish Sweet Fritters

¹/₃ *cup butter or margarine*
2 *cups warm milk*
3 *eggs, beaten*
4½ *cups all-purpose flour (approximately)*
  Fat for frying
  Powdered sugar

Combine butter or margarine and milk in a large bowl. When butter or margarine is melted, add eggs and mix well. Add enough flour to make a smooth batter. Drop by spoonfuls into deep hot fat

(375° F. on frying thermometer) and fry, turning once, until golden and cooked. Serve warm with powdered sugar. Serves 12.

Note: You may cook the fritters beforehand and keep them warm in a slow oven.

Bacon Popovers

1 *cup all-purpose flour*
½ *teaspoon salt*
2 *eggs, beaten*
1 *cup milk*
1 *tablespoon melted shortening*
3 *thin slices bacon, cooked and crumbled*

Sift flour and salt into a medium-sized bowl. Put beaten eggs into a large bowl; beat again. Add flour and ⅓ cup milk, beating several seconds. Gradually add remaining milk and shortening; beat several seconds. Put bacon into 8 greased custard cups. Add batter, filling a little less than half full. Bake in a preheated 425° F. oven 40 minutes, or until done. Serve at once. Makes 8.

Note: Popovers may be filled with creamed eggs, seafood or meat, if desired.

11

Desserts

When devising menus for breakfasts and brunches, you can take particular pleasure in choosing a light and attractive dessert, one that will be a fitting finale for the occasion.

While desserts are not traditionally served for breakfast, you can enliven an ordinary meal by including a toothsome sweet. Certainly every brunch, whether for family or friends, merits a delightful dessert.

There is a wide range of inviting and delectable pastries, puddings, cookies, cakes, ices and ice creams, as well as fruit specialties which may be served as the last course of the meal. Our word dessert derives from the French verb *desservir*, meaning "to clear the table," and at one time in Europe it was customary to offer an elaborate presentation of sweets after everything else had been removed from the dining table.

Nowadays the selection is generally limited to one dish, but you can offer two or three choices if you wish. One of the world's oldest desserts, cheesecake, which was prepared in considerable variety by the ancient Greeks, has become a very popular brunch dish. So also are light cakes prepared with fruits, or flavored with such foods as carrots, lemons, or spices.

If you did not begin the meal with a fruit course, you can always serve fresh fruits in season, either plain or flavored with some kind of alcohol, yogurt or sour cream, sweet cream, or embellished with ice cream. Baked mixed fresh or canned fruits flavored with spices, and fruit compotes, pies, and tarts are also good choices.

There are very excellent light desserts, too. These include custards, creams, sweet omelets, souffles, colorful flaming specialties, mousses, and homemade or purchased sherbets and ice creams made into coupes, sundaes, parfaits, or served in pies.

Just taste some of the marvelous desserts from this international collection.

Fruit Desserts

Here are some suggestions for making attractive and easy desserts with fruits.

Ambrosia: Sprinkle sliced navel oranges or a combination of orange and fresh pineapple slices with fruit juice, dry white wine, or champagne and grated coconut. Refrigerate three hours or longer.

Blueberries with Brandy: Sprinkle washed blueberries with brandy. Refrigerate three hours or longer. Serve topped with whipped sweet cream, vanilla ice cream, or sour cream.

Coupe de luxe: Serve brandied fruit (peaches, pineapples, or berries) in a large goblet, filling it half full; add chilled dry champagne and serve at once.

Fig-Almond Coupes: Put scoops of vanilla ice cream in stemmed dessert glasses. Top with chopped fresh or canned figs. Sprinkle with orange juice and slivered almonds.

Macedoine of Fruits: Arrange layers of fresh fruits (pineapple cubes, melon balls, sliced strawberries, peaches, bananas, or apricots) in a large glass or silver bowl. Sprinkle layers with sugar, dry white wine, or light rum. Refrigerate three hours or longer.

Melon Rings with Sherbet: Top chilled fresh melon rings with scoops of orange, lime, or pineapple sherbet. Garnish with sliced or puréed berries.

Orange-Sherbet Fruit Bowl: A good dessert for a large group. Arrange scoops of orange sherbet on a cookie sheet and freeze. Remove from freezer several minutes before serving. Put into a large chilled bowl; top with crushed pineapple or puréed berries and almond slivers.

Peach Coupes: Sprinkle sweetened sliced peaches or peach halves with dry white wine or champagne, and top with a spoonful of vanilla ice cream and a garnish of shaved sweet chocolate.

Strawberries Chantilly: Fold chilled sweetened sliced strawberries into whipped cream flavored with powdered sugar and vanilla extract or Cointreau. Serve in a large bowl or in individual dessert dishes.

Strawberries Supreme: Combine chilled whole strawberries with sweetened whipped cream. Garnish top with shaved sweet chocolate.

Turkish Lemony Yogurt Cake

This light cake, sprinkled with powdered sugar, is a good dessert after a hearty brunch.

> ½ *cup butter or margarine, softened*
> ²/₃ *cup sugar*
> 2 *eggs*
> 2 *teaspoons grated lemon rind*
> 1 *cup plain yogurt*
> 2 *cups sifted all-purpose flour*
> 2 *teaspoons baking powder*
> ½ *teaspoon baking soda*
> ½ *teaspoon salt*
>   *Powdered sugar*

Cream butter or margarine in a large bowl. Add sugar and beat until creamy and light. Add eggs, one at a time, beating after each addition. Stir in lemon rind and yogurt and beat again. Sift flour, baking powder, soda, and salt into yogurt mixture and beat until smooth. Turn into a greased 9-inch square baking dish. Bake in a preheated 350° F. oven 35 minutes, or until tester inserted into cake comes out clean. Cool 5 minutes. Turn out onto a rack and cool. Sprinkle with powdered sugar and serve while still warm, or cool. Serves about 10.

Austrian Linzer Torte

This attractive lattice-top cake is made with a rich ground almond and brandy flavored dough.

1 cup unsalted butter
1 cup sugar
2 egg yolks
2 hard-cooked eggs, sieved
  Juice of 1 lemon
2 teaspoons grated lemon rind
1 tablespoon brandy (optional)
½ pound almonds, ground
2 cups sifted all-purpose flour
1 teaspoon baking powder
1 cup raspberry or strawberry jam
  Powdered sugar

Cream butter in a large bowl. Add sugar and beat until creamy and light. Add egg yolks, sieved eggs, lemon juice and rind, and brandy, if used. Mix well. Stir in almonds, flour, and baking powder. Combine with fingers to make a smooth dough. Press ¾ of dough into a greased 9-inch layer cake pan with a removable bottom, making the bottom layer thicker than the sides. Spread bottom with ¾ cup of jam. Roll out remaining dough and cut into ⅓-inch wide strips. Arrange strips in lattice pattern over jam-covered dough. Bake in a preheated 350° F. oven 45 to 50 minutes, or until golden. Before serving, fill spaces between strips with remaining jam. Sprinkle with powdered sugar. Serves 8 to 10.

Scotch Nut Shortbread

You can make these superb cookies several days beforehand and store in a canister until ready to serve.

1 cup softened butter or margarine
½ cup sugar
¼ teaspoon salt
2½ cups sifted all-purpose flour
¼ teaspoon almond extract (optional)
½ cup finely chopped almonds or walnuts

Cream butter or margarine in a large bowl. Add sugar and beat until creamy and light. Stir in remaining ingredients; mix well. Form into a ball, and chill in refrigerator. Roll out on a floured board to ⅛-inch thickness. Cut into 2- x 2-inch lengths. Prick tops with a fork. Place on an ungreased cookie sheet. Bake in a preheated 325° F. oven about 20 minutes, or until cooked. Store in a canister until ready to serve. Makes about 4½ dozen.

Spanish Flan

The national dessert of Spain is *flan,* caramel custard or *crème caramel.* It is always good.

> 15 *tablespoons sugar*
> 2 *teaspoons water*
> 2 *cups milk*
> 4 *large eggs*
> ½ *teaspoon orange or vanilla extract*

Put 12 tablespoons (¾ cup) sugar into a heavy skillet. Add water and heat over medium heat. When sugar begins to melt, stir it and shake the pan a little, but leave over heat until mixture becomes a deep golden syrup. Pour at once into 6 custard cups or baking dish. Scald milk. Combine eggs, remaining 3 tablespoons sugar, and orange or vanilla extract in a medium-sized bowl. Pour in hot milk and beat to blend well. Pour over caramelized mixture in custard cups. Place dishes in a pan of hot water. Bake in a preheated 375° F. oven 1 hour, or until knife inserted into custard comes out clean. Remove from oven; take out from hot water; cool. Invert on individual plates and serve, or chill until ready to serve. Serves 6.

Southern Chess Pie

You can serve this lemon-flavored custard pie for breakfast or brunch.

> 1½ *cups sugar*
> 1 *tablespoon all-purpose flour*
> 1 *tablespoons white cornmeal*
> 4 *eggs*
> ⅓ *cup fresh lemon juice*
> 2 *teaspoons grated lemon rind*
> ¼ *cup butter or margarine, melted*
> 1 *unbaked 9-inch pie shell*

Combine sugar, flour, and cornmeal in a large bowl. Add eggs, one at a time, beating after each addition. Beat until light and creamy. Stir in lemon juice and rind, and butter or margarine. Turn into pie shell. Bake in a preheated 375° F. oven 35 to 40 minutes, or until knife inserted into filling comes out clean. Cool. Serve at room temperature or chill until ready to serve. Serves 6.

Down-East Blueberry Cobbler

This old-fashioned baked blueberry pudding is even better with a topping of cream, custard sauce, or ice cream!

¾ *cup sugar*
1 *egg*
3 *tablespoons melted butter or shortening*
1 *cup all-purpose flour*
2 *teaspoons baking powder*
½ *teaspoon salt*
¼ *cup milk*
2 *cups fresh or frozen blueberries*
⅛ *teaspoon ground cinnamon*

Combine ½ cup sugar and egg in a large bowl; mix well. Stir in melted butter or shortening. Sift in flour, baking powder, and salt, adding alternately with the milk. Mix well. Combine blueberries with remaining ¼ cup sugar and cinnamon. Spread evenly in a greased 12" x 8" x 2" baking dish. Top with batter, spreading evenly. Bake in a preheated 375° F. oven 30 minutes, or until tester inserted into cake comes out clean. Serve warm, with the berry side up. Top with cream, custard sauce, or vanilla ice cream, if desired. Serves 6.

Italian Citrus Granita

This flavored ice, akin to a sherbet, is slightly granular in consistency, thus the name. It is very easy to make, and there are fine crystals because it is not stirred while freezing.

4 *cups water*
2 *cups sugar*
  Juice of 6 lemons and 2 oranges (2 cups), strained
4 *teaspoons grated lemon rind*

Combine water and sugar in a medium-sized saucepan. Bring to a boil. Cook rapidly 5 minutes. Remove from heat and cool. Add lemon and orange juices and lemon rind. Mix well. Pour into 4 refrigerator ice-cube trays from which dividers have been removed, or into a large shallow dish. Freeze until firm, 3 to 4 hours in the freezer-top of a refrigerator, about 1 hour in a large freezer. Do not stir while freezing. Serve in sherbet glasses. Serves 10 to 12.

Normandy Baked Apples

These whole apples are cooked in pastry and served with cream.

> *Rich pastry for a 2-crust 9-inch pie*
> *6 medium-sized tart apples, cored and pared*
> *6 tablespoons sugar*
> *6 tablespoons butter or margarine*
> *1 teaspoon ground cinnamon*
> *1 egg, beaten*

Roll out pastry to about ⅛-inch thickness and cut into six-inch squares. Place an apple in center of six squares of pastry. Knead together the sugar and butter or margarine; add cinnamon. Form sugar-butter mixture into 6 small balls and put one ball in each apple cavity. Bring opposite points of pastry up over each apple and, with hands, mold pastry around apples to cover completely. Cut remaining pastry square into six tiny circles and place each on top of apples. Rib outsides of pastry with a fork. Brush tops with beaten egg. Arrange in a shallow baking dish. Bake in a preheated 425° F. oven 40 minutes, or until crust is golden brown and apples are cooked through. Serve warm or cold with cream or whipped cream. Serves 6.

Kentucky Bourbon Chocolate Pie

Serve this rich whiskey-flavored chocolate pie at a Derby breakfast or brunch, or at any other special-occasion meal.

> *1¼ cups sugar*
> *5 tablespoons cocoa*
> *4 tablespoons all-purpose flour*
> *¼ teaspoon salt*
> *1½ cups milk*
> *4 eggs, separated*
> *1 tablespoon butter or margarine*

1 teaspoon vanilla extract
2 tablespoons bourbon whiskey
½ teaspoon cream of tartar
8 tablespoons sugar
1 baked 9- or 10-inch pie shell

Combine sugar, cocoa, flour, and milk in top of a double boiler. Put over bubbling hot water and gradually add milk, stirring as adding. Cook over low heat, stirring frequently, until thickened and smooth. Beat egg yolks until light and creamy in a small bowl. Spoon in some of the hot chocolate mixture; mix well; add to double boiler. Cook slowly, stirring constantly, until mixture thickens. Remove from stove; stir in butter or margarine, vanilla, and whiskey. Cool. Beat egg whites with cream of tartar until almost stiff. Add sugar and beat until stiff but not dry. Spoon cooled chocolate mixture into pie shell. Top with meringue, spreading it to the edges. Bake in a preheated 350° F. oven 15 minutes. Cool and chill. Serves 6.

Spanish Orange Cups

These attractive custard-filled oranges can be prepared before-hand and refrigerated until ready to serve.

8 medium-sized oranges
8 cups orange juice
4 tablespoons cornstarch
1 cup sugar
4 egg yolks
4 glacé cherries (optional)

Slice tops off oranges, cutting off about 1 inch. Scoop out fruit and pulp, removing some of white to make a clean shell but being careful not to break the skin. Squeeze and strain juice, adding additional juice as needed to make 8 cups. Combine cornstarch, sugar, and egg yolks in a large saucepan. Mix well. Add juice and beat until smooth. Cook, stirring frequently, several minutes, until thickened and smooth. Cool. Spoon into orange shells. Chill. Top each with half a cherry. Serves 8.

234 / *The Complete International Breakfast/Brunch Cookbook*

Salzburger Nockerln

This renowned Austrian dessert, a delectable fluffy treat is called *Nockerln* (for small oval balls of many varieties), or Salzburg soufflé. It was created over 250 years ago by a chef in the Hohensalzburg palace, and is still a sure winner for a special-occasion small brunch.

1 tablespoon butter or margarine, softened
½ cup milk
1 to 2 tablespoons sugar
½ teaspoon vanilla extract
4 eggs, separated
3 tablespoons powdered sugar
1 teaspoon all-purpose flour

Butter a square or oval 8- or 9-inch baking dish. Add milk, sugar, and vanilla. Put into a preheated 375° F. oven 5 minutes. Meanwhile, beat egg whites in a large bowl until soft peaks form. Add powdered sugar, 1 spoonful at a time, beating after each addition, until mixture is thick and glossy. Beat egg yolks with flour into whites. Remove heated milk mixture from oven. With a spatula drop in three large mounds of egg mixture making them wide and high. Return to oven for 8 to 10 minutes, or until outside is golden, puffed, and creamy. Dust with powdered sugar, if desired. Serve at once. Serves 6.

Key West Lime Pie

This is an attractive light dessert for a summer brunch.

4 large eggs
1 14-ounce can sweetened condensed milk
½ cup freshly squeezed lime juice
½ teaspoon cream of tartar
6 tablespoons sugar
1 baked 9-inch pie shell

Separate eggs, putting yolks in one large bowl, three egg whites in a medium-sized bowl, and one egg white in another medium-sized bowl. Gradually add condensed milk to egg yolks, stirring as adding. Gradually mix in lime juice. Beat the single egg white and fold into milk mixture. Turn into pie shell. Beat remaining three egg whites until almost stiff; add cream of tartar and sugar; beat until stiff but not dry. Pile over filling, spreading to edges. Bake in a preheated 350° F. oven 15 minutes. Cool. Chill. Serves 6.

French Chocolate Custards

These rich small *pots de crème* are easy-to-prepare desserts that you can have ready in the refrigerator to serve when you wish.

> 2 *cups light cream*
> 6 *egg yolks*
> 2 *tablespoons sugar*
> *Dash salt*
> 6 *ounces semisweet chocolate, grated*
> 1 *teaspoon vanilla extract*
> *Whipped cream*

Heat light cream to the boiling point (when bubbles appear around the edge), in a medium-sized saucepan. Meanwhile, combine egg yolks, sugar, and salt in a small bowl; do not beat. Pour out ⅓ of hot cream, stir into egg mixture and return to cream in saucepan. Cook, stirring constantly, over medium heat until mixture thickens and spoon is coated. Stir in chocolate. Remove from heat and keep stirring until chocolate melts. Stir in vanilla. Pour into 8 small *pots de crème,* demitasse cups, or small bowls. Chill. Serve garnished with a dab of whipped cream. Serves 8.

Dutch Apple Cake

You can serve this attractive cake, topped with overlapping slices of apples, warm or cold.

> 1 *cup all-purpose flour*
> 2 *teaspoons baking powder*
> ½ *teaspoon salt*
> ½ *cup sugar*
> ⅓ *cup shortening or margarine*
> ¼ *cup milk*
> 1 *egg, beaten*
> 3 *medium-sized tart apples*
> ½ *teaspoon ground cinnamon*
> 2 *tablespoons butter or margarine, melted*

Sift flour, baking powder, salt, and ⅓ cup sugar into a large bowl. Cut in shortening or margarine with a pastry blender or two knives. Combine milk and egg; add to dry ingredients; mix well. Spread in a greased 8-inch square baking dish. Core, peel, and slice apples. Arrange in rows, overlapping, over the batter, slightly pressing down. Sprinkle with a mixture of remaining sugar and cinnamon, and then with melted butter or margarine. Bake in a preheated 375° F. oven 40 minutes, or until tester inserted into cake comes out clean. Cut into squares and serve warm or cold. Serves 6.

Strawberry-Vanilla Ice Cream Pie

You can have this pie in the freezer, ready to serve for an impromptu meal.

1 *9-inch pastry shell, baked*
1 *quart vanilla ice cream, softened*
1 *cup chopped walnuts*
1 *10-ounce package frozen strawberries, partially thawed*
 Whipped cream

Chill pastry shell. Combine ice cream and nuts; spoon half the mixture into pie shell, spreading evenly. Spread top with ¾ of the strawberries. Cover with remaining ice cream and nuts. Chill in freezer a few minutes. Top with remaining strawberries and garnish top with whipped cream. Chill in freezer until firm. When ready to serve, take out of freezer and leave at room temperature for several minutes. Serves 6.

English Poached Pears

You can serve these chilled poached pears topped with puréed raspberries and whipped cream, hot chocolate sauce, or ice cream.

12 *firm slightly underripe pears*
 Juice of 2 lemons
2 *cups sugar*
3 *cups water*
2 *teaspoons vanilla extract*
2 *10- or 12-ounce packages frozen raspberries, partially thawed*
2 *tablespoons kirsch or other liqueur*
 Whipped cream

Peel and halve pears. Scoop out cores and cut out stems. Rub with a little lemon juice to prevent darkening. Combine sugar, water, remaining lemon juice, and vanilla in a medium-sized saucepan. Bring to a boil. Cook briskly 5 minutes. Add pears and reduce heat. Simmer, covered, about 10 minutes, or until tender. Remove pears to a serving dish. Reduce syrup over high heat until thick. Pour over pears. Chill. Meanwhile, process raspberries in a blender or purée. Add kirsch or a liqueur. Serve chilled pears topped with berries and whipped cream. Serves 12.

Note: Serve pears with hot chocolate sauce or ice cream as a substitute for the berries, if desired. It is impossible to give an exact time for poaching pears, since the time depends on the texture of the pear and its ripeness.

Grapefruit Baked Alaska

These attractive individual desserts are made with a half grapefruit, a scoop of ice cream, and meringue.

4 grapefruit
¾ cup sugar
6 egg whites
½ teaspoon cream of tartar
8 small scoops hard ice cream, any flavor

Cut grapefruit into halves. Cut around each section and remove core. Sprinkle lightly with sugar and chill. Just before serving, prepare meringue. Beat egg whites with cream of tartar until stiff but moist. Gradually beat in ½ cup sugar and beat until stiff and glossy. Put a scoop of ice cream in center of each grapefruit half. Completely cover ice cream and top of grapefruit with meringue. Place at once into a preheated 475° F. oven for about 1 minute, or until lightly browned. Serve at once. Serves 8.

Jewish Honey Cake

This spicy traditional cake, called *Lebkuchen*, is superb for a large brunch.

    3 eggs
    ¾ cup sugar
    1¼ cups honey
    3 tablespoons salad oil
    ¼ cup brewed black coffee
    ½ cup almond slivers
    3½ cups all-purpose flour
    ½ teaspoon salt
    1½ teaspoons baking powder
    1 teaspoon baking soda
    ½ teaspoon ground ginger
    ¼ teaspoon ground cloves
    ¼ teaspoon ground nutmeg

Break eggs into a large bowl. Mix in sugar, honey, oil, coffee, and almonds. Sift remaining ingredients into bowl; mix well. Spoon into a greased 13″ x 9″ baking dish. Bake in a preheated 325° F. oven 1 hour, or until tester inserted into cake comes out clean. Cool and cut into slices or squares. Serves about 12.

Old-Fashioned Carrot Cake

Carrot cake is now one of the most popular American brunch desserts. This is an appealing version.

    1½ cups peanut oil or salad oil
    2 cups sugar
    4 eggs, beaten
    3 cups all-purpose flour
    2 teaspoons baking soda
    3 teaspoons baking powder
    2 teaspoons ground cinnamon
    ½ teaspoon salt
    2 cups finely grated raw carrots
    1 cup chopped walnuts

Combine oil, sugar, and eggs in a large bowl. Sift in flour, baking powder, soda, cinnamon, and salt. Mix well. Add carrots and nuts and combine thoroughly. Turn into a greased 10-inch tube pan and cook in a preheated 350° F. oven 60 minutes, or until tester inserted into cake comes out clean. Turn out onto a rack and cool. Slice when ready to serve. Serves about 14.

Jamaican Cold Rum Soufflé

This is a good dessert for a small summer brunch.

1 *envelope plain gelatin*
4 *eggs, separated*
6 *tablespoons sugar*
1 *tablespoon cornstarch*
1 *cup evaporated milk*
½ *teaspoon vanilla extract*
¼ *cup Jamaican rum*
   Pinch salt

Sprinkle gelatin over ¼ cup cold water in a small bowl to soften. Beat egg yolks with 4 tablespoons sugar in a small bowl until light and creamy. Combine cornstarch, 2 tablespoons cold water, and milk in top of a double boiler; mix well. Cook slowly, stirring, over simmering water until slightly thickened. Add beaten egg yolks, sugar, and softened gelatin; mix well. Cook slowly, stirring constantly, until mixture is smooth and thickened, or until spoon is coated. Remove from heat and stir in vanilla and rum. Beat egg whites in a large bowl until frothy; then add remaining 2 tablespoons sugar and salt, and beat until egg whites are stiff. Fold into custard and turn into a 1½-quart souffle dish. Refrigerate until set and firm, 3 hours or longer. Serves 6.

German Fruit Kuchen

You can make this fruit-topped cake with any fresh fruit in season.

¹/₃ *cup butter or margarine, softened*
¹/₃ *cup sugar*
½ *teaspoon vanilla extract*
2 *eggs*
1 *cup sifted all-purpose flour*
1 *teaspoon baking powder*
2 *tablespoons milk*
2 *cups sliced fresh fruit (peaches, strawberries, apricots, etc.)*
   Whipped cream

Cream butter or margarine in a large bowl. Add sugar and beat until light and fluffy. Add vanilla and then eggs, one at a time, beating after each addition. Sift in flour and baking powder, adding alternately with milk. Mix well. Turn into a round 9-inch cake pan lined with wax paper, and spread evenly. Bake in a preheated 350° F. oven 30 minutes, or until tester inserted into cake comes out clean. Cool 5 minutes. Turn out onto a rack and remove paper. Cool. Arrange fruit slices, sweetened with sugar, if desired, over top of cake. Garnish top with whipped cream. Chill until ready to serve. Serves 8.

Bananas Foster

This is one of the most famous and popular desserts at Brennan's in New Orleans. It's really quite simple to prepare. Wait until the rum gets hot, so you get a good flame when it's ignited. This can also be prepared over a stove burner, then brought to the table and flamed.

4 tablespoons butter
1 cup brown sugar
½ teaspoon ground cinnamon
4 tablespoons banana liqueur
4 bananas, peeled, cut in half lengthwise, then cut once across
¼ cup rum (approximately)
4 scoops vanilla ice cream

Melt butter in a flambé pan or an attractive skillet over an alcohol burner. Add sugar, cinnamon, and banana liqueur; stir to mix. Heat for a few minutes, then place the halved bananas in the sauce. Sauté until soft. Add rum and allow to heat well. Then tip the pan so that the flame from the burner causes the sauce to ignite. Allow the sauce to flame until it dies out, tipping the pan with a circular motion to prolong the flaming. Serve over vanilla ice cream: First, lift the bananas carefully out of the pan and place four pieces over each portion of ice cream, then spoon the hot sauce from the pan over the bananas and ice cream. Serve at once. Serves 4.

Old-Fashioned Strawberry Shortcake

This traditional recipe is superb for a summer brunch.

1 quart fresh strawberries
¾ cup plus 2 tablespoons sugar

2 *cups sifted all-purpose flour*
1 *tablespoon baking powder*
1 *teaspoon salt*
½ *cup shortening, butter, or margarine*
¾ *cup milk*
2 *tablespoons softened butter or margarine (approximately)*
1 *cup heavy cream*
¼ *cup powdered sugar*

Wash and hull strawberries, reserving about 6 for a garnish. Slice berries into a bowl. Cover with ¾ cup sugar; mix well and set aside. Sift flour, baking powder, 2 tablespoons sugar, and salt into a large bowl. Cut in shortening, butter or margarine with a pastry blender or two knives until very fine particles form. Pour in milk and mix quickly with a fork to combine ingredients. Turn onto a floured board or surface, knead briefly and divide dough into two halves. Pat or roll each gently into a soft large round, large enough to fit into a greased 8-inch cake pan. Spread top of each with softened butter or margarine. Put one section of dough on top of the other in the greased cake pan, and bake in a preheated 450° F. oven 15 minutes, or until golden brown and a tester inserted in the center comes out clean. Turn out onto a wire rack. Carefully cut crosswise into two halves. Put bottom half on a large plate, and cover with half the strawberries. Top with second half and remaining strawberries. Cover with whipped cream. Garnish with whole strawberries. Serves 6 to 8.

Sweet Omelet

The range of sweet omelets is wide. You can make this basic omelet and serve it plain, or fill it with orange marmalade or berry preserves before folding, then sprinkle with rum and ignite. You could also fill it with sweetened strawberries, sprinkle it with kirsch and ignite; or, fill it with sweetened brandy-flavored apples, sprinkle with sugar, and glaze under a hot broiler.

3 *large eggs, separated*
2 *teaspoons sugar*
  Pinch salt
1 *teaspoon water*
2 *teaspoons butter*
  Powdered sugar

Combine egg yolks, sugar, salt, and water in a medium-sized bowl; beat until light and creamy. Beat egg whites until stiff but not dry, and fold into egg yolk mixture. Heat butter in a heated omelet pan; add egg mixture; spoon with a spatula to spread evenly. Cook without stirring until edges are light brown. Run a knife around to loosen the edges. Fold in half and turn out onto a warm plate. Sprinkle top with powdered sugar. Serves 2.

Hungarian Pancakes with Chocolate Sauce

Prepare the pancakes beforehand and finish the dessert just before serving.

    2 eggs, beaten
    1½ cups milk
    1 tablespoon sugar
    ¼ teaspoon salt
    1 cup all-purpose flour
      Butter for frying
      Apricot, strawberry, or raspberry jam
    1 cup prepared chocolate sauce
    2 tablespoons light rum

Combine eggs, milk, sugar, salt, and flour in a medium-sized bowl; mix with a whisk until smooth. Heat a lightly greased crepe pan (7- or 8-inch). Add 3 tablespoons batter all at once, preferably from a small glass; quickly tilt pan to spread it evenly. Cook over medium heat until underside is golden. Turn over with a spatula and cook on other side. Turn out onto a pie pan and keep warm in a preheated 250° F. oven. Continue to cook other pancakes; then spread each with a thin layer of jam, and roll or fold over. Serve at once with chocolate sauce and rum, previously heated together. Sprinkle tops with chopped nuts, if desired. Serves 10 to 12.

Romanian Cheese-Filled Pancakes

    2 eggs, beaten
    2 tablespoons melted butter or margarine
    1 cup milk
    ¼ teaspoon salt
    1 cup all-purpose flour

1½ cups dry small-curd cottage cheese
½ teaspoon vanilla extract
½ cup sugar
1½ cups sour cream, at room temperature
Powdered sugar

Combine eggs, butter or margarine, milk, salt, and flour in a medium-sized bowl; mix with a whisk until smooth. Heat a lightly greased crepe pan (7- or 8-inch); add 3 tablespoons batter all at once. Tilt pan at once to spread batter evenly, then cook over medium heat until underside of pancake is golden. Turn over with a spatula; cook on other side. Turn out on a pie pan and keep warm in a preheated 250° F. oven while cooking the others.

Combine cottage cheese, drained of all liquid, vanilla, and sugar. Spread each pancake with some of cheese mixture; roll up each one, folding in sides to enclose filling. Arrange, side by side, in a shallow baking dish. Cover with sour cream, and sprinkle with powdered sugar. Bake, covered with foil, in a preheated 350° F. oven for 20 minutes. Serves 10 to 12.

Treetop Fruited Bread Pudding

This inviting pudding is a popular dessert for brunch at the attractive Treetop Restaurant of the spacious mountain resort spa, Coolfont Re+Creation, at Berkeley Springs, West Virginia. It is ideal for a large get-together.

⅔ cup seedless raisins
1½ pounds fresh white bread
2¾ quarts of milk
⅓ cup melted butter or margarine
1½ cups sugar
2 teaspoons ground cinnamon
¼ teaspoon ground nutmeg
2 teaspoons salt
12 eggs
⅔ cup fruit cocktail, sliced peaches, or fresh fruit mixture

Soak raisins in hot water to cover for 30 minutes; drain and set aside. Break bread into medium-sized pieces in an extra-large bowl. Add milk and butter or margarine. Then add sugar, cinnamon, nutmeg, and salt; mix well. Beat eggs until light and creamy. Add to bread mixture. Add raisins; mix well. Pour into a shallow, 4″ x [8″ x 16″] baking dish. Bake in a preheated 350° F. oven 1 hour. Check for doneness by gently pushing center. If springy, the pudding is done. The desired consistency is like moist brownies. To garnish, heat, drain, and spread fruit cocktail on top. Serve immediately. Serves about 25.

12

Coffee and Other Beverages

While coffee is the preferred American breakfast and brunch beverage, other drinks, especially tea and chocolate, have long been international favorites.

The oldest and most popular drink in the world is tea, native to China and enjoyed there for thousands of years. It has also been widely cultivated in India, Japan, and Southeast Asia.

Lu Yu's eighth-century *Classic of Tea* says "Mystery surrounds the origin of tea. The legend, to which most earlier Chinese readily subscribed, is that it was discovered by an emperor of the third millennium B.C., Shen Nung. He is supposed to have been burning a camellia bush, to which tea is very closely related, when he began to marvel at the aroma which assailed him. Understanding its source, he then introduced tea and its cultivation to his people."

Tea was taken so seriously by the Chinese that it became an integral part of their culture and literature. In Japan drinking tea was so important that the Tea Ceremony, *Cha-no-yo,* introduced in 729 A.D., still exists as a social institution.

Europeans began drinking tea in the early seventeenth century. Although some Englishmen condemned tea as a vice, it was the English who made the drink famous. Drinking tea for breakfast and throughout the day is still an established custom in much of the Western world.

Dutch settlers brought tea to the American colonies, where it became a prized beverage. But prized or not, a tax levied on it by the British Parliament caused havoc. As a result Americans not only stopped drinking it temporarily, but embarked on a revolution as well. Later on tea was back in vogue, and the United States's contributions to tea drinking came to include tea bags, iced tea, instant tea, and canned tea.

All tea leaves come from an evergreen tree, but they differ because of the soil, climate, and treatment of the leaves after being picked. There are three main types of tea—the most familiar, black; the light and delicate green tea; and the distinctive, partly fermented oolong. There are also scented or floral teas.

There are many ways of drinking tea. The Chinese and Japanese prefer it with no additional flavoring. Indians like spiced tea. The Russians drink it through a cube of sugar held in the mouth or sweeten it with preserves. In England tea is drunk with milk and sugar. Americans flavor it with lemon, mint, or other herbs, or sweetened with sugar or honey.

It is believed that the coffee plant, *Coffea*, was discovered in Ethiopia, perhaps as early as 500 A.D. Coffee drinking eventually became a Near Eastern custom, a tradition surrounded by ceremony. The first coffee houses were opened in Turkey hundreds of years ago. Then Turkish troops brought coffee to Eastern Europe in the seventeenth century, and a Turkish ambassador introduced coffee to the court of Louis XIV in Paris, where the drink quickly became fashionable.

During the eighteenth century London became famous for its hundreds of coffee houses called "Penny Universities" because of a one-cent admission charge. They were popular gathering places for conversation and conviviality.

Early American coffee houses resembled those of England and Daniel Webster called one, the Green Dragon in Boston, "the headquarters of the Revolution." With the Boston Tea Party in 1773, and because plantings of coffee trees in Latin America made it more available, coffee soon became a staple beverage in American homes. By the time of the Civil War, the drink was consumed in such quantity that the institution called the "coffee break" was already an everyday occurrence in many places.

Coffee has long been a symbol of hospitality the world over. Tastes in coffee drinking, however, take many forms. Near Easterners like their coffee dark and sweet, and they sometimes flavor it with spices. The Viennese top their coffee with whipped cream. The French and Italians prefer a dark-roasted pulverized coffee. In many countries the drink is flavored with alcohol. American cowboys used to demand that their coffee be, "hot, black and strong enough to walk." In Louisiana the coffee is flavored with chicory, and Cajuns like it "Black as the devil, hot as hell, pure as an angel, sweet as love." Certainly, iced coffee is a traditional summer drink all over America.

There are more than a hundred kinds and varieties of coffee which come from many countries; they differ in flavor, body and aroma. Some are good in themselves; others do better when blended. Some are more prized then others. It's the roasting that gives coffee beans their familiar dark brown color.

The kind of coffee you buy and make is a matter of taste, of personal choice, but always use a fresh grind, fresh cold water, proper measurements, and perfectly clean equipment.

Chocolate is another popular favorite morning drink from Aztec times to the present. *Xoxoc-atl*, as it was originally called, is one of Mexico's great culinary gifts to the world.

Conquistadores first tasted chocolate during the Spanish invasion of Mexico. Montezuma and his courtiers drank unbelievable quantities of a vanilla-flavored drink, so precious that only men of high rank were permitted to enjoy it. The variations were green, honeyed, bright red, orange-colored, rose-colored, black, and white chocolate.

Cacao beans, the Spanish discovered, came from a perennial evergreen, botanically called *theobroma* or "food of the Gods." The word cocoa first appeared in print in Dr. Johnson's Dictionary in 1775. No one knows whether the spelling error was his, or a typesetter's.

Cortez brought cacao beans to the Spanish court, and the Aztec drink was made more palatable by the addition of sugar. By the mid-1600s Europeans had become so enchanted with the New World beverage that chocolate shops became the rage of the Continent.

Chocolate was first imported to the American colonies in the mid-1700s by Massachusetts traders. Although the price was high, chocolate drinks became popular and were widely used during the protests against the tax on tea. Chocolate, rich and stimulating, was thought to be very nourishing as well as delicious.

You can make excellent breakfast and brunch beverages with the many kinds of chocolate or cocoa available. Here are some excellent recipes for coffee, tea, and chocolate.

French Café au Lait

This national breakfast drink of France is served with flaky croissants or other breads.

> 1½ *cups strong, hot, freshly brewed coffee*
> 1½ *cups hot, rich milk*

Using two pots, pour simultaneously into coffee cups. Makes 4 servings.

Viennese Coffee

As lovers of good coffee, the Viennese enjoy their world-renowned drink served with whipped cream, or *Schlagobers.*
Brew extra-strength coffee, sweeten to taste, add hot milk, if desired, and top with whipped cream.

Café Royal

Put a lump of sugar into a demitasse cup half-filled with very strong coffee. Fill the cup slowly with brandy so it will stay on top. Light the brandy and serve.

Italian Espresso

This well-known beverage is made with a very dark pulverized coffee brewed in a two-tiered *macchinetta,* the Italian-style drip pot. You can also make it in a regular drip coffeemaker with either a French or Italian dark roast coffee that is very, very finely ground.

> 8 *tablespoons Italian-roast coffee*
> 1½ *cups water*

Make according to directions of coffee maker. Serve in demitasse cups with sugar, or Roman style with a twist of lemon. Do not use cream. Makes 4 servings.

Italian Caffé Cappuccino

This drink gets its name from its color, which is the same as the robes of the Capuchin monks.

Make Italian Espresso. Pour equal amounts of hot Espresso and hot milk into tall or regular cups. Sprinkle the top of each with ground cinnamon or nutmeg.

Spanish Mocha

4½ cups hot coffee
4½ cups hot chocolate
  Sugar to taste
  Ground cinnamon

Combine ingredients in a saucepan and heat. Do not boil. Beat with a rotary beater until frothy. Serve garnished with ground cinnamon. Makes 12 servings.

Café à l'Orange

Add a dash of curaçao to each cup of strong, black coffee. Serve with a cinnamon stick in each cup.

Irish Coffee

This famous Irish drink, sometimes served as dessert, has become a great American favorite. According to the Irish it should be made with cream rich as an Irish brogue, coffee strong as a friendly hand, sugar sweet as the tongue of a rogue, and whiskey smooth as the wit of the land.

To make, put a jigger of Irish whiskey into a warmed, stemmed Irish coffee goblet or wine glass. Add 2 teaspoons sugar and fill glass ²/₃ full with hot strong coffee. Top to brim with whipped cream. Do not stir. Drink the hot coffee and whiskey through the coolness of the cream.

Café Brûlot

There are many versions of this traditional New Orleans drink, which is also called *Café Brûlot Diabolique*. It is black coffee laced with brandy, sometimes a liqueur, and flavored with spices. It is served flaming from a large bowl or chafing dish, and is ladled into *brûlot* cups. This recipe is from Antoine's restaurant.

1 *1-inch stick cinnamon*
8 *whole cloves*
   Peel of 1 lemon, cut into thin shreds
6 *lumps sugar*
4 *jiggers brandy*
4 *cups demitasse coffee*

Put cinnamon, cloves, lemon, and sugar into a chafing dish. Put brandy into a ladle, ignite, pour over ingredients; stir; gradually add coffee and continue to stir until flame fades. Serve in *brûlot* or demitasse cups. Serves 4.

Coffee with Liqueurs

You can make many flavorful coffees by adding a liqueur to the hot brew. Fill a demitasse cup about three-fourths full with strong hot coffee. Add a dash or more of Tia Maria (Spanish), Kahlúa (Mexican), Kirsch (Swiss), or Amaretto, Curacao, Grand Marnier, Cointreau, Cognac, Anisette, or any other liqueur.

American Spiced Ice Coffee

Here is an interesting version of this popular American summer drink.

3 *cups strong hot coffee*
4 *whole cloves*
2 *cinnamon sticks*
½ *teaspoon ground nutmeg*

Pour coffee over spices in a large bowl. Let stand one hour. Strain over ice cubes in 4 tall glasses. Serve with cream and sugar, if desired. Serves 4.

Brazilian Coffee

2 *squares (2 ounces) unsweetened chocolate, grated*
1 *cup strong coffee*
¼ *cup sugar*
3 *cups scalded light cream or milk*
   Whipped cream

Combine chocolate and coffee in top of a double boiler over

simmering water. Mix until well blended. Add sugar. Slowly add cream or milk; mix well. Remove from heat. Beat until frothy. Serve in cups topped with whipped cream. Makes 4 servings.

Note: You can serve this drink cold topped with vanilla ice cream, if desired.

Near Eastern Coffee

In the Near East, strong dark coffee served in tiny cups about the size of an egg shell, and called Turkish or Arabic coffee, is drunk in great quantity. The coffee is made in a special utensil called an *ibrik*, made of brass or copper with a long handle, no spout and no cover. You serve the coffee sweet, medium, or unsweetened.

   1½ cups water
   4 teaspoons sugar (approximately)
   4 tablespoons finely pulverized coffee

Pour water into a *ibrik* or saucepan. Add sugar; bring to a boil. Stir in coffee. Bring to a boil. Allow brew to froth up three times. Remove from heat and add a few drops cold water. Spoon some of foam into each cup; pour in coffee. Makes 4 servings.

Note: Add a cardamom seed to each cup, if desired.

English Tea

Tea has long been the traditional English breakfast beverage and remains so today. It should be made in a China pot so the tea will steep and all the fine flavors and aromas will not escape. Fill the teapot with boiling water to heat it before you make the tea. Then empty it, and put in the tea leaves. The usual amount is 1 teaspoon of leaves per serving cup; for a stronger drink, use a little more. The water must be boiling, a round bubbling boil, when you pour it over the tea leaves in the pot. Put on the lid and cover with a tea cozy, if desired, to hold in the heat while the tea steeps. Allow about 5 minutes for the steeping. Pour and drink.

American Iced Tea

Place 2 teaspoons tea leaves for each cup of cold water in a pitcher or glass container. Cover with water. Refrigerate, covered, for 24 hours. Strain and serve in tall glasses over ice cubes. Garnish with a thin slice of lemon or mint leaves, if desired.

Oriental Jasmine Tea

In the Orient, green (unfermented) and oolong (semifermented) teas are preferred. They are delicate drinks with pleasing aromas. A particularly good one is Jasmine Tea, oolong leaves scented with jasmine petals. You boil the leaves in water and serve the drink plain.

Moroccan Mint Tea

Mint tea is the national drink of Morocco and is traditionally made and served by the men in the family. It is poured from a metal pot into small glasses decorated with colored rings and arranged on a tray.

> 1 tablespoon green tea
> 1 large bunch fresh mint leaves
> ¼ cup sugar (approximately)

Preheat teapot by rinsing with ½ cup hot water. Put tea into pot; add mint leaves and sugar. Cover with boiling water (about 4 cups) and let steep 3 to 5 minutes, stirring a little at the end. Pour into glasses. Makes 6 servings. According to Moroccans, courtesy requires that each guest drink three glasses.

Clyde's Own Hollywood Hot

This stimulating beverage is a specialty of Clyde's Restaurant in Tysons Corner, Virginia.

To make it, pour hot tea into brandy snifters. Add a generous dash or jigger of Grand Marnier. Serve garnished with an orange slice.

Mexican Chocolate

Steaming cups of hot chocolate have been popular for breakfast in Mexico for centuries. They are beaten with a *molinillo,* an attractive carved wooden beater.

> 1 2-ounce cake Mexican chocolate or, 2 1-ounce squares unsweetened
> chocolate, 2 tablespoons sugar, 1 teaspoon ground cinnamon, and
> pinch salt
> 4 cups milk

Combine ingredients in a heavy saucepan and cook until chocolate melts. Remove from heat and beat until smooth and frothy. Pour into cups or serve from a pitcher. Makes 4 servings.

Note: Mexican chocolate contains the necessary sugar and cinnamon. For more froth, you can add an egg to the ingredients.

Swiss Hot Chocolate

2 *squares (2 ounces) unsweetened chocolate*
½ *cup sugar*
Dash salt
⅓ *cup hot water*
2 *cups milk*
Whipped cream

Melt chocolate in top of a double boiler over simmering water. Add sugar, salt, and hot water; stir well. Cook 1 or 2 minutes. Gradually add milk and heat through; remove from stove. Beat with a rotary beater until frothy. Serve topped with whipped cream. Makes 4 servings.

Hot Cocoa For a Crowd

1¼ *cups cocoa*
1½ *cups sugar*
¾ *teaspoon salt*
1¾ *cups hot water*
4 *quarts milk*
1 *tablespoon vanilla extract*

Combine cocoa, sugar, and salt in a large saucepan. Pour in hot water. Boil, stirring, 2 minutes. Reduce heat and add milk, stirring as adding. Leave on the stove long enough to heat through. Remove from the stove; add vanilla; beat with a rotary beater until frothy. Serve garnished with whipped cream or a dish of ground cinnamon, if desired. Makes about 20 servings.

Metric Measure Conversion Table

Metric Measure Conversion Table
(Approximations)

When You Know (U.S.)	Multiply by	To Find (Metric)
	WEIGHT	
ounces	28	grams
pounds	0.45	kilograms
	VOLUME	
teaspoons	5	milliliters
tablespoons	15	milliliters
fluid ounces	30	milliliters
cups	0.24	liters
pints	0.47	liters
quarts	0.95	liters
	TEMPERATURE	
degrees Fahrenheit (F°)	subtract 32° and multiply the remainder by 5/9 or .556	degrees Celsius or Centigrade (C°)

Index

255